Shakespeare's
Early Tragedies

Shakespeare's Early Tragedies

Nicholas Brooke

METHUEN & CO LTD

First published 1968
by Methuen and Co Ltd
11 New Fetter Lane, London EC4
© 1968 Nicholas Brooke
Printed in Great Britain by
Richard Clay (The Chaucer Press) Ltd.,
Bungay, Suffolk

SBN 416 19340 4

Distributed in the U.S.A. by
Barnes & Noble Inc.

for

Clifford and Gabriele Leech

Contents

Foreword

Some parts of the first three essays have appeared in print before, and I am grateful to the editors and publishers of *Critical Quarterly*, and of *Gemini Books 2 : Shakespeare : The Tragedies*, ed. C. Leech, for permission to reprint them here.

Quotations and line references are, for the plays discussed, to the new Arden Shakespeare where available, that is for *Titus Andronicus*, ed. J. C. Maxwell, *Richard II*, ed. P. Ure, and *Julius Caesar*, ed. T. S. Dorsch: I am indebted to their editors for their commentaries and introductions as well as for their texts. For *Richard III*, *Romeo and Juliet*, and *Hamlet* I have used the Collins Tudor Shakespeare, ed. P. Alexander, and found particular help for all the plays in the New Cambridge Shakespeare, ed. J. Dover Wilson. References to other Shakespeare plays are always to Alexander's edition.

I owe a great debt, too, to innumerable other critics and scholars who have written on Shakespeare: it would be impossible to record this in detail, and I have used footnotes only sparingly for specific points; the books and essays which I have found most interesting are listed in the selective bibliography, though it should be said that some of the more recent items were published after I had drafted my own discussion of the plays.

Most of these essays originated as lectures in the University of Durham, given at the suggestion of Professor Clifford Leech: it is a pleasure to recall the encouragement, and the criticism, that made working with him there such a memorable experience. I am grateful too to students in Durham and in the University of East Anglia with whom I have discussed these plays.

Foreword

Finally, I must acknowledge the patience of my family during the years in which, on and off, I have been pre-occupied with this book, and especially my wife and our younger son, Thomas, who have lately laboured prodigiously to compile the index.

July, 1968

Introduction

It has for some time seemed an established fact that Shakespeare's greatest plays were his tragedies, and that the period of his greatest tragedies began with *Hamlet* and ended with *Macbeth*. This has been so generally agreed in the past hundred years that it has come to seem an irrefutable judgement; perhaps it is in fact so, I certainly do not intend to challenge it in this book. But it did not always seem so transparently clear, or at least did not once seem to rest on so absolute a distinction; it was not in fact given final identity before Bradley's *Shakespearean Tragedy* appeared in 1904. German criticism and German philosophy of the nineteenth century, the work especially of Hegel and Nietzsche, assured the pre-eminence of tragedy, and especially of Greek tragedy; it was Bradley's achievement to transfer this allegiance decisively to Shakespeare. In his modification of Hegel's theories to fit the English case, he established strong grounds for believing that tragedy is not just a dramatic genre, but, in its true form, a distinctive and peculiarly fine experience.

It is, I think, rather curious how easily this discrimination has been assimilated: it seems to have become possible for every schoolchild to distinguish 'true tragedy' from any other play which ends with the death of the hero. Some may have doubts whether *Antony and Cleopatra* ought not to be admitted to the distinguished group, though Bradley determined with particular care that it should not. But no one, so far as I know, has proposed that any tragedy before *Hamlet* should be regarded in the same light. The earlier plays are often treated as merely that: exercises prior to the great achievement that was to follow. Yet I said that this, which has become so clear, was not always so: Whately compared *Richard III* and *Macbeth* in the eighteenth century, and saw the superiority of the later play; but he did it, a hundred and fifty years after Shakespeare's death, with an air of discovery; and he certainly did not determine that because *Macbeth* was a superior play, *Richard III* was therefore an uninteresting one. And in comedy, no such distinction has yet been established: no doubt there are marks of maturity in *As You Like It* that are lacking in *Love's Labour's Lost*; it would not be difficult to point them out; but they are not such as to ensure general agreement that the later play is in an altogether different class. But then, no one has had an intuition of a definable 'comic experience' by which one may know 'true comedy' from any other kind.

The theatre itself does not seem to have been more discriminating in tragedy than in comedy. *Hamlet* is altogether Shakespeare's most successful play; but after that it is not clear that the later plays come off better than the earlier, and it is in fact quite clear that *Richard III* generally fares better than *Macbeth*. I do not suggest that this is an adequate basis for judgement; but it does, at least, raise problems. If true tragedy is known by the tragic experience, where is that experience to be tested (it is an ancient riddle), in the theatre or in the library? It is, I think, seldom precisely found in the theatre, where the play at large is often a richer experience than its ending; which may, in fact, strike one as no more than apt. And the identity of true tragedy was established in a century that never forgot Lamb's claim that Shakespeare's tragedies ought not to be performed. Bradley, it is true, did not share Lamb's conviction, and treated the stage with far greater respect; yet in *Shakespearean Tragedy* he speaks constantly of the 'book' and addresses the 'reader'. I do not claim any special theatrical insights in the essays that follow, and they are of course the result of a close study of the text; but I hope it will appear that that study, an imaginative one by necessity, is governed by an imagination trained to think of the stage. At the least it will be seen that I write of the play and the audience. I am not convinced any longer that there is a single homogeneous tragic experience that can be used to distinguish true tragedy from a lower kind;

nor that a dramatic criticism based on this concept is a valid one for the later plays, let alone the earlier ones.

I am, however, convinced that the long settled opinion on this matter has had a depressing effect on the study of the early tragedies. There are, of course, plenty of exceptions to this, and the bibliography names several, but generally speaking they have been viewed critically as prentice work, and examined for handy comparisons to illumine the quality of later achievements. Thus passages are cited to show the stiffness of the verse against the flexibility of the 'mature style' (as if Shakespeare had at any time only one style at command); or the 'conventional' nature of their imagery compared to the free play of the associative faculty later on (a distinction which suggests a preference for unconscious creation most inappropriate to Shakespeare's superb control at any stage of his career).

So my first, and strongest, aim in this book is to look at these plays for what they are, in themselves, and not for what we might with hindsight predict from them for the later plays which already have their due share, not just of attention, but of estimation. And when I say 'in themselves', I mean individually; I want to look at what each is uniquely as a single play, and by no means to draw them together into a closely-knit group, nor – even worse – to make them a chain leading from 'immature' towards 'mature'. It will be clear from what I have already said that I have no general theory of tragedy to propound. In fact, rather the reverse. It seems to me that within the very loose term 'tragedy' there is a range of possibility, of positive variety, such as we expect to find in 'comedy'. Between *Twelfth Night* and *The Alchemist*, *Volpone* and *The Way of the World*, or *The Importance of Being Earnest* and *The Caretaker* there is virtually no common ground, and to find some and to try to bring the plays together on that, could only be achieved at the expense of terribly mutilating the plays themselves. This does not mean that there are no distinct resemblances and connections to be noted, but that noting them must always sub-serve the central interest in what each play in itself is. Once one looks at the plays I am considering with this point in mind, they appear to be almost as different from one another as were the

4 *Shakespeare's Early Tragedies*

comedies I catalogued. That *Titus Andronicus* and *Romeo and Juliet* are not like one another will be readily agreed, possibly even too readily. *Richard III* and *Richard II* are so alike in name, and are so much more often considered as histories than as tragedies, that their likeness might seem to be pre-empted. Some difference from the others may derive from their status as histories: although both have strong formal characteristics, neither shows any trace of the classical five-Act structure which Shakespeare thought appropriate for *Titus* and *Romeo and Juliet*. But otherwise the *Richards* have almost nothing in common at all, and it may seem strange, but it is true, that of the two it is *Richard II* which is by far the more concerned with blood, and so in that respect the more closely related to *Titus*.

The same is, of course, true of the later tragedies, that they are very strikingly different from one another; and it is a truth which is still partially obscured by the bracket 'great tragedies'. When we consider the plays in this way, we do not see a single continuous chain evolving a single notion of tragedy. *King Lear* is, nowadays, probably the best-known of Shakespeare's tragedies, or at least the most highly regarded; *Titus Andronicus* is still the least known; yet they have more in common with each other probably than either has with any other of Shakespeare's plays. The same is true of *Richard III* and *Macbeth*. There are points of likeness between *Romeo and Juliet* and *Othello*, and even *Antony and Cleopatra*, but although all three can be said to be concerned with love it is surely most remarkable how different they are from each other. These parallels are tenuous enough, but they may serve to suggest that, for Shakespeare, tragedy was never one thing, and that he may have deliberately explored the range of very different kinds of play that end aptly in death, sometimes rehandling in later years themes which he had tackled very early in his career. For the themes of a play, and the kinds of people and event with which it deals, are its core and centre of interest; they may be properly fulfilled in a tragic conclusion without that conclusion being the *raison d'être* of their existence. The ending of a good play is always in some sense felt to be inevitable; but the inevitability of the end of *Lear*, the continuous movement towards an exhausted death which the play has, is a very different thing from the inevitability of *Hamlet*'s end which seems rather to be brought about by accident in the last few minutes of the play. *Hamlet*, of course, has not been neglected, and it has often been considered by itself. It seemed, however, wrong to stop short of it, and possibly right to approach it afresh with a frame of reference (earlier rather than later plays) slightly different from usual. Much of what I had said about earlier plays seemed to be relevant to aspects of this one that are sometimes regarded as problematic; but it would have been inconsistent merely to have added an appendix on these, and my discussion of *Hamlet* has much the same proportions as my essays on its predecessors. If it is rather longer than them, that is largely because the play is longer and more complex. And if further explanation is needed for its presence here, it should no doubt be the usual one, that, like so many other people, I wanted to have my say about it.

Until we free them from the monolithic idea of Tragedy, and regard them simply on their own account, we are not likely to understand very well how, in fact, these early plays should be related to the later tragedies. In fact many of the main lines of modern critical investigation, into iterative imagery or control of tone for instance, began with examination of the later plays, and assumed that what was found to be so characteristic of them must have grown to this obscure but brilliant unity from a more random use before. The truth of this matter I believe to be the opposite: these characteristics are actually less 'obvious', though by no means less important, in the later plays than in the earlier; they have become more flexible no doubt, more subsumed in a general unity of tone, but they have their origin in the fertile, if rather too self-conscious, experimentation of Shakespeare's early plays. For he was not then simply experimenting in what could be done with modes of dramatic experience already established on the English stage: with the popular tradition leading back through *Cambises* to the moralities, or the more recent sophistication of Lyly, Greene, Peele, Kyd, and, especially of course, Marlowe; nor simply adding to that his own knowledge (as it would seem to have been) of a more classical tradition in Latin, Italian, and

French plays. He was also, I believe, experimenting in the dramatic possibilities of the already highly sophisticated forms of Elizabethan verse: the use of emblematic imagery – of established relations between an image and its significance which include a precise definition of value, commonly of moral value (the difference, for instance, between describing a woman's lips as 'cherries' or as 'rubies' is an evaluative one); and, equally obtrusive, the observation of a stylistic decorum, of formally distinguishable modes of utterance which are equally distinctions of significance and value. The supreme achievement of Elizabethan poetry was *The Faerie Queene*, of which the first three books were printed in 1590; and it is difficult not to suppose that Shakespeare's conception of poetry sprang from Spenser, though I am certainly not concerned here to demonstrate any specific 'influence'.

The deliberate use on the stage of forms evolved specifically for non-dramatic verse may well sound unpromising. But it is already clear in *The Rape of Lucrece* that for Shakespeare the Spenserian mode has powerfully dramatic possibilities, and *Titus Andronicus* has for some time been recognized as very closely related to *Lucrece*. And it is clear that sharply distinguished modes of utterance can, of themselves, make a dramatic contrast; as, for instance, the contrast between Hamlet's own soliloquies and his speech in the character of Pyrrhus. This, it seems to me, is still an important problem in current performances of the plays. The argument about delivery of Shakespearean speech is too often reduced to a crude contrast between the remoteness of Edwardian metrical declamation and the vitality of contemporary speech. Neither, as a fixed norm, is in the least appropriate. Shakespeare's range is from a prose which must have been very close to Elizabethan speech, through more formal kinds of prose, blank verse that is close to speech or to prose, and so on up to a verse that is very remote indeed from prose or any form of common speech, whether or not it is enclosed in rhyme. In different circumstances he may either set extremes in violent contrast, or carefully modulate one into another (as, for instance, in the opening of *Hamlet*). The problem is a real and difficult one, partly at least because the relationship these varied modes of utterance had to common speech in the 1590s is lost both to actors and audiences today, simply because the language has changed so considerably; nothing now sounds so artificial as the most obvious colloquialisms of Elizabethan English. None the less, the solution must be found *within* the very varied rhythm and rhetorical pitch of Shakespeare's writing, and not by trying to ignore them: if it were more generally understood that that variety is functional in the plays, its recognition as a fully viable dramatic medium might be more confidently established. It is also clear, and had been so to dramatists before Shakespeare took it up (to Marlowe most notably) that emblem imagery, being a visual representation of moral ideas (a 'figuring foorth' as Sidney put it) can be related to the visual composition on the stage: thus Richard II reversing the sacramental order of coronation while Bolingbroke sits silent on the throne is patently an emblem of the blasphemy of usurpation, supported in the verse by references to Pilate, Judas, and the crucifixion.

These are matters of technique which have struck me, in thinking about these plays, as being especially conspicuous, and with that, significant. In them I tend to find illumination both of the basic concerns of the plays, and of the range of variation with which they are presented. About them, therefore, I have a good deal to say; and they recur in different forms in each of the six plays I am considering, so that I do, partly, trace development here; but even here, it is in the end with variety *more* than development that I am struck, and on that I hope my stress has fallen. In other respects I do not have a specific programme of dramatic criticism to propound, any more than I have a theory of tragedy; but there are of course principles that govern the selection of points to discuss or to pass over. Much of this is more or less subconscious, the results of considering these plays now and not at some other moment of history. And it is this of course which both requires and ensures the continued activity of criticism in relation to works so generally known as Shakespeare's. Indeed, particularly with them, for they are beyond dispute the central literary and dramatic fact of our inheritance. I do not imply by

B

this a deliberate searching into the question of how Brecht or Beckett may illuminate Shakespeare: from such an inquiry we might get useful but narrow insights; still less do I propose the impertinent question 'What is Shakespeare's relevance today?' Our finding him interesting, vitally interesting, guarantees the relevance; and the question to be asked is clearly not 'What is the relevance', but 'What is the interest?' The exploration, that is to say, proceeds into the work as it seems to be in itself, for that way alone offers hope of enlarging our prospects, and even of discovering relevances we would not have expected. The quality of the interest revealed must in fact depend on the capacity of the critic, considering Shakespeare, to be of interest to his contemporaries.

It follows, then, that while I am of course trying to point to what seem to me the matters of most central interest in these plays, I do not for a moment make the monstrous claim of treating them comprehensively, and there are times when I specifically mention matters I have not properly discussed, though far more often I simply pass them over in silence. Economy of space, the tediousness of infinite detail, or the mere sense that I have already said more than enough may often account for these omissions. But there can also be another reason. It must be clear from what I have already said, and it is an obvious point of experience anyhow, that there may be matters in which Shakespeare took considerable interest, and very probably (it does not quite follow) his contemporaries did also, which nevertheless do not immediately interest me or – it does not follow at all – us. Some such matters we can simply overlook; others we are obliged to recognize and acknowledge for they do, obviously, affect the form and shape of the play.

In them, at least, our interest may remain primarily historical, which is always and properly a part of our interest in the literature of the past. And there is another form of historical concern of which we ought to be aware, the concerns of recent periods of history which affected their criticism, and thus the traditional reading of Shakespeare which governs our preconceptions. Two major issues of this kind strike me as belonging to the recent past and as still tending to confuse the present: these are, successively, 'character' and 'order'. About character more than enough has been said in the past forty years. It was a concern of Shakespearean criticism for the eighteenth century, and the prime concern of the nineteenth. It would be ludicrous to pretend now that we are not concerned with the individual qualities of people; but individuality and mere difference are quite distinct things. Our interest in character is not the same as the Victorian, and that was not at all the same as Shakespeare's. A distinct idea of 'character' as distinguishing people from each other was in fact a development of the seventeenth century; and that development certainly owed something to Shakespeare, especially to his later works. But at any rate in these earlier plays his concern seems to me more often with the common roots of human experience and behaviour than with what makes one person different from another. I do not mean that the *dramatis personae* are all the same: Titus and Aaron are not at all the same; but the interest developed in their differences is not primarily such as we should recognize as one of character. It is because there can easily be confusion about this that I do sometimes go into it when discussing the plays.

Concern with 'order' is a different and rather more recent thing. As a dominant theme in Shakespearean criticism it dates from between the wars and was at first closely related to the political interests of that time and so most often recognized in the English history plays. The form of the interest was, I think, somewhat determined by the time in which it was developed: for it *tends* (I am conscious of dangerously large generalization) to enunciate a military, or at least a drill squad conception of order; committed, that is to say, to stressing the subordination of individuals to larger entities – the very opposite, in fact, of the earlier concern with character. It is a concern which seems to me characteristic of the 1930s when writers as various as Yeats, Eliot, Huxley, Waugh, Auden all sought to submit their personalities to systematic religions. And when the taste for austere definition found expression in the architecture of the Bauhaus; or when, finally, the symbolic climax of political concern was the clash of Fascism and Communism in the Spanish Civil War.

Shakespeare, certainly, *was* concerned with order, and the Tudor despotism created out of the medieval tradition an image not too far removed from that of more modern doctrines of the supremacy of the State. In the history plays, Shakespeare presents this image very clearly. But two qualifications should be made: first, that his allegiance to it was never a simple matter, and even so early as in *Richard III* it seems to me that radical questionings do arise. Secondly, his intuition of order is profoundly involved with an idea of harmony, of music, which (in *The Merchant of Venice* for instance) is often far removed from any political conceptions. It follows that I think the idea of order ought to be treated with more care, and more scepticism, than it commonly is. And this can be illustrated by noting that the context from which Shakespeare's concept of order is usually quoted, Ulysses' speech in Act I, scene iii, of *Troilus and Cressida*, is one in which it is exposed for radical questioning both as to its cosmic existence, and as to its value.

I should perhaps say a word about my procedure in these essays. A play does not necessarily depend on a strong narrative interest, and it may take very little account of the time sequence of the events it represents. But it is, even more than other literary forms, committed to a sequence of time in its representation. In the theatre events (actions and/or speeches) follow each other, and there is no going back. A play's significance evolves, and becomes known as a completed whole only with its last action which may simply fulfil what has gone before, or may establish a final modification. This, and not mere pedestrianism, is why my discussions tend to proceed by following the sequence of scenes in the text. As far as Acts are concerned, I have used the Folio divisions for convenience of reference, and in several places I have commented where they seem to me to be significant structural units calling for recognition as such. Despite what I have said about the process of a play, the attention I give to the parts is naturally by no means even. Generally speaking I dwell at greater length on the earlier than on the later Acts, for in them are established the bearings from which the play proceeds. The ways in which those bearings are established is often of great significance to what they are, and thus justify considerable detail in the analysis; it would be both tedious and unnecessary to maintain such detail throughout. Once the main lines of development are established I would rather hand the play back to my reader, noticing only substantially fresh developments besides the main bearings of the working-out of the process whose initiation I have detailed. For sometimes dwelling on detail I make no apology, though it may occasionally seem to promote subtleties out of keeping with the solid and sharp definitions which the theatre needs. The fact is that the establishing of such solidity and sharpness, as distinct from amorphous generalities, is itself a subtle achievement, and though in the theatre we may be more aware of the result than of the subtlety with which it is achieved, in reflecting on how it is done we are bound to observe the subtlest means as well as the broadest. It is also not the case, whatever Henry James thought, that the theatre is incapable of subtlety; to that charge, all Shakespeare's work is a sufficient answer. It is, of course, always possible to introduce irrelevant subtlety, and no doubt I am sometimes guilty of this; but in the face of Shakespeare's quality, *over*subtlety, properly speaking, is not possible.

I have not devoted much space to problems of authorship or date. The precise sequence of these plays is not known; we can confidently say that *Titus* and *Richard III* came first, but not which is the earlier of the two. Both were certainly written by 1594, and *Romeo* and *Richard II* followed in the two years after that, though again we cannot be quite certain in what order. The dating of *Julius Caesar* in 1599 is pretty clear, and *Hamlet* within a year or two after is certainly the latest of all. As for authorship, I have regarded them all as entirely by Shakespeare. In any case, the important question is not the unity of the author, but of the play, and each of these seems to me to reveal on examination an elaborate and carefully controlled structure reflected in an equivalent control of language. If anyone but Shakespeare were known to have written them they would properly be regarded as masterpieces; and if the fact that Shakespeare wrote even greater plays later were allowed to depress our estimate of these, it should also rule out of serious consideration almost all the rest of English literature.

Titus Andronicus
[1593?][1]

I

Titus Andronicus has for a long time been the most unpopular of all Shakespeare's plays: but its general execration dates only from the eighteenth century. In Shakespeare's lifetime it was very popular indeed. When it was at least twenty years old, in 1614, Ben Jonson commented ironically on its lasting reputation in the Induction to *Bartholomew Fair*:

> He that will swear *Jeronimo* [i.e. *The Spanish Tragedy*] or *Andronicus* are the best plays yet, shall pass unexcepted at, here, as a man whose judgement shows it is constant, and hath stood still, these five and twenty, or thirty years.[2]

That is only the most considerable of many references attesting both to its popularity, and its old-fangledness. The Restoration could still stomach the play, and Ravenscroft's 'improved' version (1687) held the stage regularly until 1725. But that seems to have been the end; thereafter it had scarcely been seen at all on the professional stage until the well-known revival at Stratford-on-Avon in 1955, produced by Peter Brook, with Laurence Olivier as Titus and Anthony Quayle as Aaron. Otherwise it survived

---

1 Although there is evidence to date *Titus Andronicus* in 1593–4, a general belief that it should be Shakespeare's earliest play has led to arguments for an earlier date. I shall argue that it is close to *Lucrece* in poetic as well as in Ovidian reference, and see no reason why it should not have been also close in time. But see J. C. Maxwell's discussion in *Titus Andronicus*, 1953.

2 ed. E. A. Horsman, 1960, Induction, ll. 107–10.

three nights in London in the mid-nineteenth century, nine at the
Old Vic, as part of a complete cycle of all the plays between
the wars, and a few more recently. The Stratford revival was,
however, a different matter: it coincided with some revival of
interest among scholarly critics, though this hardly impinged on
the newspapers who ascribed its success entirely to magical
powers in actor and producer. This, I think, was quite wrong:
only at one point can I recall the producer departing from the text
noticeably, when he brought the ritual murder on to the stage;
and the significance of this might well have escaped a modern
audience if this had not been done.

Taste and sentiment in the eighteenth century recoiled from a
play which was so obviously 'good' in neither. Ravenscroft indeed, introducing his improvements, described the original as a
'rubbish heap', and said that he had been told that Shakespeare
did not write it. Theobald, in the early eighteenth century,
accepted that gladly: in both, the wish was plainly father to the
thought; and so it continued to be for almost all editors in the
eighteenth and nineteenth centuries. Early in the twentieth J. M.
Robertson, the supreme disintegrator of Shakespeare's texts, did a
very thorough job on *Titus*, and found contributions in it from
almost every known Elizabethan dramatist. This, however,
proved a *reductio ad absurdum*, and since then the field has narrowed
to Peele. Dover Wilson, in the Cambridge New Shakespeare
edition (1948) believed that Shakespeare revised and expanded a
play of Peele's; J. C. Maxwell, in the new Arden Shakespeare
edition (1953), suggested that Peele wrote Act I of a play which
Shakespeare planned. Critical judgement still fathered scholarly
opinion: Dover Wilson thought the play 'rottenly planned', and
so ascribed it to Peele (who couldn't construct); Maxwell thought
it 'admirably planned' and so ascribed it to Shakespeare (who
could). It is plain that we need a truce to all this conjecture:
scholarly statements about authorship have the weight to crush
critical inquiry; and when they are based on nothing but critical
opinion, the circle is vicious indeed. Francis Meres in 1598 listed
the play as Shakespeare's; Heminge and Condell, his literary
executors, printed the play as his in 1623. There is no good

evidence to question this, and I shall proceed on the working assumption that the play is entirely Shakespeare's; indeed, it will become apparent that the play seems to me to have a coherence and unity of structure and writing scarcely possible in casual collaboration.

II

The unpleasantness of the play has become proverbial, and it is certainly obvious. Lavinia (off stage, but only just) is raped, has her tongue cut out and her hands cut off: in this condition she is led on stage by her satisfied violaters, and stands there while her Uncle Marcus descants on what he sees in elaborate rhetoric:

> Why dost not speak to me?
> Alas, a crimson river of warm blood,
> Like to a bubbling fountain stirr'd with wind,
> Doth rise and fall between thy rosed lips,
> Coming and going with thy honey breath.
> But, sure, some Tereus hath deflow'red thee,
> And, lest thou should'st detect him, cut thy tongue.
> Ah, now thou turn'st away thy face for shame,
> And, notwithstanding all this loss of blood,
> As from a conduit with three issuing spouts,
> Yet do thy cheeks look red as Titan's face
> Blushing to be encount'red with a cloud. (II. iv. 21–32)

This is certainly unpleasing, in its baroque development of bloodiness: 'a crimson river of warm blood, like to a bubbling fountain stirr'd with wind' or, 'a conduit with three issuing spouts'. Lavinia is turned to stone in the formalized language of the poetry; and yet the vision is the more horrible for occasional reminders that she *is* alive, for instance '*warm* blood'.

That is only the beginning of the extreme horrors on the stage: Titus, in Act III, cuts off his own hand; Lavinia picks it off the stage with her teeth (because she has no hands), and finally Titus, with 'gentle' Lavinia's help, cooks up the Empress's sons in a pie, and causes her to eat it.

This is bloody stuff indeed; add to it the evident truth that

Marcus' speech quoted above is static, undramatic, not at all the stuff of which stage plays are made; and add to that the oft-repeated statement that the structure of the play at large is chaotic – and all in all there would seem to be a sufficient case against it.

I shall return to the structural point later; it seems best to begin now at the crux of the problem of taste, which I take to be this speech of Marcus', and consider more carefully what it is. First of all, I have called attention to the fact that the verse, however formal, is not frigid. One can point as well to:

> Yet do thy cheeks look red as Titan's face
> Blushing to be encount'red with a cloud.

Here, 'encount'red' means firstly only 'meet', and then 'be covered up'; but it is also the standard word for the accosting of a prostitute, and it is that source which is the root of Lavinia's blush, the shame which (however complete her innocence may seem) drove Lucrece to suicide. Such writing is certainly not the frigid blundering of a hack. Nor is it the work of somebody being funny, as Dover Wilson believed. The basis for his contention about this passage is the close parallel between it and two stanzas of *The Rape of Lucrece* (1594). Lucrece, also raped, has just knifed herself in the presence of her husband and all the nobility of Rome:

> Stone-still, astonish'd with this deadly deed,
> Stood Collatine and all his lordly crew;
> Till Lucrece' father, that beholds her bleed,
> Himself on her self-slaught'red body threw,
> And from the purple fountain Brutus drew
>   The murd'rous knife, and, as it left the place,
>   Her blood, in poor revenge, held it in chase;
>
> And bubbling from her breast, it doth divide
> In two slow rivers, that the crimson blood
> Circles her body in on every side,
> Who like a late-sack'd island vastly stood
> Bare and unpeopled in this fearful flood.
>   Some of her blood still pure and red remain'd,
>   And some look'd black, and that false Tarquin stain'd.
>
>   (1730–43)

Comparing this with Marcus' speech in *Titus*, Dover Wilson remarks that *Lucrece* is a period piece, 'nevertheless the unquestion-
able product of a serious artistic impulse'; whereas he sees the
other as 'a bundle of ill-matched conceits held together by sticky
sentimentalism'. 'Is it not clear,' he asks, 'that the whole speech is
caricature?'[1]

To me it does not seem in the least clear; but there is, certainly,
a difference. The conceits of *Lucrece* can be developed more freely,
because the narrative poem is not restrained by physical facts;
hence the emblematic mingling of red blood and black. This kind
of thing is not so freely available in *Titus*, because here the visual
imagination is restricted to what is seen, on the stage; and on the
stage, all blood is red. I can sympathize, too, with Dover Wilson's
impression of 'sticky sentimentalism': *The Rape of Lucrece* is
written in a carefully (and, as Hazlitt remarked, coldly) detached
tone of narration, in which the personal situation is kept remote
from our feelings; whereas in *Titus* the problems arise, it seems to
me, from trying to fuse *that* tone, with a living situation on the
stage, that of an uncle addressing his deflowered niece. Hence in
Lucrece even the relation of her father to Lucrece is formally represented and does not become absurd; but in *Titus* the pronoun
'thy' has immediate personal force: the speech is punctuated by
personal addresses – 'Why dost not speak to me', 'Shall I speak for
thee', and so on – which disconcertingly wrench the formal development of the poetry back to the personal application.

So that, if we reject Dover Wilson's theory of burlesque (in this
context; I shall return to it in other ways later), but accept his
general criticism of the two passages, the fact of this parallel with
Lucrece (it is only the most considerable of several) remains important, for it is suggestive of what Shakespeare is attempting in
Titus Andronicus. I have remarked on the red and black blood,
which is not a physical fact (however superstitiously believed);
and in *Lucrece* one does not mistake it for fact. It is the clearest
instance in this passage of what is obvious everywhere in the
poem, that the images are emblematic, and that emblems are made

---

1 *Titus Andronicus*, ed. J. Dover Wilson, Cambridge, 1948, Introduction, pp. liii-liv.

out of the figures of the poem. Shakespeare's Lucrece is, in poetry,
the figure Sidney described from a painting:

> . . . such a kinde of difference, as betwixt the meaner sort of
> Painters (who counterfet onely such faces as are sette before
> them) and the more excellent, who having no law but wit,
> bestow that in cullours upon you which is fittest for the eye to
> see: as the constant though lamenting looke of *Lucrecia,* when
> she punished in her selfe an others fault. Wherein he painted not
> *Lucrecia,* whom he never sawe, but painteth the outwarde
> beauty of such a vertue.   (*An Apologie for Poetrie*)

The human figure in Shakespeare's narratives (even in the erotic
Venus and Adonis) is only slightly more definitely a thing of flesh
than the allegorical projections of *The Faerie Queene* (which can
also become, in its own way, highly erotic); and, in fact, both of
Shakespeare's verse narratives get very close to allegory. In such
a poem, the 'narrative' becomes anything but 'story-telling': it
develops an interpretation and commentary through emblematic
elaboration; it calls for the reader's alert judgement, and hence the
detached tone which I commented on.

This is what is happening in *Titus Andronicus.* Marcus' speech is
an attempt to adapt the techniques of *The Rape of Lucrece* to the
stage (and not a wholly successful one). It is, therefore, a comment
on the action, and realizing that, one can see its place in the play
more clearly. The speech occurs at the very end of Act II, an Act
which has developed the major crime against Lavinia (and a
number of other crimes too), and so this stands in the place of a
choric commentary on that crime, establishing its significance to
the play by making an emblem of the mutilated woman. This
function would have been clear, if the speech could have been
labelled 'chorus', and allowed a divine knowledge of all events.
As it is, the speech is not only partially disguised as dramatic
utterance (the disguise is more opaque for readers than audience:
an actor is obliged to speak it out as a set piece); it also has the
complication that knowledge has to be passed off as Marcus'
guesswork. This produces the clumsy sequence of rhetorical
guesses: 'But, sure, some Tereus hath deflow'red thee' – he is,

rather absurdly, right first time; and the guess and the commentary have to be worked into the stage situation of Uncle and Niece, so that the passage I quoted is preluded by 'Why dost not speak to me', and succeeded by 'Shall I speak for thee? shall I say 'tis so'.

The 'sentimentality' of which Dover Wilson complained, derives entirely, I suggest, from the juxtaposition of the narrative manner with these snatches of dialogue, forcing too immediate a personal application on the lines. If one omits them, and reads only the main matter, it is not sentimental at all. In tone, it is precisely like *The Rape of Lucrece*, granted only the diffusion of blank verse; the advantage, for such formal writing, is certainly with the formality of a rhymed stanza.

Recognizing the *kind* of poetry in which this speech is composed has important corollaries for considering the play as a whole. This speech itself lies nearer to non-dramatic poetry than anything else in the play, because its function is to develop a major theme out of the central action; in this it resembles Clarence's dream of human guilt, the slimy bottom of the deep, in *Richard III*. But it is evident, here, that the use of poetry that Shakespeare is experimenting with in *Titus* is similar to that in *Lucrece*, itself derived from Spenser's achievement in *The Faerie Queene*: formal in structure and tone, relying on emblems to fuse imagery and moral idea, and responding to Ciceronian ideas of decorum in matters of style, related to the form of emblem used. Such an adaptation of what is essentially non-dramatic verse to the stage involves difficulties, as we have already seen, and we should expect to see more of this elsewhere. But on the whole we should expect to find variations of style and tone as large and deliberate as those which occur in *The Faerie Queene*, for instance between Book II and Book VI, or, more startlingly, between the two halves of Canto vi of *Mutabilitie*, contrasting the modes of epic and pastoral. In such a context one would expect not only the poetic language to have a deliberate formality, but to find that echoed as well in a formality of dramatic structure.

This I shall try to demonstrate. There is also another legacy of emblematic verse to the stage, the use of the stage picture as a visible emblem. This I have suggested is poor Lavinia's case, dumb and unmoving like the wood-cuts in an emblem book, while Marcus provides the interpretative verses that were usually printed beneath. It is certainly effective, even though here embarrassing; but it is characteristic of the use of the stage in this play. Titus grovelling on the floor while the State of Rome passes by in III. i; or leaving the stage at the end of the same scene, headed for Revenge's cave, bearing the heads of his dead sons while Lavinia carries his own hand in her teeth; or in IV. iii shooting arrows to the stars – all these, and many more, are visual images of a kind that may be more familiar in descriptive verse than actually *seen* on a stage; but they are powerfully effective in establishing emblems of the play's significance. They lead naturally into the emblematic punishment allotted to Aaron:

> Set him breast-deep in earth, and famish him. (V. iii. 179)

and to the strange, and moving conclusion which the discovery of the first quarto[1] restored to the play:

> Her [Tamora's] life was beastly and devoid of pity;
> And being dead, let birds on her take pity.   (199–200)

That final reference to pitiless birds is not fortuitous: it makes the last in a chain of references to Ovid's account of the rape of Philomel, which first becomes explicit in Marcus' speech under discussion:

> But, sure, some Tereus hath deflow'red thee,
> And, lest thou should'st detect him, cut thy tongue.
> (II. iv. 26–7)

Tereus raped his sister-in-law, Philomel, and cut out her tongue to prevent her revealing the truth to his wife, Progne. Philomel, however, sewed the story into a sampler, and then helped Progne to achieve a beastly revenge. In Ovid's tale, they are all metamorphosed into birds. This initial reference is not casual: it is developed later in the speech:

---

1 In 1904. Editions of Shakespeare (such as the Oxford and the Globe) which first appeared before this date reproduce the botched-up ending found in later Quartos and the Folio.

Fair Philomel, why, she but lost her tongue,
And in a tedious sampler sew'd her mind:
But, lovely niece, that mean is cut from thee;
A craftier Tereus, cousin, hast thou met,
And he hath cut those pretty fingers off,
That could have better sew'd than Philomel.
O, had the monster seen those lily hands
Tremble like aspen-leaves upon a lute,
And make the silken strings delight to kiss them,
He would not then have touch'd them for his life. (38–47)

In that, there is nothing funny in the least. Ovid is used again in
IV. i to identify the criminals, and at the denouement Titus explicitly states:

For worse than Philomel you us'd my daughter,
And worse than Progne I will be reveng'd.
                               (V. ii. 194–5)

This thread of reference to Ovid is by no means merely an
exhibition of classical erudition; nor is Ovid used as a source for
the action (apart from a few details): it serves to interpret the
action, and to unify the play's structure. Eugene M. Waith[1] has
shown that Golding, and other Elizabethans, regarded Ovid's tale
as moralizing the deterioration of men and women, under the
stress of revengeful passion, into beasts; and Ovid himself spoke
of 'a plan that was to confound the issues of right and wrong'[2]
when the victim outdoes her violator in bestiality.

This is the central theme of Shakespeare's play; and the
character of Marcus' speech, whatever its limitations, is finally to
be understood in this translation of the events of the second Act
into a thematic statement of the play's formal concern. I have
milked the speech pretty well dry, in order to illustrate this, and to
establish the kind of unity which the play has; a unity which
transcends all questions of divided authorship, and utterly repudiates the idea of a mere burlesque.

---

1 'The Metamorphosis of Violence in *Titus Andronicus*', *Shakespeare Survey*, 10, 1957,
pp. 39–49.
2 *The Metamorphoses of Ovid*, trans. Mary M. Innes, 1955 (*Penguin Classics*).

III

A deliberate choice of tone and control of action is certainly striking at the beginning of the first Act. Saturninus and Bassianus are shown in the full pomp of a Roman election to the Emperorship: a ceremonial scene, centred on the crown itself, held by Marcus Andronicus 'aloft', that is, on the upper stage with the other tribunes, while the candidates and their followers enter one from each of the stage doors to complete the symmetrical composition:

> Princes, that strive by factions and by friends
> Ambitiously for rule and empery,
> Know that the people of Rome, for whom we stand
> A special party, have by common voice,
> In election for the Roman empery,
> Chosen Andronicus, surnamed Pius
> For many good and great deserts to Rome.
> A nobler man, a braver warrior,
> Lives not this day within the city walls:
> He by the senate is accited home
> From weary wars against the barbarous Goths,
> That with his sons, a terror to our foes,
> Hath yok'd a nation strong, train'd up in arms.
>
> (I. i. 18–30)

The ceremonial staging is echoed in the pomp of utterance. The verse is not distinguished, but its stiffness is a consequence of function, not mere inexperience. Rome has always for Shakespeare the emotive suggestion of political greatness, and also of political curiosity: his interest in a society different from Tudor England is manifest here in the presentation of a fusion of democracy with Imperial power that pre-figures the political interest of *Julius Caesar* or *Coriolanus*.

The pomp of Rome is contrasted with 'weary wars against the barbarous Goths', and this opposition echoes throughout the first Act, finding its sharpest statement towards the end, when Marcus pleads with Titus:

> Thou art a Roman; be not barbarous. (378)

That is the theme: the contrast of the 'Roman' nobility of Man,
and the 'Gothic' barbarity; or in common Elizabethan terms,
between man proper, and man-near-beast: these are the terms
which dominate Act II, and emerge at the end of Act I where
Titus issues his invitation

> To hunt the panther and the hart with me (493)

– two emblematic beasts that shadow Tamora and Lavinia.

But before the play can arrive at even that degree of explicit-
ness, a great deal of exposition is required, and with that Act I
proceeds rapidly. First of all, there is the ceremonial build-up for
Titus' elaborately magnificent entrance to the tomb:

> O sacred receptacle of my joys,
> Sweet cell of virtue and nobility.   (92–3)

So far, the impressive staging, theatrical effectiveness and the
political interest have struck one. Now something else intrudes:
the tomb suggests a morbid aspect to Roman greatness (like
Coriolanus' preoccupation with his wounds); Lucius extends that
feeling:

> Give us the proudest prisoner of the Goths,
> That we may hew his limbs, and on a pile
> *Ad manes fratrum* sacrifice his flesh,
> Before this earthy prison of their bones,
> That so the shadows be not unappeas'd,
> Nor we disturb'd with prodigies on earth. (96–101)

The high style is maintained, reinforced with Latin; but the effect is
strongly coloured by the colloquial 'hew his limbs', a vivid intrusion that is sustained in the contrast between 'his flesh' and 'their
bones'. A latent brutality is strongly felt: this Roman, Titus'
eldest son, is almost barbarous himself. When Tamora has
pleaded eloquently for *her* son, and Titus has refused mercy (with
the splendidly inadequate words 'Patient yourself, madam'), he
claims the death of Alarbus as a ritual murder:

> Religiously they ask a sacrifice.   (124)

C

But religion yields to a cruder revenge as Lucius repeats his phrase:

> Let's hew his limbs till they be clean consum'd. (129)

Tamora exclaims at this 'cruel, irreligious piety', and one of her surviving sons comments:

> Was never Scythia half so barbarous! (131)

and another retorts:

> Oppose not Scythia to ambitious Rome. (132)

Scythia was for the Elizabethans, as for the Romans, the land beyond the fringe of civilization, full of wild beasts. Titus' claim to religious revenge gives cause for a bloody retort, and the tragic irony of this thinly disguised Roman barbarity is stressed on Lucius' re-entry:

> See, lord and father, how we have perform'd
> Our Roman rites: Alarbus' limbs are lopp'd . . .
> (142–3)

Lucius matches his previous 'hew'd' with the equally brutal 'lopp'd': and it is these two words which Marcus brings up again to describe the mutilated Lavinia at the end of Act II:

> Speak, gentle niece, what stern ungentle hands
> Hath lopp'd and hew'd and made thy body bare . . .
> (II. iv. 16–17)

This analysis makes it clear, I hope, that the shifts of tone and diction are deliberate, repeated, and echoed significantly. The root of the tragedy revealed here is not simply the meeting of Roman and Barbarian, but the emergence of barbarity in the Romans themselves, of the beast in (the noblest) Man. Further, though the Goths will turn out to be barbarous indeed, they are at this point able to score a dignified retort; and thus to hint one of the play's strongest developments, when the villainous Aaron blazes out in Act IV with more humanity than either his Roman or Gothic superiors.

This first hint of the tragic pattern must be registered, for there

are other shifts of tone to follow, and another (more obvious)
tragic blunder to be established. Titus is offered the Empery, and
declines it; but he accepts the role of arbitrator between Saturninus and Bassianus. So far, both their utterances have been
colourlessly dignified; now, as Titus proceeds to blind acceptance
of primogeniture (the political question had obvious relevance to
the problems of Elizabeth's successor), an effective dramatic irony
is developed in the violent and stupid interruptions from Saturninus, contrasting with Bassianus' moderation:

> SATURNINUS: Andronicus, would thou were shipp'd to hell,
> Rather than rob me of the people's hearts!
> LUCIUS: Proud Saturnine, interrupter of the good
> That noble-minded Titus means to thee!
> TITUS: Content thee, prince; I will restore to thee
> The people's hearts, and wean them from
> themselves.
> BASSIANUS: Andronicus, I do not flatter thee,
> But honour thee, and will do till I die:
> My faction if thou strengthen with thy friends,
> I will most thankful be; and thanks to men
> Of noble minds is honourable meed.
>
> (206–16)

Titus persists in appointing the boor Saturninus to a post for
which he is so patently unfit, and the tragic consequences of this
blunder immediately unfold. Saturninus offers to marry Lavinia, a
gesture which Titus accepts. But the next irony emerges in
Saturninus' evident lechery for Tamora:

> A goodly lady, trust me, of the hue
> That I would choose, were I to choose anew.
>
> (261–2)

Capell marked this '*Aside*'; but the couplet marks it as a formal
compliment, containing the pressure of concealed feeling. The
trap springs at once: Bassianus claims Lavinia as his betrothed and
carries her off with the support of Titus' family; one of his sons,
Mutius, covers their exit, and the formal tone of the scene is
violently changed:

TITUS: What, villain boy,
           Barr'st me my way in Rome?   (290–1)

The brutality already apparent in the play is now revealed in Titus
himself: the barbarity within the Roman has come out, and that
theme is now associated with the obvious blunder of electing
Saturninus.

How much of a blunder that is, is rapidly revealed. Saturninus
immediately determines to marry Tamora, and rejects Titus in-
sultingly; the relations of the principal characters are now established. Titus begins to recognize his situation and yields to
Marcus' entreaties to bury Mutius honourably ('Thou art a
Roman; be not barbarous'). The formal utterance yields to another
striking change of tone:

ALL: No man shed tears for noble Mutius;
           He lives in fame that died in virtue's cause.
MARCUS: My lord, to step out of these dreary dumps,
           How comes it that the subtle Queen of Goths
           Is of a sudden thus advanc'd in Rome?
TITUS: I know not, Marcus, but I know it is:
           Whether by device or no, the heavens can tell.
           Is she not then beholding to the man
           That brought her for this high good turn so far?
                                                  (389–97)

Marcus' 'dreary dumps' are suddenly colloquial, the tone of a
private conversation. Titus is reduced from pomp and circum-
stance to rejection and despair, and the bare recognition is impressively uttered: 'I know not, Marcus, but I know it is.' From
that knowledge he builds up a pathetic suggestion of hope which
anticipates his coming madness. At this point the Folio text adds a
line (which may have originated in an actor – Burbage?) stressing
the unhinged optimism:

           Yes, and will nobly him remunerate.   (398)

Even here, this is absurdly unlikely, and is immediately rendered
impossible by further revelations of Saturninus and Tamora.

Saturninus lapses continually from the high imperial tone to mere boorishness:

> So, Bassianus, you have play'd your prize:
> God give you joy, sir, of your gallant bride.
>
> (399–400)

Bassianus remains patient, and so does Titus; so Tamora has to intervene to restore the imperial voice, explaining the principles of political discretion in a long aside to her husband (442–55): 'Dissemble all your griefs and discontents', 'I'll find a day to massacre them all'. Saturninus is persuaded, and imitates her tone to end the act in gracious acceptance of Titus' invitation 'To hunt the panther and the hart with me'.

The roles and relationships of all the principal characters have now been established, with the exception of Aaron who remains on stage to explain himself in soliloquy. And simultaneously the play's central theme, the dignity of man opposed to vengeful bestiality, has been clearly defined. No doubt Act I is crowded and involved (it has taken some time to analyse); but it is neither confused nor slip-shod. On the contrary, it is remarkable for deliberate control; perhaps *too* deliberate: each 'discovery' (in Aristotle's sense) comes pat upon its anticipation (e.g. the revelation of Saturninus' boorishness at the moment when Titus decides to elect him). And the structural control is reflected in the language, in the shifts of tone, as well as in the implanting of ideas essential to the subsequent development. The weakness of this Act, then, is in over-elaboration, excessive self-consciousness. The discoveries are brilliant, but there are too many of them. It is also true that the stress on brutality tends to overlay the more subtle development I have tried to reveal, but this is not necessarily a criticism. Only two murders are committed, but the tale of Titus' innumerable sons extends this violence over the whole Act, and the obsessive effect is endorsed by the stress on ritual murder, 'our Roman rites'. In 1590 blood feud was by no means uncommon; and in this respect the Roman play had a reference to Elizabethan England which is no longer part of our society. Violence, however, is another matter.

Act I ends with the general direction '*Exeunt*'. The Folio then begins the second Act with 'Flourish. Enter Aaron alone.' It is obvious, as Maxwell says, that the flourish belongs to the Emperor's exit, and not to the entry of a slave. The error results from splitting up the direction in the Quarto which has no Act divisions: 'Exeunt. sound trumpets, manet *Moore*.' This must indicate continuous stage performance, whereas the Folio's Acts need have no relevance whatever to the theatre. But in this case, the trumpets and the general clearance of the stage do seem to bring an Act to its close, and it seems to me that the play is worked out on a more or less classical basis of five Acts. There is no interval, but Aaron's soliloquy has clearly the function (among others) of choric comment:

> Now climbeth Tamora Olympus' top,
> Safe out of fortune's shot, and sits aloft,
> Secure of thunder's crack or lightning flash,
> Advanc'd above pale envy's threat'ning reach.
>
> (II. i. 1–4)

The tone is a new one: its vaunting hyperbole immediately suggests Marlowe, and this heroic pitch is sustained in the simile of the sun which

> Gallops the zodiac in his glistering coach.   (7)

The self-address to which Aaron proceeds is also like Marlowe, as well as Richard of Gloucester in *3 Henry VI* or *Richard III*:

> Then, Aaron, arm thy heart, and fit thy thoughts,
> To mount aloft with thy imperial mistress.   (12–13)

And more like Marlowe still is the revelation of Aaron's sexual relations with Tamora, who is

> faster bound to Aaron's charming eyes
> Than is Prometheus tied to Caucasus.   (16–17)

The heroic tone of Tamburlaine is clearly echoed here, and it establishes the theme of Ambition; Tamora is, like Marlowe's

hero, 'above pale envy', free to soar unchecked because a monarch
is above the law. Further, Aaron aspires to freedom, like the Jew
of Malta, by placing himself outside the moral law:

> Away with slavish weeds and servile thoughts!
> I will be bright, and shine in pearl and gold. . .
>
> (18–19)

Aaron's exultant speech adds a new theme to the tragic foundations of the play that I have already noticed – the ethos of
Marlowe's heroes,[1] of contempt for human littleness, centred here
on Tamora's fortunes, and her relations with Aaron:

> To wait, said I? to wanton with this queen,
> This goddess, this Semiramis, this nymph,
> This siren, that will charm Rome's Saturnine,
> And see his shipwrack and his commonweal's.
>
> (21–4)

As *The Comedy of Errors* multiplied its comic situations far beyond
Plautus, so did *Titus Andronicus* multiply its tragic themes.

Aaron's speech is about lust, but in splendidly imaginative
terms. The pitch lowers abruptly on the entry of Tamora's sons,
Chiron and Demetrius, wrangling over their 'love' for Lavinia.
Aaron's rebuke deflates them:

> This petty brabble will undo us all   (62)

and later:

> Why, then, it seems some certain snatch or so
> Would serve your turns.   (95–6)

The splendours of Marlowan ambition are dramatically translated
into merely bestial lust in the radical change of tone.

V

So far, developing straight out of Aaron's soliloquy, the scene has
been unlocalized. J. C. Maxwell in the new Arden edition

---

1 I discussed this relationship in 'Marlowe as Provocative Agent in Shakespeare's
Early Plays', *Shakespeare Survey*, 14, 1961; see especially pp. 35–7.

abolished editorial scene headings, and the effective use of the Elizabethan stage became clear. The old Arden edition headed the scenes of Act II as follows:

i: Rome: Before the Palace.
ii: A Forest.
iii: A lonely part of the Forest.
iv: Another part of the Forest.

It would be ludicrous, even with a revolving stage, to attempt three distinct forest scenes; and in fact the effectiveness of this sequence very much depends on the use of an entirely unlocalized stage: a formal shift from 'Rome' to 'Forest' would destroy the unity of the Act. The real transition is indicated in the end of Act I:

> To-morrow, and it please your majesty
> To hunt the panther and the hart with me,
> With horn and hound we'll give your grace bonjour.
>
> (I. i. 492–4)

The play is shifting from Rome to a pastoral setting. The initial encounter between Aaron and Tamora's sons has no specific 'place', and when locality does become significant, it is very clearly indicated:

> My lords, a solemn hunting is in hand;
> There will the lovely Roman ladies troop:
> The forest walks are wide and spacious,
> And many unfrequented plots there are
> Fitted by kind for rape and villainy:
> Single you thither then this dainty doe,
> And strike her home by force, if not by words.
>
> (II. i. 112–18)

The significant change of setting is made even clearer in

> The emperor's court is like the house of Fame,
> The palace full of tongues, of eyes and ears:
> The woods are ruthless, dreadful, deaf, and dull.
>
> (126–8)

Where the locality is definitely given, it is done with the force of an image, seen emblematically, like the settings in *The Faerie Queene*: the forest is 'Fitted by kind for rape and villainy' and the 'solemn hunting' may become a chase for Lavinia, the doe (as Titus' reference to hart and panther had already suggested). Such a direct apprehension of nature in moral terms is familiar as the mode of Elizabethan non-dramatic writing: it depends on visual imagination, but not on too literal a seeing of particular landscapes. It might seem ill-fitted to the stage, but only if a now old-fashioned theatre with literal-minded scene painting is involved. An unlocalized stage can employ this tradition with great effect: in the theatre visual imagination is stronger than in narrative poetry, but no less effective as emblem. But if painted backcloths are used, or implied in the stage directions, or the play is read as if it were a modern novel, all this becomes merely absurd.

How absurd becomes clear as the Act develops. Titus gives the scene the pastoral charm of a hunt:

> The hunt is up, the morn is bright and grey,
> The fields are fragrant and the woods are green.
> Uncouple here and let us make a bay,
> And wake the emperor and his lovely bride,
> And rouse the prince, and ring a hunter's peal,
> That all the court may echo with the noise.
>
> (II. ii. 1–6)

This proposes a different view from Aaron's, and Tamora follows with an even more interestingly divergent account:

> My lovely Aaron, wherefore look'st thou sad
> When everything doth make a gleeful boast?
> The birds chant melody on every bush,
> The snake lies rolled in the cheerful sun,
> The green leaves quiver with the cooling wind,
> And make a chequer'd shadow on the ground;
> Under their sweet shade, Aaron, let us sit. . .
>
> (II. iii. 10–16)
> We may, each wreathed in the other's arms,
> Our pastimes done, possess a golden slumber,

> While hounds and horns and sweet melodious birds
> Be unto us as is a nurse's song
> Of lullaby to bring her babe asleep.   (25–9)

Dover Wilson (pp. xi–xii) saw this as 'the finest and tenderest passage of any length in the play', but wondered by what strange freak it was placed on the lips of Tamora the tiger. In this, I think, he was mistaking the point, as well as overlooking the nature of the 'pastimes' which Tamora envisages before the brilliantly paradoxical image of post-coital innocence closes her idyll. The nurse image, as well as other lines here, are echoed from *Venus and Adonis*, where the same setting is used as an emblem of lust. Aaron contradicts the vision abruptly:

> Madam, though Venus govern your desires,
> Saturn is dominator over mine.   (30–1)

He goes on to re-interpret the emblems:

> What signifies my deadly-standing eye,
> My silence and my cloudy melancholy,
> My fleece of woolly hair that now uncurls
> Even as an adder when she doth unroll
> To do some fatal execution?
> No, madam, these are no venereal signs:
> Vengeance is in my heart, death in my hand,
> Blood and revenge are hammering in my head.
>
>   (32–9)

The lamb reveals itself as an adder biting, whereas for Tamora the snake rolled in the cheerful sun transposed into the sleeping babe: the emblems are not of love, but of lust and revenge, and Aaron goes on to develop the Philomel theme.

Act II might be aptly called 'variations on a pastoral theme'. Bassianus and Lavinia, with incautious irony, refer to Tamora as Diana (a rather different huntress), and conclude:

> let her joy her raven-coloured love;
> This valley fits the purpose passing well.   (83–4)

And the climax of this movement is reached in Tamora's revised version of the prospect:

Have I not reason, think you, to look pale?
These two have tic'd me hither to this place:
A barren detested vale you see it is;
The trees, though summer, yet forlorn and lean,
O'ercome with moss and baleful mistletoe:
Here never shines the sun: here nothing breeds,
Unless the nightly owl or fatal raven:
And when they show'd me this abhorred pit,
They told me, here, at dead time of the night,
A thousand fiends, a thousand hissing snakes,
Ten thousand swelling toads, as many urchins,
Would make such fearful and confused cries,
As any mortal body hearing it
Should straight fall mad, or else die suddenly.

(91–104)

This was still the same 'scene' ('a lonely part of the forest') as
Tamora's earlier erotic vision. But it is not a scene at all: it is a
descant on 'nature' accompanying and interpreting, in the poetry,
the dramatic action; Nature that is at once the paradise garden and
a barren detested vale, as Man is at once noble and bestial.

When the stylistic contrast of Acts I and II is understood in
this way, one can no longer suppose it to derive from a change of
authorship. Its rhetorical sophistication tends to make of the
action a formalized spectacle; but the action itself is sufficiently
dramatic to preclude this becoming dull.

VI

As in Act I, effective use is made of surprise. The 'gentle' Lavinia
enters with her husband and taunts Tamora for her lust:

'Tis thought you have a goodly gift in horning,
And to be doubted that your Moor and you
Are singled forth to try experiments. (II. iii. 67–9)

The vulgarity of tone is at once cheap, stupid, and dangerous. It
is as unexpected as Lucius-the-Roman's barbarity in Act I. And it
is as convincing: it would be sentimental indeed to look for a nice
little heroine in this play. Lavinia, here, has the beastliness of con-

scious virtue, and her vindictiveness anticipates the later action. She is to be dumb and helpless, and careless *readers* may therefore forget her presence in later Acts; but she is, like Ovid's Philomel, to be *active* in the vile revenge. Even in Lavinia, the paradise garden is also a barren detested vale.

The balance of response in this scene is very nicely controlled: Tamora the taunted reacts by destroying Bassianus; Lavinia the taunter is reduced to desperate pleading, not for her life, but for death. What she gets is deflowering, lopping, and hewing. Tamora's nature is fully revealed:

No grace? no womanhood? Ah, beastly creature.   (182)

Lavinia is brought back to the stage at the end of the Act to the accompaniment of the brutal jokes of satisfied lust:

CHIRON: Go home, call for sweet water, wash thy hands.
DEMETRIUS: She hath no tongue to call, nor hands to wash;
              And so let's leave her to her silent walks.
CHIRON: And 'twere my cause, I should go hang myself.
DEMETRIUS: If thou hadst hands to help thee knit the cord.
                                                 (II. iv. 6–10)

The beastliness of man tends towards a sense of horrid farce.

That is the main development of Act II; it is alternated with the less interesting fate of Titus' sons in Aaron's trap. The twin disasters for Titus' family are achieved simultaneously (Lavinia off-stage, while Quintus and Martius are on stage), and it is left to Marcus to conclude the Act with the choric speech I discussed at the beginning of this chapter. Like Aaron, at the beginning of the Act, Marcus is left alone to deliver a speech in a radically different style, whose choric function is clear, both to comment on the action of the last Act and to anticipate the next. But there are two differences. Firstly, Aaron's speech was more fully concerned with anticipation than retrospection, whereas Marcus's largely looks back over achieved events; so that whereas Aaron's serves to link Act II on to Act I and make their development continuous, Marcus's serves rather to finish off Act II, and make a break in the action. He brings a whole part of the play to an end. Secondly, whereas Aaron really was alone, Marcus is not: Lavinia's presence is, as I pointed out, in some ways an embarrassment. But Marcus' reference to her is as emblematic as Tamora's to the forest glade: the mutilated body represents the revelation of the Act, of human beastliness, and the sheer destructiveness beneath the shining cheerfulness of nature.

Thus so far the play is very closely integrated: Act I establishes the dramatic situation with a thematic stress on Roman nobility versus barbarity; Act II develops that into the criminal action, with its thematic stress on the duality of nature, paradise, and hell. Hell-mouth itself is compared to the pit which Titus' sons fall into:

> . . . this fell devouring receptacle,
> As hateful as Cocytus' misty mouth.
>
> (II. iii. 235–6)

The unity of each Act is ensured in a manner, like Spenser's, of dominant verse tones: Act I is heroic, whereas Act II is pastoral; complexity of idea being indicated by abrupt changes of tone within the general norm. The two Acts are to be taken together as the first part of the play, and so must not be allowed to fall apart because of their stylistic contrast. Hence the use of Aaron's speech to link them, and Marcus' final summary. But such extreme use of decorum does always (as in *The Faerie Queene*) tend to disunity; and there is some awkwardness in adapting the poetic technique to dramatic utterance. This first part of the play is superbly organized, and surprisingly complex in its development; it is also very deliberate in every move of action and speech, and perhaps the deliberation is sometimes too apparent.

VII

The next movement is indicated at the end of Marcus' speech:

> Do not draw back, for we will mourn with thee:
> O, could our mourning ease thy misery!
>
> (II. iv. 56–7)

The dominant tone of Act III is elegiac: Titus on his knees before
the State of Rome, ignored by them, and left half crazy with self-
pity; and then Titus seeing Lavinia and descanting in a manner
not unlike Richard II's laments; finally all the Andronici together
as a chorus of despair. Elegy may seem to promise something even
less dramatic than pastoral and in a sense this is true: Act III
achieves a kind of stasis at the centre of the play, a pivot in the
structure between the two main sequences of action, the beastly
crimes before and the even more bestial revenge after. Thus its
central action is hardly active at all, though superbly dramatic: the
extreme change of mood when Titus caps the climax of Marcus'
lament with a burst of laughter:

> MARCUS: Ah, now no more will I control thy griefs.
>   Rent off thy silver hair, thy other hand
>   Gnawing with thy teeth; and be this dismal sight
>   The closing up of our most wretched eyes.
>   Now is a time to storm; why art thou still?
> TITUS: Ha, ha, ha!
> MARCUS: Why dost thou laugh? it fits not with this hour.
> TITUS: Why, I have not another tear to shed.
>
>   (III. i. 259–66)

That tears lie near to laughter is a cliché frequently experienced
in the strained gaiety of funerals; it is a double experience as
appropriate in its way to dramatic elegy as the duality of nature is
to pastoral. This moment is the dramatic centre of the Act, indeed
of the whole play, the point at which suffering drives Titus from
passive grief to insane activity. It is anticipated, indeed provoked,
by the grotesquely comic presentation of the lurid action in which
Aaron persuades Titus to lose his hand. The offer of his sons' lives
draws from Titus a barely sane recollection of the emblems of
Act II:

> O gracious emperor! O gentle Aaron!
> Did ever raven sing so like a lark
> That gives sweet tidings of the sun's uprise?
> With all my heart I'll send the emperor my hand.
>
>   (157–60)

The grotesque edge, here, develops into open farce as the Andronici fall to wrangling over whose hand should be cut off, allowing Aaron to point the absurdity:

> Nay, come, agree whose hand shall go along,
> For fear they die before their pardon come. (174–5)

For Dover Wilson this is an instance of Shakespeare making fun of the melodramatic genre, and certainly our laughter sets us outside the action, seeing its mere absurdity. But this detached perception is not equivalent to repudiation: Chaucer's Troylus, safely removed to an outer sphere, sees the suffering actions of men in which he has been engaged, as matter for laughter. The suffering remains real enough; and so here, though the action which provokes the laughter and the suffering is heightened and improbable the responses of Marcus, Lucius, and Titus are probable enough. Almost more probable than Aaron's; and we are brought to see that we share our laughter with his exultant wickedness:

> O, how this villainy
> Doth fat me with the very thoughts of it!
> Let fools do good, and fair men call for grace,
> Aaron will have his soul black like his face. (202–5)

Aaron, I said, was placed outside the restrictive laws of life by his association with the empress, and still more by his conscious commitment to villainy; the enjoying laughter of this villainy is a further emancipation from the inhibitions of squeamish feelings. In this recognition Shakespeare is drawing on the experience of his predecessors, of Marlowe (in particular *The Jew of Malta*) and of popular drama leading back through the Vice of morality plays into the grotesque comedy of the miracle cycles[1]; and the figure of Aaron is very closely related to Shakespeare's own Richard of Gloucester. With this range of popular tradition behind him, it is not surprising that Aaron stands out from the play with a vitality no other figure can rival.

---

1 See A. P. Rossiter: *English Drama from Early Times to the Elizabethans*, 1950, pp. 157–60.

The laughter here then is partly destructive of the solemnity (and thus far a relief), but partly the most horrible, and most profoundly real thing in the scene: for it is the laughter of witnesses to a mad house, or the Dance of Death: the point at which human civilization and dignity crumbles into farce, and becomes simply monstrous. It is thus a prelude to the more intense laughter of Titus sixty lines later, which marks his transition from object of sympathy to total alienation. Alienation of mind, because he is seen to be insane; alienation of sympathy, because he puts himself beyond the range of our approval. This is, effectively, his metamorphosis from man into beast, his noble nature transformed to a barren detested vale, where he searches for satisfaction:

Then which way shall I find Revenge's cave? (270)

It follows that, contrary to the expectations of tragedy which Shakespeare himself established in later plays, the end here is a spectacle of human degeneracy by which we may be appalled, but from which our sympathy is largely excluded. Here again I think Shakespeare is borrowing from an earlier dramatist's experience: Hieronimo, in Kyd's *Spanish Tragedy*, makes a similar declaration of intent to revenge in his famous 'Vindicta mihi' speech in Act III, scene xiii; and like Titus's, Hieronimo's conscious repudiation of orthodox approval alienates him from the audience's full sympathy.[1] It is true that Hieronimo is madder before this scene than after it; but his restored coherence of mind is devoted to a violent action more deeply insane than his simple confusion before. Sympathy was not a usual expectation of early Tudor tragedy, whether academic like *Gorboduc* or popular like *Cambises*. The difference is that Shakespeare, taking a hint from Kyd, makes this alienation a central idea in his play: that men may be driven by suffering, not to the ennoblement of Victorian belief, but to become sub-human revengers. Man metamorphosed into beast suffers too the collapse of human dignity into the farce of insanity that I have discussed.

---

1 For a rather different view, see Philip Edwards' discussion in his Introduction, pp. lviii–lx, to *The Spanish Tragedy*, 1959.

This, then, is the dramatic achievement of Act III: its climax is in the superb dramatic irony of Titus' laughter when Marcus appeals for tears. Irony in the relations of the brothers becomes inevitable, for Marcus remains a touchstone of sanity and normal judgement, and must henceforth be excluded from Titus' plans. Retrospectively, we can perceive the ironic misunderstanding of Lavinia's kissing Titus after l. 249: Marcus sees it as a gesture of comfort, but when Titus breaks his silence we discover it to have been a kiss of complicity, like Philomel inducing Progne to revenge. 'Gentle' Lavinia is the agent of Titus' metamorphosis, and she is his bestial accomplice in Revenge. The roots of bestiality we have seen in them both in the first two Acts; that is what emerges now as they leave the stage bearing the emblems of their purpose, the heads of Titus' sons, his hand between Lavinia's teeth. The scene ends with Lucius alone, announcing a more conventional and respectable revenge: he will collect an army to attack Rome, destroy Saturnine and Tamora, and so restore the order which we have seen so profoundly disturbed.

VIII

Lucius' soliloquy would seem a natural conclusion to the Act, with the same kind of choric function I found in Aaron's and Marcus's before. It is an exceptionally short Act, but its function of pivot between the two main sections of the play makes that intelligible. In the Folio, however, it was slightly enlarged by the addition of III. ii which had not appeared in the Quartos. Dover Wilson and J. C. Maxwell[1] believed it to have been part of the original play, accidentally omitted from the first Quarto; this may be so, but a number of points incline me to believe with earlier editors that it was in fact a later addition. In the carefully worked structure that I have been analysing it appears to have no specific function, other than exploration of the psychology of manic obsession, which the play does not seem generally to be much concerned with. More suspiciously, it employs exactly the same

---

[1] In the Cambridge and Arden editions respectively.

D

characters as IV. i; this not only looks like a rather clumsy way of forming an addition, but also is very unlike Shakespeare's normal method of varying his successive scenes; further, it is very unusual, Acts or no Acts, for Shakespeare (or any other Elizabethan) to construct a play so that continuous playing would be impossible. Here, III. ii ends with Titus, Marcus, Lavinia, and the boy Lucius leaving the stage to read a book, and IV. i opens with exactly the same characters entering. We have seen that Acts I and II were designed for continuous playing, and there is no other necessary break in the play; an interval after Act III would not be unreasonable, but it seems unlikely that it would have been made necessary.

On the other hand, to regard it as an addition is not to diminish its quality. It is well known as one of the best written scenes in the play; but it is also rather different from anything else. It develops, brilliantly, Titus' insanity: he is hysterically angry when Marcus offers to kill a fly, but when Marcus suggests that the fly reminds him of Aaron, Titus bursts out:

> O, O, O!
> Then pardon me for reprehending thee,
> For thou hast done a charitable deed.
> Give me thy knife, I will insult on him . . .
>
> (III. ii. 68–71)

The obsessive mind is superbly revealed, but this type of direct psychological observation is unique in the play. It reminds me of the additions to *The Spanish Tragedy*, especially the 'Painter scene', which shows similar interest in Hieronimo's insanity, again unlike Kyd's original scenes. That was probably written about 1600 and it seems to me likely that the 'Fly scene' in *Titus* dates from the same period, witnessing a change of interest in the old plays, when Shakespeare undertook a new version of the old *Hamlet*.

This is not to say that Shakespeare did not write the scene; only that it probably was not part of his original play. It may well be that it is not correctly placed in the Folio; placed after III. i it seems to reopen the lamentations as if the decisive turn to action had not been made: it might more plausibly be substituted for the

end of IV. i,[1] Titus turning to a feast after discovering the identity
of Lavinia's assailants.[2]

IX

Act IV, scene i, opens with a vivid reminder that Lavinia is linked
with Titus in obsession: the boy Lucius runs frightened away
from her intent pursuit. Her purpose is to reveal her fate, and its
perpetrators, which she achieves by indicating Ovid's *Metamorphosis* in the library. Thus the Philomel theme is recapitulated,
and brings from Titus another recollection of the emblems of
Act II:

> Lavinia, wert thou thus surpris'd, sweet girl,
> Ravish'd and wrong'd, as Philomela was,
> Forc'd in the ruthless, vast, and gloomy woods?
> See, see!
> Ay, such a place there is, where we did hunt, –
> O, had we never, never hunted there, –
> Pattern'd by that the poet here describes,
> By nature made for murthers and for rapes.
>
> (IV. i. 51–8)

Titus develops the beast emblems with hints of learning from
Ovid what to do. His hysterical manner becomes a cloak for his
intention, deceiving Marcus by an irony similar to the misunderstanding of Lavinia's kiss in III. i: the boy offers to stab Chiron
and Demetrius, and Titus replies:

> No, boy, not so: I'll teach thee another course.
> Lavinia, come. Marcus, look to my house. (119–20)

Titus means the cannibal banquet; but Marcus, thus excluded from
the party, misunderstands:

> But yet so just that he will not revenge.
> Revenge the heavens for old Andronicus!
>
> (128–9)

---

1 If my memory is correct, Peter Brook placed it there at Stratford in 1955.
2 For a fuller discussion of this problem, see my article: 'The Intrusive Fly: A Note
on Act III, scene ii, of *Titus Andronicus*', *Filološki Pregled*, I–II, 1964, pp. 99–102.

Like Hieronimo, Titus *ought* to leave vengeance to the heavens:
that would be 'just'. But it is important here to feel Titus' withdrawal from justice, what Ovid called 'a plan that was to confound
completely the issues of right and wrong'. We follow his revenge
with an interest that is quite separate from moral approval; the
more clearly so because it is contrasted with Lucius' independent
plan for justified rebellion against the tyrant.[1]

The hint of justice from the heavens is, however, fulfilled in
crazy form in IV. iii when Titus delivers his threatening letters by
shooting them on arrows over the walls, so that they drop on
Saturninus from the skies. The scene is at once farcical and tragic
as an expression of human impotence; but out of its mad gesture
grows the reputation for irritating but harmless lunacy which
enables Titus to trap Tamora in Act V. In the meantime, Titus'
deterioration into bestiality in one sense, or his mad assumption of
divinity in another, are both counterpointed by the brilliant development of Aaron in IV. ii. While the play seems to be breaking
into fantasies of angels and devils, Aaron remains uncompro-
misingly human: not, of course, 'good', or in any way senti-
mentalized, but with a solid reality lacking in the other figures:

> Pray to the devils; the gods have given us over.
>
> (IV. ii. 48)

His speech has a far more flexible speech rhythm which at once
distinguishes him:

> Ay, just; a verse in Horace; right, you have it.
> [*Aside.*] Now, what a thing it is to be an ass!
>
> (24-5)

And this quality emerges in action when the empress's black baby
is revealed. Aaron displays a magnificent contempt for the lives
and worries of any one else:

CHIRON: I blush to think upon this ignomy.
AARON: Why, there's the privilege your beauty bears.
Fie, treacherous hue, that will betray with blushing

---

1 The justification of rebellion against an obvious tyrant is not questioned either here
or in *Richard III*; *Richard II* is a very different matter.

> The close enacts and counsels of thy heart!
> Here's a young lad fram'd of another leer:
> Look how the black slave smiles upon the father,
> As who should say, 'Old lad, I am thine own.'
>   (115-21)

Paternal pride issues uninhibitedly into action to preserve the baby's life:

> Two may keep counsel when the third's away:
> Go to the empress; tell her this I said.   [*He kills her*.
> 'Wheak, wheak!'
> So cries a pig prepared to the spit.   (144-7)

Titus was metamorphosed into a beast; Aaron has no metamorphosis, he develops as a beast straight from the earth to which he will finally be condemned. But in this instinctual assurance of behaviour there is a power which seems impressively sane when contrasted with the derisive fantasy of what follows, Titus shooting arrows at the stars, loaded with evasive challenges to the emperor. With such superbly speakable words, it is not surprising that Aaron tends to dominate the end of the play. In the implied disturbance of values in this Act, this reversal of expectation is brilliantly effective; but as Titus is so firmly distanced from our sympathy, the human vitality of Aaron becomes a force that threatens the ultimate balance of the play. He is not simply part of the spectacle, and cannot be contained within the emblematic pattern of his punishment:

> Set him breast-deep in earth, and famish him;
> There let him stand and rave and cry for food.
> If any one relieves or pities him,
> For the offence he dies.   (V. iii. 179-82)

Aaron repudiates the pity:

> I am no baby, I, that with base prayers
> I should repent the evils I have done . . .
> If one good deed in all my life I did,
> I do repent it from my very soul.   (185-90)

The quality of Aaron is something discovered in human experience, and learnt from Marlowe; he has a force that seriously disturbs the spectacle of tragedy in the play, of a kind that is more widely explored in *Richard III*. But scarcely more deeply, even there; a quality of humanity that cannot be absorbed in emblematic schemata has ultimately to be realized in the tragic hero himself before the tragic balance can be fully assured. In the tragic heroes from Richard II onwards, including Brutus, one can see an emergent wickedness that involves a wider range of our response.

x

Act IV ends with Saturninus and Tamora discussing Lucius' revolt, and the danger to Rome. This is sanity of another (and duller) kind than Aaron's. It leads to a clear stage, but not to a decisive Act ending. Act V opens with Lucius himself, and the revenge action is rapidly developed. There seem here to be signs of planning by Acts, IV being concerned with the plans for revenge, V with their execution. But it is by no means so clear as earlier divisions, and the play should surely be continuous here, so that Lucius and his Goths enter immediately after Saturninus and Tamora have left. My conclusion is that the play was planned in five Acts, with the last two probably continuous, as the first two certainly were; thus there are really two main movements to the play, with Act III standing between them as a pivot, with the central metamorphosis. Before that, Titus was noble man, Aaron a beast; after Act III Titus deteriorates into mad beast, while Aaron displays a kind of nobility: the issues of right and wrong are indeed confused.

But in Act V orthodox order has, of course, to be restored. That Lucius now represents (his brutality in Act I is long since forgotten), contrasted in scene i with the exultant villainy of Aaron. Scene ii carries the farcical development to its farthest limits, with Tamora disguised as the allegorical figure of Revenge in a mad game of pretence whose effectiveness is barely related to plausibility. But once Titus has killed Tamora's sons, his whirling

words return to sanity in unfolding his plans and returning once
again to Philomel and Progne:

> For worse than Philomel you us'd my daughter,
> And worse than Progne I will be reveng'd.
>
> (V. ii. 194–5)

The final holocaust, in V. iii, like that of *The Spanish Tragedy*,
brings the farce back towards the reality of tragedy rather in the
manner of a masque, or a modern ballet. Kyd actually uses a
dance, where in *Titus* it is more like grotesque comedy, with Titus
dressed as a cook; in both it is the shock of death itself that re-
stores a sense of reality to the stylized enactment of unleashed
destructiveness. In these early plays the heaping of bodies on the
stage is achieved in harmony with the formal development before;
it is only later, in such dramatists as Webster, that the attempt to
combine the universal destruction with realistic plausibility
threatens tragedy with laughter that is out of place. Shakespeare
only avoids this danger in his more naturalistic tragedies, *Julius
Caesar* and *Hamlet*, by the intensely moving speeches that succeed
the deaths.

Once the holocaust is achieved, Marcus takes charge and re-
stores the political Order of Act I; Lucius is declared emperor,
and passes judgement on Aaron whose unrepentance stands alone
to question the complacence of the conventional ending. But
Lucius' last speech is unexpected, leaving the play with a final
stress on the images of nature that have dominated it:

> As for that ravenous tiger, Tamora,
> No funeral rite, nor man in mourning weed,
> No mournful bell shall ring her burial;
> But throw her forth to beasts and birds to prey.
> Her life was beastly and devoid of pity;
> And being dead, let birds on her take pity.
>
> (V. iii. 195–200)

Faced with a damaged page in his copy, the printer of the second
Quarto filled in with a conventional couplet on political order:

> Then afterwards to order well the state,
> That like events may ne'er it ruinate.

That sentiment (in less excruciating verse) is what one would expect; it calls attention to the strange quality of what Shakespeare actually wrote, creating a final emblem of the beast in man which can destroy humanity and substitute barbarity.

XI

The transformation of Tamora from dramatic character into emblem for the play is once again like Spenser's usage in *The Faerie Queene*, most conspicuously at the end of the fabliau of Malbecco and Hellenore, when Malbecco in jealous fury throws himself over the cliff:

> Yet can he neuer dye, but dying liues,
>   And doth himselfe with sorrow new sustaine,
>   That death and life attonce vnto him giues,
>   And painefull pleasure turnes to pleasing paine.
>   There dwels he euer, miserable swaine,
>   Hatefull both to him selfe, and euery wight;
>   Where he through priuy griefe, and horrour vaine,
>   Is woxen so deform'd, that he has quight
> Forgot he was a man, and *Gealosie* is hight.
>
> (Variorum, ed. F. M. Padelford, Baltimore, 1934,
Book III, Canto X, Stanza lx)

I have emphasized this poetic stylization in *Titus*, for it is the unifying element in the play. Its ambitious multiplicity of tragic patterns – the political order destroyed and restored; the destructive sequence of revenges; the Marlowan aspirations of Aaron – all these are concentrated on the central interpretative theme of tragedy as the emergence of the beast in man. The alienation of sympathy inherent in this idea requires of the audience the same judicial detachment obvious in *The Rape of Lucrece*; but at the same time, to grasp the significance of this, we must be exposed to the shock of physical horror. The matching of these opposed reactions is not overall successful, just as it is not locally successful in Marcus' speech at the end of Act II. But though it may have been the violence which gave *Titus* its initial popularity, it is not a simple matter of serving a popular taste: the play is governed by an imaginative intelligence which later found the blinding of Gloucester necessary to the tragedy of Lear.

The experimental use of non-dramatic poetic technique has some brilliant successes: the emblematic view of nature in Act II is given greatly enhanced vividness by the sense of characters really seeing what they describe; and Titus shooting arrows at the stars, which in a narrative poem would be a literal incident, develops on the stage the complex sense of being at once a real protest against tragic life, a mad gesture, and a farcical impotence. On the other hand, reference to *The Faerie Queene* implies a limitation on the actor's use of human personality which only Aaron escapes. But this should not prevent our responding to innumerable points of individual experience: Titus' shock in Act I at Saturninus' rejection of him; Tamora's anger in Act II when Lavinia and Bassianus taunt her, and Lavinia pleading afterwards; the brutal humour of Chiron and Demetrius releasing their victim, Aaron with his black baby, and so on. They are many, and diverse, and they occur in unexpected places turning our attention in strange directions – towards Tamora and Aaron as well as Lavinia and Titus, and sometimes away from the latter in revulsion: and all these forming part of the tragic structure I have analysed.

There is, in fact, a tremendous inventiveness and intelligence active in this often despised play. It is, obviously, experimental in character, and in many ways it does not succeed. But it is characterized by a remarkable linguistic and dramatic vitality, and the reference I made above to *Lear* may serve to indicate how fertile these experiments ultimately proved.

Richard III
[1593?]

I

The theatrical success of the role of Richard himself has tended to obscure the fact that his play presents any important critical problems. It was a very early play, the earliest of those which have consistently held the stage; and if it seemed dull in parts, or inconsistent, or in any way puzzling, that was easily accounted for by Shakespeare's immaturity. The fact that it is a work of outstanding technical virtuosity, in words and stagecraft, has not always been given the stress it needs; still less that the elaborate patterns worked out in it give it an exceptionally firm sense of structural unity.[1] It was treated in the eighteenth century as a tragedy, and compared (unfavourably, of course) with *Macbeth*; in the nineteenth century it was hardly allowed the tragic dignity, but rather regarded as melodrama, a prototype for *The Red Barn*, and fit matter for Lewis Carroll's parody. But the play thus criticized was scarcely the one that Shakespeare wrote: Colley Cibber's version was first acted at Drury Lane in July 1700, and though the proportion of Shakespeare's words gradually increased, Cibber's arrangement of material dominated stage versions until very recently indeed.[2] It concentrated exclusively on Richard himself; omitted scenes in which he did not appear, minimized Margaret's role (which was often cut entirely), and drastically pruned the formalized pattern-

1 This has been fully argued by A. P. Rossiter in *Angel with Horns*, 1961.
2 See Clifford Leech: 'Shakespeare, Cibber, and The Tudor Myth', in *Shakespearian Essays*, ed. A. Thaler and N. Sanders, *Tennessee Studies in Literature*, 1964.

ing of language which is so conspicuous a feature of the play, on the grounds that it was undramatic. This selective procedure is still often followed, most notably in Sir Laurence Olivier's film. And although the critics usually did read Shakespeare's text, their attention was for two centuries as selective as the actors'.

Recent critical history, and even more recent theatrical history, have however offered us a totally different view of the play, stressing the elements which Cibber excised: the tendency to ritual, the formalized staging and language, are held to be devices for binding together and rounding off the epically conceived sequence of moral-history plays about the Wars of the Roses. This attitude is not altogether irreconcilable with Cibber's activities, for it likewise assumes that the play is not viable as an independent unit, but is only intelligible when played in series with its predecessors. The dominant role of Richard can be assimilated if he is seen as the instrument of divine retribution on a guilty society; but the notion that his career has any significance as tragedy is nowadays rarely expressed. The usual attitude seems to be that the play results from a rather uncomfortable fusion of two distinct purposes: a formal conclusion to the series on the one hand, and a lively melodrama about Richard himself on the other.

I am not concerned to deny that the formal aspects of the play develop from 2 and 3 *Henry VI*, nor that it is intended to conclude an impressive sequence. But it does not seem to me to be dependent on that sequence for its own quality, and it does seem to me to have its own most interesting unity. I want to argue here that the play, once deprived of its moral-history, was deprived of any adequate opposition to Richard; so that his stature, which Cibber might seem to have enhanced, was in fact diminished, and the decline from tragedy to melodrama became inevitable. On the other hand, concentration on the moral-history has tended to divert attention from the centrality of Richard's disturbing vitality in the play, and so has tended also to produce an unintelligent and boring play. My assertion is, therefore, that the two aspects of the play require each other, and that the contrast between them is not a technical accident which Shakespeare should have been concerned to minimize, but an important structural device, elaborated

to its maximum effect in the use of contrasting linguistic and
dramatic modes, with a consequence which can properly be called
tragic.

II

Such a contrast is by no means new in this play. As the series of
histories moves towards its conclusion, we become aware of a
mounting weight of ritual on the stage; an echoing series of
scenes in patterned form and patterned speech lead on from 2 and
3 *Henry VI* into the highly formalized structure and writing of
Richard III itself. This mounting tide of ritual is punctuated by
actions of violence – battles, murders, executions; a sequence
which itself becomes by repetition a pattern, a kind of anti-ritual
of chaotic violence, which is inclined towards grotesque comedy
in Richard's famous comment on Hastings:

> Chop off his head – something we will determine.
> (III. i. 193)

Simultaneously, as the actions of men accumulate in destruction,
the lamentations of women mount in chorus from the solo voice of
Margaret in Act I to the assembly of weeping dowagers in Act IV:

> I had an Edward, till a Richard kill'd him;
> I had a husband, till a Richard kill'd him:
> Thou hadst an Edward, till a Richard kill'd him;
> Thou hadst a Richard, till a Richard kill'd him.
> (IV. iv. 40–3)

And so on – as we may easily feel – for far too long. Too long
because, among other reasons, we cannot for the life of us remember who these Edwards were, though we remember well
enough who the Richard is that concludes every line. The theory
runs that seeing *Richard III* in series with the other histories
would give this jingle new significance, for we should then know
all the references. This I do not believe; not simply because in
practice (e.g. at Stratford in 1964) it hardly works out that way,
but because it seems to me that the form of language itself pre-

cludes such precise intelligence. Even if we have studied the cast lists and the genealogical table and carried our knowledge fresh to the performance of this scene, as Margaret speaks we shall forget the detailed identifications: the names roll on in ritualized accumulation until their whole weight is laid on the single focus, Richard:

> From forth the kennel of thy womb hath crept
> A hell-hound that doth hunt us all to death.   (47–8)

The ritual repetition piles up the roll of the accusing dead in *un*-particularized accumulation to convert Richard from his natural state of man into that of a sub-human figure of evil. In this process the identical names fit easily; it is the more singular titles that are awkward to assimilate. We forget the Harrys and the Edwards; but Rivers, Vaughan, and Grey stick out. Shakespeare absorbs them adroitly into the anonymous pattern by an exceptional use of rhyme:

> And the beholders of this frantic play,
> Th' adulterate Hastings, Rivers, Vaughan, Grey . . .
> (68–9)

The jingling rhyme distracts attention from the names and makes even them part of the sing-song litany, the generalized accumulation of death. The intensity of the ritual incantation was first developed from more ordinary blank verse through couplets in Margaret's asides.

This technical device clinches the function of language I have been dwelling on: it is to generalize and to de-humanize the sense of events; not to recapitulate our knowledge of detail, but to transcend the detail in creation of a larger pattern in which individuals lose their independence and identity. Just as the litany of the church overwhelms us with the *number* of evils from which the good Lord should deliver us, rather than calls our attention to their separate identities. One aspect of the rhetoric of the play finds its climax here, not in imitation of Seneca, but in echo of liturgical forms, such as the ancient 'Ubi sunt' theme to which Margaret proceeds:

Where is thy husband now? Where be thy brothers?
Where be thy two sons? Wherein dost thou joy?   (92–3)

And so on.

I have somewhat laboured this rather obvious point, because awareness of it seems to me necessary to what I want to say about the play. It is this aggregation of events into a generalized momentum which seems to me to represent the fundamental sense of 'history' in the play; and it is this development which links it most closely to *Henry VI*. None of Shakespeare's histories, not even 1 *Henry VI*, is a mere chronicle; but *Richard III* is the most remote of them all from mere chronicling. The events are there, but in unfamiliar proportions, so that (for instance) the murder of Clarence is more conspicuous than that of the boy princes. Interpretation is always more prominent than event: Richard's coronation is not shown, so that the stress remains on the blasphemous parody of election by which he reaches the throne. History, the legacy from the earlier plays, becomes an order of chaos, a ritual of destruction that grows in power until it destroys the destroyer, Richard himself. Strictly speaking it is not Margaret and her pupils who destroy Richard, it is Richmond; and Richmond is something which they decidedly are not, an unequivocally 'good' character. But it is quite impossible to see him as Richard's 'mighty opposite' in the dramatic conflict of the play: the force that builds up against Richard till his fall becomes inevitable is not Richmond, but the ritual of history, the swelling chorus of a more-than-human force. Richmond is a *tertium quid*, the inheritor of the new land when the conflicting forces have destroyed each other.

History, therefore, becomes imaginatively felt as an impersonal force rolling on beyond the lives of individual men, who are thereby belittled and cannot achieve the stature of a tragic figure. It is against this weight that Richard's personality is pitted, with impressive wit and force. The conflict in the play becomes therefore almost a matter of conflicting genres, for the historical and the tragic as shown here represent radically contrasting ideas of value – history has no place for tragedy, and in the end we must balance one against the other.

III

The first need is to explore the technical means by which Richard is thus isolated from the ritual sense of the play, in order to define the significance of this isolation. For it is not, I think, simply a matter of his being a different character; nor is our response to him a simple matter. One way of accounting for our fascination with so repulsive a figure is indeed simple enough: it is psychologically fairly obvious that while we can delight in the machinations of a clever dog who cocks a snook at all rectitude, authority, and religion, we can simultaneously be complacently satisfied when he is properly punished in the end. This is a simple and familiar ambivalence; but how Shakespeare establishes this double delight, and what he constructs out of it, call for more precise attention to the play, and particularly to the different kinds of utterance found there.

I have pointed to the generalizing ritual patterns of words in IV. iv; that is the furthest the play goes in formality of speech. In contrast, I quoted also Richard's 'Chop off his head', a shockingly *informal* treatment of an (obviously) serious matter. Opposite as those two utterances are, it is Margaret's which is closer to the play's norm, which is more insistently rhetorical than that of any other; ejaculations of the flexibility of private speech are almost confined to Richard himself. Even with him they are not common, but by virtue of their repeated surprise come to seem characteristic of his personality. Accepting his mother's blessing in II. ii, he continues aside:

> And make me die a good old man!
> That is the butt end of a mother's blessing;
> I marvel that her Grace did leave it out.
>
> (II. ii. 109–11)

It is not a gentlemanly tone, but it adds a dimension to the scene, not only by its caustic wit, but also by momentarily introducing a mundane level far from the rhetorical pitch at which the scene has been proceeding. The effect is the same in III. v when Richard recalls his mother as he plans to rumour her adultery:

> Yet touch this sparingly, as 'twere far off;
> Because, my lord, you know my mother lives.
>
> (III. v. 93–4)

The sentiment is hardly touching, because it is so inevitably ironic: but the possibility of sentiment is glanced at, more sharply than in all the wailing of the queens.

This punctuation of rhetorical formality with sudden penetrations of the mundanely human adds, by itself, a whole critical dimension to the play; and it is something peculiarly associated with Richard himself. He makes the contrast felt in the end of I. i:

> Which done, God take King Edward to his mercy,
> And leave the world for me to bustle in!   (I. i. 151–2)

God's mercy versus the world, formal language versus 'bustle'; and, one may now add, the formal structure of the play versus Richard. That awareness is sustained in I. ii, the *tour de force* of the wooing of Anne, which I shall discuss later. The scene is surprisingly convincing; but it is also a performance. And it must be a very good performance, or it does not work. The words are virtuoso, so must the acting be. The tendency of all Richards that I have seen is to do what Lamb condemned in Cooke's performance: to make the underlying villainy obvious all the time.[1] That is what Olivier did, and the scene lost all power. But the full descriptive notes which survive on Kean's performance make it clear that he did not do this.[2] He made the scene brilliantly persuasive, the charm real, and he triumphed. So that when he was alone on the stage after Anne's departure, and blew the gaff on his performance, the audience felt a sense of shock. A shock, of course, not of total surprise, but of recognition, of what had been always known yet almost forgotten.

Almost forgotten, but never quite: the scene was always rhetorical in an obtrusive if brilliant way. A spectacle of persuasion, not quite persuasion itself, however brilliantly based on

---

1 See *Lamb's Criticism*, ed. E. M. W. Tillyard, 1923, pp. 52–3.
2 See *Oxberry's 1822 Edition of King Richard III, with the Descriptive Notes Recording Edmund Kean's Performance Made by James H. Hackett*, ed. A. S. Donner, 1959.

psychological observation. This is what is made clear in Richard's soliloquy:

> Was ever woman in this humour woo'd?
> Was ever woman in this humour won?
>
> (I. ii. 227–8)

These lines are a parody of the rhetorical performance he has just given, and the point is enforced by the characteristically abrupt switch to direct speech which follows:

> I'll have her; but I will not keep her long. (229)

The abrupt change of utterance makes a sharp critical comment on the whole mode of the scene; in a way, on the whole play. The rhetorical mode in which *Richard III* is so ostentatiously written, and the formal structure which matches it, are not the result of Shakespeare uncritically doing his best in a given theatrical fashion (Senecan or otherwise): the rhetorical mode is known and placed, both for its splendour and its falsity, within the play. The distance which I have noted in general terms between Richard's interjections and the general tone of the play, can here be seen as directly critical exposure. A distinction is felt which is finally made explicit in Margaret's advice on how to curse:

> Think that thy babes were sweeter than they were,
> And he that slew them fouler than he is.
> Bett'ring thy loss makes the bad-causer worse;
> Revolving this will teach thee how to curse.
>
> (IV. iv. 120–3)

The relationship between rhetoric and reality could not be more plainly stated; that the words are put in Margaret's mouth confirms her as the only antagonist comparable to Richard himself. Elsewhere the agent of this critical exposure is, almost always, Richard alone; and this fact as much as any other sets him apart from the other actors and, what is more, sets him in a favourable light to other people's disadvantage. It is not a question of whether he is better or worse than other people, but simply that he is more real.

This sense of him makes everyone else mere actors in a play. It

E

is one aspect of the rhetorical mode that it confines the actors within its limitations, from which only Richard and Margaret stand apart. In a sense this is ironical, because Richard himself is the supreme actor. From the actor's point of view, this is not one role, but many: the ardent wooer, the honest blunt puritan at the court of King Edward, the witty uncle with his nephew York, the devout scholar with his clerical tutors, and so on – it is a long list. It is this protean quality which makes him so theatrically brilliant, provided that the actor, like Kean, gives every role its full value, and does not, like Cooke, attempt the super-subtlety of reducing them all to one.

This condition in Richard's part has a further consequence. In *his* performance, the difference between 'being' and 'acting' is very clear; and it is when he is with others on the stage that he is acting, as (each in their single roles) so are they. Thus, as I said, it is with him alone that a dimension of reality is felt. It follows that his relation to the audience – to us – is essentially different from anyone else's and this is established in his very first speech, in the unusual manner of opening a play with the solo appearance of the leading actor.

Unusual, that is to say, for Shakespeare. Marlowe had opened *The Jew of Malta* and *Dr Faustus* with soliloquies from the heroes; but each of their speeches follows a prologue, so that they are already within the play. Richard's speech is itself a prologue as well as a soliloquy from the hero, though to some extent it shifts from the one into the other; from:

> Now is the winter of our discontent
> Made glorious summer by this sun of York;
>
> (I. i. 1–2)

into:

> But I – that am not shap'd for sportive tricks . . . (14)

This is not, however, soliloquy in the sense of the speaker talking to himself: it is an address to the audience, not so much taking them into his confidence as describing himself. This mode of initial self-description is, of course, taken over here from the old tradition of the morality play. But it is a mistake, I think, to suppose that Shakespeare uses it simply because this is an early play following familiar conventions. He did not do it in any other play, and it is very rare among his contemporaries; nor does he follow it in this play with similar speeches for any other character. In other words, this should be seen as a deliberately bold technique used for specific purposes in establishing the distinctive character of *this* play.

The first effect to note is that it supplies, very economically, a traditional role for Richard from the moralities, that of the Vice: a sardonic humorist, by origin a kind of clown, who attracted to himself the attributes of anti-Christ bent on the mocking destruction of accepted virtues: a singularly welcome figure whenever virtue becomes tedious or oppressive; but one in whom the audience's delight is always coupled with condemnation. This, of course, is Richard's role, as he claims in III. i:

> Thus, like the formal vice, Iniquity,
> I moralize two meanings in one word.
> (III. i. 82–3)

The Vice was commonly the star of a morality play, what the audience most wanted to see. He had, like other kinds of clown, a special relationship with the audience, a kind of sly ironic confidence insinuated between them and the other players; and this is also Richard's. Like most ironists, he secures the audience 'on his side', and yet involves us even further when (again like most ironists) he betrays our trust, and turns out to be way beyond us, leaving us embarrassed as Baudelaire did: 'Vous! hypocrite lecteur: mon semblable! mon frère!' Our condemnation of his evil is involved in recognition of our brotherhood with it.

This relationship between Richard and the audience is given a special emphasis because, as I said, he alone is given the morality address, he alone has any direct contact with the audience at all. It follows that, in the technical construction of the play, Richard is set apart from the other actors, not just in character, nor just in mode of speech, but also in theatrical mode. Everyone else is distanced from the audience, is in a sense taking part in a play within a play of which Richard is the presenter. We are forced to know them as actors acting just as, when Richard joins them, he is (more obviously) an actor acting; and the consequence of this alienation (the Brechtian term is appropriate) is a carefully imposed limitation on the sympathy or approval that other figures can have. The audience can never become closely involved with Anne or Elizabeth, Hastings or Buckingham. It is this critical detachment which is enforced in the unusually sustained rhetorical language of the play. The result is that the whole play is set in a perspective which I have compared to that of a play within a play: we have, continually revived by Richard's rare but very telling asides, a double view of what is happening: we view the patterns of formal development for themselves, and we know them for an artefact, a coldly formal order *imposed* on the warmer but less orderly matter of human life. If this alienation were less marked, we could more easily detach ourselves from Richard in sympathy for his victims.

IV

Richard is isolated, I said, from the patterned speech, and therefore from the patterned structure of the play. That *Richard III* is the most patterned of all Shakespeare's plays is a fact so obvious that it scarcely seems to need demonstration; but the precise form and function of its patterns are more difficult to describe. The last Act employs visual symmetry as a final emblem of what has been already established as the play's structure. Richard and Richmond pitch their tents on opposite sides of the stage, and the ghosts of Richard's victims address first one and then the other in ritualized succession, damning Richard and blessing Richmond. The image would seem too simple and crude if it were not for two things: first, that this *does* emerge as an emblem of the play, whose symmetry has become increasingly plain in the previous scenes; and second, that this scene itself is not quite so simple as my description of it.

From IV. iv onwards the sense of symmetry is peculiarly strong. The cursing queens in IV. iv echo Margaret's previous

appearance in I. iii. Richard's subsequent wooing of the princess
Elizabeth through her mother is a startling reprise of his wooing
of Anne in I. ii, and his comment when it is done:

> Relenting fool, and shallow, changing woman
>
> (IV. iv. 431)

is only a more direct statement of his comment on Anne:

> Was ever woman in this humour woo'd?
> Was ever woman in this humour won? (I. ii. 227–8)

But there is the difference that in the later scene his success is
equivocal (it is implied, though not stated, that the ex-queen was
double-crossing him). In addition, Buckingham's brief appearance
before his execution (V. i) completes the sequence of cameos of
Richard's victims which punctuate the action from Clarence's
murder in I. iv, through Rivers, Vaughan, and Grey in III. iii and
Hastings in III. iv, and Tyrrel's account of the murdered princes
in IV. iii. To this sequence Richard's own doom (conscience-
troubled, like the others) is an obvious climax. Further, the
ghosts in V. iii are represented as a simultaneous dream for
Richard and Richmond, and thus enact an echo of the dream
which Clarence, so impressively, describes in I. iv. The whole of
the end of the play is referred to the opening of I. i: Richard's

> Now is the winter of our discontent
> Made glorious summer by this sun of York
>
> (I. i. 1–2)

is recalled by Richmond's stress on the setting sun:

> The weary sun hath made a golden set,
> And by the bright tract of his fiery car
> Gives token of a goodly day to-morrow.
>
> (V. iii. 19–21)

and by Richard's recognition that for him it will never rise again:

> Tell the clock there. Give me a calendar.
> Who saw the sun to-day?
> RATCLIFF: Not I, my lord.

RICHARD: Then he disdains to shine; for by the book
                He should have brav'd the east an hour ago.
                A black day will it be to somebody.

                                                        (276–80)

In this way the symmetrical staging of tents, sleeping rivals, and echoing ghosts achieves a consummation of the symmetry of the whole play, and is not the rather crude device it might seem out of context.

But symmetry does not only establish likeness and pattern: it can also be the basis for establishing subtle difference. This is the case with the two wooing scenes: Richard repeats, in the second, very much the same performance as he gave in the first, including the justification of his admitted murders as inspired by love. But whereas with Anne that argument is made to prevail when seemingly pressed to the point of self-destruction, with Elizabeth it is subtly transposed through the claim of political necessity into the mutual safety of the disputants:

                In her consists my happiness and thine;
                Without her, follows to myself and thee,
                Herself, the land, and many a Christian soul,
                Death, desolation, ruin, and decay . . .
                Plead what I will be, not what I have been;
                Not my deserts, but what I will deserve.
                Urge the necessity and state of times,
                And be not peevish-fond in great designs.
Q. ELIZABETH: Shall I be tempted of the devil thus?

                                                        (IV. iv. 406–18)

It seems that she will, but whether to give her daughter to Richard or to Richmond is an ambiguity that makes of her a 'changing woman' in a sense beyond Richard's understanding.

It is also true that the tents and ghosts in V. iii, besides enacting the play's structural symmetry, are not quite so simple in themselves as I suggested. The ghosts make of the opposed kings figures very nearly identified with Angel and Devil. Richard has, of course, often been seen as devil in the play, but ironically he is never less so than here: Anne has revealed earlier that he has a

conscience which makes his nights hideous with bad dreams; that
is how he interprets this one:

> My conscience hath a thousand several tongues,
> And every tongue brings in a several tale,
> And every tale condemns me for a villain.
>
> (V. iii. 193–5)

Villain he is, but not devil. And recognizing that Richard is not a
devil lends support to the unease we are apt to feel about the
angelic figure of Richmond. This does not arise simply from
human distrust of angel-figures (though that often is felt about
Richmond, and not without reason), but rather because the supernatural forces recognized in the play have never before been
unequivocally divine. The ghosts' addresses to Richmond are the
first sign of blessing we have had: before this, appeals to God
have always been curses, a dubious form of prayer. Anne in I. ii
cursed Richard:

> O, cursed be the hand that made these holes!
> Cursed the heart that had the heart to do it!
> Cursed the blood that let this blood from hence!
>
> (I. ii. 14–16)

but she proceeded to curse his offspring:

> If ever he have child, abortive be it,
> Prodigious, and untimely brought to light . . . (21–2)

and so finally his wife:

> If ever he have wife, let her be made
> More miserable by the death of him
> Than I am by my young lord and thee! (26–8)

The irony, that she is cursing herself, for she will soon become his
wife, she fully expounds shortly before her death (IV. i. 66–87).
    Such cursing is itself apt to be as evil as what it attacks. This is
made plain with Margaret, whose own wickedness is constantly
remembered as rival to Richard's:

> The curse my noble father laid on thee,
> When thou didst crown his warlike brows with paper

And with thy scorns drew'st rivers from his eyes,
And then to dry them gav'st the Duke a clout
Steep'd in the faultless blood of pretty Rutland –
His curses then from bitterness of soul
Denounc'd against thee are all fall'n upon thee;
And God, not we, hath plagu'd thy bloody deed.
Q. ELIZABETH: So just is God to right the innocent.
(I. iii. 173–81)

But, of course, nobody in this play (until Richmond appears) is
innocent; and it *is* 'we' who plague the bloody deeds. Whether it
is *also* God is not, in the circumstances, clear. Clarence ('poor,
simple soul') assumes that it is not:

If God will be avenged for the deed,
O, know you yet He doth it publicly.
Take not the quarrel from His pow'rful arm;
He needs no indirect or lawless course
To cut off those that have offended Him.
(I. iv. 212–16)

The ultimate irony may be that it is God as well as Richard and his
hired murderers who plague Clarence and the rest; but, if so, He
certainly does use indirect and lawless courses.

The fact is that Margaret, whose tremendous curses predict the
main pattern of events in the play, is a semi-supernatural figure,
but not a divine one. She is a sufficiently indirect course; Richard
is still more totally lawless.

v

It is, then, easy to see how the end of the play brings an overall
symmetry into active presentation on the stage; and in this end
remembers its beginning, both in the echoes of the sun image, and
in the ghosts who recall not only Clarence's dream, but in their
own persons the sequence of crimes envisaged in Act I and
carried out through the length of the play. The actual end is a solo

speech from Richmond, as the beginning was a soliloquy from Richard. The difference is again as significant as the likeness: Richmond's speech is addressed to a stage audience, and only to us through them; Richard speaks directly to us, the theatre audience.

It is then, strikingly, Richard *solus* with which the play begins. The solitary figure is presented to us (or, more accurately, presents himself) before the sense of symmetrical patterning is established. But even this point is not quite so simple, for Richard's speech divides, as I said, into two distinct parts, of which it is the second (ll. 14–41) which presents himself:

> But I – that am not shap'd for sportive tricks . . .
>
> (I. i. 14)

This does indeed set out the solitariness of the figure, and virtually makes an emblem of himself:

> Why, I, in this weak piping time of peace,
> Have no delight to pass away the time,
> Unless to spy my shadow in the sun
> And descant on mine own deformity.   (24–7)

Richard's shadow in the sun is both the image of his deformed body as he can see it on the ground (since he has no looking-glass) *and* an emblem of the shadow he casts on the 'sun of York'. At that point, the second part of the speech is firmly linked to the first, the general prologue for the play:

> Now is the winter of our discontent
> Made glorious summer by this sun of York;
> And all the clouds that lour'd upon our house
> In the deep bosom of the ocean buried.   (1–4)

There may be a slight hint of Richard's distinctive utterance here in the use of a pun to enforce the figurative sense of 'sun' as King Edward, the son of the dead York: but on the whole it is choric language, and thus Richard's speech combines in one unit the formal indications of a prologue with the self-description of the

Vice; contains, in fact, within forty lines, the structural basis on which the play is developed.

The rest of the first scene elaborates the 'villainy' on which Richard is 'determined': quibbling with prophecies, dreams and such about the letter G, taken for his brother George (instead of himself, Gloucester). Thus Clarence is easily led towards *his* dream of drowning, the first of Richard's victims, no longer the 'clouds that lour'd upon our house' but now the members of that house itself being 'In the deep bosom of the ocean buried'. The performance establishes at once both that Richard *is* a performer, and the exuberance with which he performs:

> Nought to do with Mistress Shore! I tell thee, fellow,
> He that doth naught with her, excepting one,
> Were best to do it secretly alone.
> BRAKENBURY: What one, my lord?
> GLOUCESTER: Her husband, knave! Wouldst thou betray me?   (98–102)

That is a public joke, in the sense that it is accessible to Richard's audience on the stage. Much of his wit is more obscurely ironic, available only to us, his other audience; for instance:

> We are not safe, Clarence; we are not safe.   (70)

More elaborately, he makes his farewell an ironic comment on his plot:

> Well, your imprisonment shall not be long;
> I will deliver or else lie for you.   (114–15)

The form of 'lie' which Richard will tell we already know; the play on 'deliver' is glossed by one of Clarence's murderers in I. iv:

> Why, so he doth, when he delivers you
> From this earth's thraldom to the joys of heaven.
>   (I. iv. 245–6)

The irony here is being used as a structural device, to establish anticipation and echo between related scenes. It reaches one stage further in Richard's few lines alone after Clarence's exit:

Simple, plain Clarence, I do love thee so
That I will shortly send thy soul to heaven,
If heaven will take the present at our hands.

(I. i. 118–20)

They are, of course, strange hands for heaven to accept presents
from; that it should do so is not (despite Clarence's belief) a new
idea (it is suggested in the Homilies), but Richard makes us aware
of it in its most unpleasant aspect. The ultimate irony in these
lines, however, is no longer even accessible to Richard, but only
to the audience: that is, that heaven does in fact accept Clarence at
Richard's hands, but not as a present: the price is to be paid in
Act V.

Irony as a structural device is even more apparent in the opening of the next scene, still involved in the relations between the
human and the supernatural, but no longer confined to Richard's
utterance, and now totally divorced from the element of joking.
Anne, standing by Henry VI's corpse, utters the curse I quoted
before, which is to fall upon her, as we already realize from
Richard's declared intention to marry her at the end of I. i. The
structural form of the play is beginning to open wider, from its
beginning in Richard's solo appearance. The first pattern established was of a very close relationship between Richard's plan for
Clarence and its enactment immediately afterwards; this, like the
symmetry of V. iii, might seem crude if one did not grasp that its
obviousness was very much of a piece with the rhetorical language
– an equivalence between language and structure that is the
opposite of an art to hide art. As in *Titus Andronicus* the function
of this art is not to deceive the audience that the events presented
are actually happening, but on the contrary to display them with
critical detachment, rather than become involved.

At the end of I. i Richard's soliloquy, matching the opening
speech of the scene, seems to conclude a sequence; at the same
time he enlarges the pattern by two further anticipations – of his
marriage to Anne, and of the death of Edward. The second extends the structural pattern through to II. ii; the first leads more
immediately into the wooing scene, but this in itself is a far more
elaborate fulfilment of the anticipation than was the trapping of

Clarence. I have already remarked that the ironic structure is now functioning beyond Richard himself, in the curse Ann unwittingly lays upon herself. The scene is conducted in extremely formal rhetorical patterns, matched by the rhetorical implications of the stage situation – Anne and Richard addressing each other from either side of Henry VI's corpse:

> O, gentlemen, see, see! Dead Henry's wounds
> Open their congeal'd mouths and bleed afresh.
> Blush, blush, thou lump of foul deformity,
> For 'tis thy presence that exhales this blood
> From cold and empty veins where no blood dwells;
> Thy deeds inhuman and unnatural
> Provokes this deluge most unnatural.   (I. ii. 55–61)

The pattern of matching lines established in the repetition of key words emerges with 'blood' in ll. 58–9, and is more strongly marked in 'unnatural' in the next two lines. It is extended into the dialogue between the two, in units that vary in length:

	Lady, you know no rules of charity,
	Which renders good for bad, blessings for curses.
ANNE:	Villain, thou knowest nor law of God nor man:
	No beast so fierce but knows some touch of pity.
GLOUCESTER:	But I know none, and therefore am no beast.
ANNE:	O wonderful, when devils tell the truth!
GLOUCESTER:	More wonderful when angels are so angry.
	Vouchsafe, divine perfection of a woman,
	Of these supposed crimes to give me leave
	By circumstance but to acquit myself.
ANNE:	Vouchsafe, diffus'd infection of a man,
	Of these known evils but to give me leave
	By circumstance to accuse thy cursed self.
	(68–80)

The whole dialogue is a triumph of rhetoric, superbly varied in pace as the balancing lines are longer or shorter: this passage opens with paired lines, goes on to singles, and ends with triplets. Elsewhere the range extends from half lines to the longer solo speeches – Anne's just before this passage, and Richard's later leading to the climax when he produces his sword, which she refuses, followed by a rapid sequence of short lines to his opposite offer of the ring – which she accepts. But to call the scene a triumph of rhetoric is not to deny its psychological plausibility: the grieving widow trapped into a reversal of feeling is a familiar and well-attested theme (the widow of Ephesus, for example), and Richard's performance is built on that. He proceeds first to intensify her hatred, leading towards the emotional climax in which he can bring off the peripeteia with sword and ring. All this, of course, takes place in front of the corpse of a man Richard had murdered: the association is very clearly made between the attitudes and lust for power of the Machiavel and a perverted sexuality, violently cruel and destructive. Once he has achieved domination he loses all interest in Anne – we hear later of his nightmares that keep her awake in bed, but never of his making love to her. His 'angry mood' is satisfied by murder and decapitation. The collocation suggests the novels of de Sade, but there is one obvious difference: in Shakespeare this observed relationship is presented as part of the highly patterned structure, distanced by the formal patterning of language; whereas in Sade's work the clinical observation and ironic presentation seem to be an imperfect mask for obsession with the evil he analyses. There is certainly no trace of such obsession in the writing of this play: its sexual current, prominent in this scene and equally so later in the wooing of Queen Elizabeth for her daughter, is elsewhere frequently felt, but very much as an undercurrent. In this scene Richard recalls Margaret's sadistic treatment of his brother and his father, an incident from *Henry VI* which is several times remembered in the play; and it is Richard likewise who comments on Edward's sensuality and sums up the time in his image of grim-visag'd war, who, now smoothed out,

> capers nimbly in a lady's chamber
> To the lascivious pleasing of a lute.

                                         (I. i. 12–13)

Puritanism is elsewhere on Richard's tongue: he harps on Mistress Shore, and on Hastings' dealings with her as well as Edward's, and he insinuates a closeness between her and Elizabeth, the 'lusty widow' Edward had married.

But although the sexuality of the Machiavel, and its sadistic and puritanical reflexes, are continually felt in the play, this never constitutes a main theme here (as it does in *Titus Andronicus*). It is, even in the scene with Anne, kept firmly at a distance, by the verbal patterning I discussed. Richard brings this scene to an end with a soliloquy which begins by analysing the strangeness of his triumph, and leads into a recapitulation of his opening speech:

> And will she yet abase her eyes on me . . .
> On me, whose all not equals Edward's moiety?
> On me, that halts and am misshapen thus? . . .
> I'll be at charges for a looking-glass,
> And entertain a score or two of tailors
> To study fashions to adorn my body . . .
> Shine out, fair sun, till I have bought a glass,
> That I may see my shadow as I pass.   (I ii. 246–63)

Here, in these echoes of the play's opening, a stronger sense of formal closure to a sequence is felt; his soliloquy after I. i had seemed to mark such a closure, but this replaces it as a far more conclusive cadence. The larger pattern opens out of the smaller, and this progressive enlarging of the pattern continues very markedly in I. iii. Three actions have now been postulated, none of them complete: the murder of Clarence, the wooing of Anne, and the death of Edward. Before the first of these is accomplished, scene iii takes the forms of patterned language established in scene ii and carries them considerably further, until Margaret has predicted the largest pattern of all, almost (but not quite) the entire action of the play.

VI

The scene opens with the quarrelling of the court factions, which comes to a head between Richard and Queen Elizabeth; at this point Margaret enters, more like a ghost than a character in the

play. I have already commented that she alone shares with
Richard the distinction of being detached from the other characters: but her detachment is of a different kind. Whereas Richard,
however often he is called a devil, is in fact made more humanly
real to us, Margaret's affiliation is more supernatural. Her presence is a fiction of Shakespeare's for historically she died in exile
before most of the events of this play took place. Richard refers to
the historical facts:

> Wert thou not banished on pain of death?
> Q. MARGARET: I was; but I do find more pain in banishment
> Than death can yield me here by my abode.
> (I. iii. 166–8)

Which does not explain why she has not been put to death. Her
ambiguous existence is clearly deliberate; in both her appearances,
here and in IV. iv, she enters silently and unobserved and only
later comes forward into the dialogue. She is, thus, not quite a
ghost, but nearly so, a semi-supernatural figure, but by no means
a divine one. Her status is as equivocal as that of many later
Shakespearean prophets, the soothsayers in the Roman plays, or
the ghost in *Hamlet*, or even the witches in *Macbeth*. That is going
too far, but Richard is not altogether wide of the mark when he
calls her 'foul wrinkled witch'. Prophecy in Shakespeare is always
fulfilled (that is its dramatic function) but prophets are not always
(or indeed often) as saintly as Henry VI, and he was a holy fool.
But it was he who foretold Richmond's ultimate victory (as
Richard tells us later): a divine agent is outside Margaret's vision.
Her role is not in fact mere prophecy: it is cursing. The ironic
function of the curse – fulfilled, but evil – has already been demonstrated with Anne: it is Richard who opens the sequence here.
With Margaret's entry his quarrel with Elizabeth moves back into
past events, on which the unseen ex-queen provides a ritualizing
commentary:

> Out, devil! I do remember them too well:
> Thou kill'dst my husband Henry in the Tower,
> And Edward, my poor son, at Tewksbury. (117–19)

When she comes forward, Richard recalls the central atrocity she committed against his brother and father which I quoted earlier (173–80). It is evident that York's curse on that occasion has been fulfilled – but, as I said before, it is far less evident that the fulfilment was God's doing. Margaret is ironical about it:

> Did York's dread curse prevail so much with heaven
> That Henry's death, my lovely Edward's death,
> Their kingdom's loss, my woeful banishment,
> Should all but answer for that peevish brat?
> Can curses pierce the clouds and enter heaven?
> Why then, give way, dull clouds, to my quick curses!
>
> (190–5)

She has already re-established the formal patterning of speech which Richard used with Anne in I. ii; she carries it a stage further as her curse unfolds, into the antiphonal manner whose ultimate development I analysed in IV. iv:

> Though not by war, by surfeit die your king,
> As ours by murder, to make him a king!
> Edward thy son, that now is Prince of Wales,
> For Edward our son, that was Prince of Wales,
> Die in his youth by like untimely violence!
> Thyself a queen, for me that was a queen,
> Outlive thy glory, like my wretched self . . .
> Long die thy happy days before thy death;
> And, after many length'ned hours of grief,
> Die neither mother, wife, not England's Queen!
> Rivers and Dorset, you were standers by,
> And so wast thou, Lord Hastings, when my son
> Was stabb'd with bloody daggers. God, I pray him,
> That none of you may live his natural age,
> But by some unlook'd accident cut off!   (196–213)

Richard himself, of course, will accomplish all these things; she turns next on him:

> RICHARD: Have done thy charm, thou hateful wither'd hag.
> MARGARET: And leave out thee? Stay, dog, for thou shalt
>   hear me.

If heaven have any grievous plague in store
Exceeding those that I can wish upon thee,
O, let them keep it till thy sins be ripe,
And then hurl down their indignation
On thee, the troubler of the poor world's peace!
The worm of conscience still be-gnaw thy
    soul . . .
No sleep close up that deadly eye of thine,
Unless it be while some tormenting dream
Affrights thee with a hell of ugly devils!

                                        (214–26)

The list of disasters given before provides much of the plot of the
play; these lines give us its structural shape. Richard's sins are
'ripe' when he ascends the throne, and it is at that point that he is
left in final isolation, as Buckingham fails him; and after his last
apparent triumph, the wooing of Elizabeth, the messengers of
disaster come rushing in. The 'worm of conscience' gnaws him
before the end, and he never sleeps without hideous dreams.

Margaret goes on to pick up Richard's original pun on 'sun':

And turns the sun to shade – alas! alas!
Witness my son, now in the shade of death . . .

                                        (267–8)

The ironies of cursing are given final stress by Buckingham:

                            curses never pass
        The lips of those that breathe them in the air.
MARGARET: I will not think but they ascend the sky
        And there awake God's gentle-sleeping peace.
        O Buckingham, take heed of yonder dog!

                                        (286–90)

Meaning, of course, Richard, not God. The irony certainly rebounds on Buckingham, for her prediction is fulfilled; but in a
sense it finally rebounds on her too – for the only act that is unquestionably God's is the sending of Richmond, and that Margaret
could not foretell although (significantly) her late sainted husband
could. Irony, on such a scale as this, becomes a motif as important
as the sense of symmetry it attacks. Its structural function is to

F

relate the symmetric pattern to the challenging figure of Richard, and by doing so to question both.

VII

The opening out of successively larger patterns one from within another is now firmly established, and the working out of Margaret's curse provides the main pattern of events, the structural shape, and one major theme, that of guilt and conscience. The other figures in this scene have not the independence which I defined as Richard's, nor the half-supernatural power of Margaret. But they are all guilty. The world in which Richard operates is guilt-ridden. This opening of the largest pattern is immediately followed by the completion of the earliest one with the murder of Clarence. Hence his famous speech about his dream is a comment on guilt and conscience:

> O Lord, methought what pain it was to drown,
> What dreadful noise of waters in my ears,
> What sights of ugly death within my eyes!
> Methoughts I saw a thousand fearful wrecks,
> A thousand men that fishes gnaw'd upon,
> Wedges of gold, great anchors, heaps of pearl,
> Inestimable stones, unvalued jewels,
> All scatt'red in the bottom of the sea;
> Some lay in dead men's skulls, and in the holes
> Where eyes did once inhabit there were crept,
> As 'twere in scorn of eyes, reflecting gems,
> That woo'd the slimy bottom of the deep
> And mock'd the dead bones that lay scatt'red by.
>
> (I. iv. 21–33)

The strange and very potent image of the last five lines recurs elsewhere in Shakespeare, most vividly in *The Tempest*:

> Full fathom five thy father lies;
>   Of his bones are coral made;
> Those are pearls that were his eyes . . .
>
> (I. ii. 396–8)

Here, in *Richard III*, it involves a kind of imaginative poetry not found elsewhere in the play, and so it has often been called intrusive and irrelevant. Death by drowning echoes, in fact, Richard's opening lines, and there are other references to it later, though never again in such conspicuous form. The shining brilliance set in dead men's skulls on the slimy bottom seems to me too perfect an image of the play to be set aside as mere decoration: I would rather take it as a kind of choric speech, commenting on the state of things represented in the last scene (including, with 'woo'd', the sexual references I discussed), as much as on Clarence's own guilt.

He proceeds to a further dream, or rather to a further part of the same dream, where he is explicitly accused by his own conscience and by the ghosts of those he has wronged:

> O, then began the tempest to my soul!
> I pass'd, methought, the melancholy flood
> With that sour ferryman which poets write of,
> Unto the kingdom of perpetual night.
> The first that there did greet my stranger soul
> Was my great father-in-law, renowned Warwick,
> Who spake aloud 'What scourge for perjury
> Can this dark monarchy afford false Clarence?'

> (44–51)

And so on: this speech prefigures, in the vividness of the dream, the fulfilment of Margaret's prophecy, as these ghosts precisely prefigure the ghosts that haunt Richard in V. iii. The difficulty in recognizing this speech as choric is that Clarence speaks it only of his own experience; its general application is not made immediately apparent, other than by juxtaposition with the last scene. This, I think, is a technical clumsiness, akin to the problems raised by Marcus' speech at the end of Act II of *Titus Andronicus*. Shakespeare avoids the embarrassment of Marcus addressing his dumb niece, but at the expense of detaching this poetry too far from the general situation to which it, most effectively, applies. But if we have grasped the inter-relatedness of the evolving patterns of the play, we should not miss the bearings of this speech.

The scene switches abruptly from this high choric pitch to its opposite in grotesque comedy, with the murderers. But the theme is still conscience:

1 MURDERER:	How dost thou feel thyself now?
2 MURDERER:	Faith, some certain dregs of conscience are yet within me.
1 MURDERER:	Remember our reward, when the deed's done.
2 MURDERER:	Zounds, he dies; I had forgot the reward.
1 MURDERER:	Where's thy conscience now?
2 MURDERER:	O, in the Duke of Gloucester's purse!

(122–7)

But out of the cynical joke, the reality of conscience does emerge for the 2nd Murderer:

> How fain, like Pilate, would I wash my hands
> Of this most grievous murder!   (270–1)

If Richard's detachment from the main play can sometimes set him in a favourable light, we have also to recognize that he achieves his domination precisely by repudiation of this conscience which returns to torture him in Act V. In seeing this morality-pattern of guilt and conscience reflected at both ends of the scale, in a profoundly imaginative poetry and in comic prose, we move perhaps deeper into the heart of the play. Beyond the social and political level, we have already had with Margaret a strong hint of the supernatural operating in the structural patterns that extend beyond the wills of men; but its nature was at least dubious. Here, in the murderer's allusion to Pilate as well as in Clarence's prayers, there is a strong hint that the final resolution will be Christian. Clarence's dream was, in fact, of a classical, and therefore mythological, hell; for Richard later it is translated into a Biblical, and therefore theological, damnation.

Clarence's murder accomplishes the first of Richard's plans, the first pattern of the play, though the scene is simultaneously used for larger references. Of the patterns initiated in the first two scenes, only the death of Edward remains to be accomplished, and that is the business of the first two scenes of Act II. The structural ironies are sustained in Buckingham's self-curse, a kind of echo of Anne's in I. ii:

> Whenever Buckingham doth turn his hate
> Upon your Grace, but with all duteous love
> Doth cherish you and yours, God punish me
> With hate in those where I expect most love!
> When I have most need to employ a friend,
> And most assured that he is a friend,
> Deep, hollow, treacherous, and full of guile,
> Be he unto me. This do I beg of God . . . (II. i. 32–9)

An invitation which Richard punctually accepts in IV. ii. A similar but more subtle irony arises at the end of this scene: Richard characteristically declares of Clarence's death:

> Mark'd you not
> How that the guilty kindred of the Queen
> Look'd pale when they did hear of Clarence' death?
> O, they did urge it still unto the King!
> God will revenge it. (134–8)

Since this is said to Buckingham, the 'friend' is already 'Deep, hollow, treacherous, and full of guile'; but the irony really reflects on Richard himself, and that is reinforced when the last phrase is echoed only fifteen lines later (although in the next 'scene') by Clarence's young son:

> God will revenge it; whom I will importune
> With earnest prayers all to that effect.
> (II. ii. 14–15)

Edward's actual death leads to an intensification of the antiphonal mode of lament. Here it is between Elizabeth, the old Duchess of York and Clarence's children:

Q. ELIZABETH: Ah for my husband, for my dear Lord Edward!

CHILDREN: Ah for our father, for our dear Lord Clarence!

DUCHESS: Alas for both, both mine, Edward and Clarence! (71–3)

In IV. i Anne is added to the weeping queens, and this pattern is completed in IV. iv with Margaret's second entry. Here, in II. ii, the two main plans – Richard's plot and Margaret's curse – meet for the first time in Edward's natural death. They march together through the second part of the play (II. iv–IV. iii), and this is anticipated in a brief dialogue between Buckingham and Richard at the end of II. ii, planning to remove Rivers, Vaughan, and Grey. There, for the first time, the progress of the play is interrupted by the short scene (II. iii) between the citizens, providing a totally different perspective from the intensive concentration on the noble contestants. Its choric function – a kind of entr'acte (there seems little justification for a five Act division of this play, as there usually does not in the histories) is intensified towards the end when they echo the major images from Richard's and Clarence's speeches in Act I:

> When clouds are seen, wise men put on their cloaks;
> When great leaves fall, then winter is at hand;
> When the sun sets, who doth not look for night? . . .
> By a divine instinct men's minds mistrust
> Ensuing danger; as by proof we see
> The water swell before a boist'rous storm.
> But leave it all to God.   (II. iii. 32–45)

In the last part of the play – from IV. iv onwards – the fulfilment of Margaret's witch-like curse goes beyond the scope of Richard's human plan, to encompass his isolation, fall, and death: but at this point, as I have shown, a larger pattern still is revealed, as God releases Richmond off the sea (the reverse of death by drowning), something that outgoes what Margaret could foretell.

Thus the first and last parts of the play are pivoted about its central section: in the opening sequence its structural characteristics of symmetry and irony are very clearly expounded; and, no less clearly, they are fulfilled in the last sequence.

VIII

The actual patterns evolved in the play are not, then, one but several; which is why its structure, though felt to be highly

organized, proves complicated to analyse. They involve a multiplicity of themes at least as ambitious as those of *Titus Andronicus*.
The simplest is the sequence of little tragedies that leads from
Clarence, through Rivers, Vaughan, and Grey, to Hastings,
Buckingham, and finally Richard himself. This is not merely a
sequence, because all the others form part of the structure which
Richard builds up against himself. He steadily intensifies his own
alienation from other men, and develops with his own rising
power simultaneously the force that will destroy him. At the
moment of his highest triumph, the grasping of the crown, the
first messenger of disaster brings news of rebellion, and his last
ally, Buckingham, withdraws his support. That this is fatal to
Buckingham does not make it less so for Richard: his isolation
must eventually unite all men against him.

That conclusion is moralistic. Richard, I said, is aligned with the
old Vice, who was a kind of clown. Many of the attributes of the
clown remain with Richard, including his anarchic anti-moralism;
but here the clown has become a tragic figure, given a new intensity from the Elizabethan image of the Machiavel, and from
association with Marlowe's representatives of the ambition for
human self-sufficiency, the will to dominate. In this he has some
resemblance to Aaron in *Titus*; but his kinship with humanity is
established by means quite different from Aaron's paternal affec-
tions. Richard is the condemned outsider, rising to power by
sheer force of will. The power to rise is as impressive as the
ultimate fall is inevitable; and the force of Richard's will is not
necessarily diminished by the final irony that it may itself be the
instrument of a greater Will.

The moral pattern involves the theme of guilt and conscience so
strongly marked in the formal balance of the first and last Acts.
One could, no doubt, extend this catalogue in several directions:
but finally, subsuming all the rest, the multiplicity of structural
patterns finding its equivalent utterance in highly patterned
language and verse insist on a dominant sense of patterning as
such. As each evolves out of the other, they reach progressively
further beyond the lives of individual men, or even of such a semi-
human figure as Margaret, so that human self-assertion is

ironically mocked, and the larger sense of pattern becomes established as the idea of history, terrifying in its very largeness and
inevitability. The irony in fact works both ways: if it mocks the
human, it also questions the divine. Like Marlowe's *Dr Faustus*
it is a play of overt Christian orthodoxy with very evident
sceptical implications. But Shakespeare's orthodoxy is both more
firmly and more massively established.

This returns me finally to the point from which I began: to
reflection that in this play History represents a crushing weight of
retribution. A pattern which becomes a vast ritual of destructive
vengeance; and the closer it approaches to ritual, the stronger
become its associations with the supernatural. This supernatural
order emerges in Act V as a manifestation of the Divine Will,
destroying Richard and substituting the unequivocally angelic
Richmond. So that in the end the ironist himself is subject to a
greater irony, that he has functioned as an instrument of destruction in the world of guilt.[1] This divine pattern is explicitly Christian; one cannot help reflecting that it is, at the same time,
repulsive.

What emerges in this revelation of a Christian order behind the
seeming chaos of human affairs is a final sanction to the formal
structure and the formal language of the play. The rhetorical
norm which can rise to the forms of ritual establishes this sense of
predestination on which the whole theory of Tudor history is
built. It provides a framework in which men and women become
mere actors, but it provides also a fitting ceremonial conclusion to
the sequence of plays. Its obtrusiveness in the play, however,
accounts for more than this, not simply because of the multiplicity
of other patterns I have discussed, but also because this final development of the formal Order in the series of plays produces
its own anti-body, Richard himself.

Every point I made to show Richard's dissociation from the
body of the play tends also to dissociate him from the orderly
pattern. And when one remembers that this included a critical
awareness of rhetorical falsity, and a human dimension that is his

---

[1] See A. P. Rossiter, *op. cit.*

alone, one can glimpse, I think, why this play does in the end move us with some sense of tragedy. Within this gigantic machine of order there is no place for the human will; we are oppressed by the same sense of helplessness as can be induced by a rolling mill, or the rolling weight of the ocean. Mankind, here, is no more than dead skulls on the slimy bottom of the deep; and if any jewel shines in the eyeless socket, it is not Richmond, but Richard himself. To be good, is to submit to the crushing weight; the only resistance possible is the way of deliberate evil. I said that Richard derived his role from the Vice of the moralities; there is a sense in which he becomes in the end Mankind as well (though not, of course, Everyman): the human representative, bolder than ourselves, resisting oppression, and being destroyed. The world not only seems, but is, the poorer for his loss.

Which is, of course, a perverse conclusion, however true. Shakespeare's histories have been shown to be supremely orthodox in the pattern they display; but it seems to me that in *Richard III* Shakespeare admits the challenging scepticism of Marlowe to a place in his play, and in so doing discovers the tragic dilemma of his own orthodoxy: the orderly predestinate scheme destroys the dignity of man. The result is in no sense a sentimentalizing of Richard. It is, however (as A. P. Rossiter insisted), supremely ambivalent: a simultaneous perception of two utterly different and opposed scales of value, the historical and the tragic. The sense of History and the sense of Order here become synonymous: even at the political level history is larger than the individual man; at the metaphysical pitch mankind loses all significance. Such a view of history is hostile to any sense of tragedy. But in this play the one does not eclipse the other: they are clearly distinguished and simultaneously developed into maximum contrast and conflict. The tragic conflict, what lifts the play above melodrama or the mere narrative of a well-merited fall, is not offered within the character of Richard, but in the character of the play itself, in the conflict of dramatic modes that it presents. And in this we may see the morally and physically deformed Richard as an emblem of the tragic enfeeblement of man.

Romeo and Juliet
[1595]

I

There is no doubt that *Romeo and Juliet* was known on the stage before April 1597, for in that month Danter's printing presses were destroyed, and he had already produced the 'bad quarto' edition using a text pirated from the play in performance. How much earlier it was written we have no sure means of telling. It has been suggested that the mock-play of Pyramus and Thisbe in *A Midsummer Night's Dream* was, as part of the joke, a self-parody of *Romeo and Juliet*, which may be true though it is far from clear. If it is true, then *Romeo* was possibly written in 1595 which puts it not only before *Richard II*, but also between *Love's Labour's Lost* and *A Midsummer Night's Dream*, possibly not far removed in time from *The Two Gentlemen of Verona*. Such a placing suggests its romance theme, its persistently lyrical tone, and the accentuated formality of its structure and language. There is here not merely the controlled variety of tones which we have seen in earlier tragedies, but even the use of varied verse forms including even entire sonnets (for the chorus, and for the first encounter of Romeo and Juliet themselves). It is obvious that the experience of the non-dramatic sonnets is involved here, and in fact the play can partly be seen as a dramatic exploration of the world of the love sonnet, in much the same sense that *Titus Andronicus* is a dramatic exploration of the world of *The Rape of Lucrece*. In almost every other respect it is its unlikeness to *Titus* that is obvious. That was political, brutal, hysterical, farcical; this is domestic, romantic, comic (not farcical), and there is no interest whatever in insanity. The contrast, in fact, is so complete, both with *Titus* on the one hand, and with *Richard III* on the other, that it would seem clearly to be deliberate, the exploration of three very different kinds of dramatic experience linked only superficially by the term 'tragedy'. It is only in technique that one can see a likeness; I noted in *Titus* the multiplication of tragic themes, the highly self-conscious organization and control of utterance, and in these respects there is a marked resemblance to *Romeo*. The tragic themes are again multiplied, and the range of verse and prose is both wider and more obvious. In other words, we have here the same experimental ambitiousness and fertility of invention in a quite different genre: the tragedy of romance, or of love.

This suggests another likeness to *Titus Andronicus*: I suggested there, that although the theme could be exclusively tragic in implication (and became so in *Lear*), it was so contained within the strongly formal framework and verse that we have no difficulty in imagining comedies being written at the same time: there is no temptation to imagine Shakespeare committed to the world of his play. This is even more true of *Romeo*, which in many ways seems to be a formal exercise in romantic tragedy, given the kind of overt formality of structure and verse which rather suggests the order of a stately dance; it is not perhaps surprising that this quality in Shakespeare's play has encouraged the production of a number of ballets in the past hundred years – it is probably, in fact, more often seen on the stage nowadays as a ballet than as a play. It is a moving play, certainly, but it is also detached; it does not encourage a deep emotional involvement in the audience; so that its feeling is of the reverse side of the same coin as romance comedy. And this quality, so far from being obscured, is emphasized: much of the play is actually comedy, close in kind to *The Two Gentlemen*, with which it could almost be a twin birth, the comic and tragic variations on the same theme.

Almost, but not quite; for *Romeo* is the stronger, and deeper, of the two. The formal structure is strongly emphasized; but it is also continually questioned, and penetrated – so that we are made to perceive more than it will of itself reveal, to grasp the move-

ments of experience which lie beneath the formal surface. The
spectacle of the formal tragedy is worked out in the highly
artificial tomb scenes which complement the earlier bedroom
scenes; and if both are located, as I suppose, on the inner stage,
then this parallelism will be the more obvious. Between them,
these two sequences fulfil precisely the Prologue's anticipation of
a 'death-marked love', and the elaborate poetry spoken in the
tomb insists on the formality of structure. So that this conclusion,
though the climax of the play, can be moving only in a detached,
contained way. The most moving scene in the play, in a sense, is
not this final pavan of death at all, but the death of Mercutio in
Act III, scene i, which is in prose, and the sequel to a passage of
very trivial comedy:

MERCUTIO: I am hurt.
A plague a both your houses! I am sped.
Is he gone and hath nothing?
BENVOLIO: What, art thou hurt?
MERCUTIO: Ay, ay, a scratch, a scratch; marry, 'tis enough.
Where is my page? Go, villain, fetch a surgeon.
ROMEO: Courage, man; the hurt cannot be much.
MERCUTIO: No, 'tis not so deep as a well, nor so wide as a
church door, but 'tis enough, 'twill serve. Ask for me to-
morrow, and you shall find me a grave man. I am peppered,
I warrant, for this world. A plague a both your houses!
Zounds, a dog, a rat, a mouse, a cat, to scratch a man to
death! A braggart, a rogue, a villain, that fights by the book
of arithmetic! Why the devil came you between us? I was
hurt under your arm.
ROMEO: I thought all for the best.
MERCUTIO: Help me into some house, Benvolio, or I shall
faint.
A plague a both your houses!
They have made worms' meat of me.
I have it, and soundly too – Your houses!
(III. i. 87–105)

It is not quite clear that Mercutio's last lines should be printed as
verse: the imprint of metre within them is very faint, and they are
far more obviously a continuation of his prose utterance. What is

clear is that Romeo's lines have an undisturbed rhythm that is far more closely related to the verse in which he proceeds after Mercutio's exit. And this smooth obliviousness, the feebleness of 'I thought all for the best', is shocking in its obtuseness. It is 'not his fault' Mercutio died, yet he stands terribly reproved; reproved by prose. That is to say, the fanciful world of poetic romance which is fulfilled by a poetic death is reproved by a prosaic one; as poetry is apt to be reproved by life (the point of Keats' agonized self-questionings in his letters, and in *The Fall of Hyperion*). And that Romeo is circumscribed by such a fanciful structure has already been amply demonstrated: by Mercutio himself, mocking the sonneteer's view of life, and, even more interestingly, by Juliet: 'You kiss by th' book.'

But Romeo has not altogether stood apart from the play in this; it is not simply himself that is reproved. The whole play is challenged and re-directed by this scene. The genre in which it is conceived is set sharply against a sense of actuality as Mercutio dies the way men do die – accidentally, irrelevantly, ridiculously; in a word, prosaically. All this is focused in one of Shakespeare's most (justly) celebrated puns:

> Ask for me to-morrow, and you shall find me a
> grave man.

It is witty, and it is also painful; it cracks open a world of courtly wit, to reveal at once a perception of death, and of seriousness.

II

The shock of this scene is used to precipitate a change of key in the play: it becomes immediately more serious, and decisively tragic where before it had been predominantly comic. This is felt, not merely in the immediate consequence of Romeo killing Tybalt and being therefore banished, but also in Juliet's next entry which presents passion with a new intensity quite removed from the innocent romantic stuff we have had earlier:

> Gallop apace, you fiery-footed steeds
> Towards Phoebus' lodging; such a waggoner

As Phaethon would whip you to the west,
And bring in cloudy night immediately.
Spread thy close curtain, love-performing night,
That runaways' eyes may wink, and Romeo
Leap to these arms, untalk'd of and unseen.

(III. ii. 1–7)

There is not, of course, the faintest question of comparing this to
prose: it is at the furthest remove from that; and being so, it
sustains the formal poetic structure of the play. But however
patently 'poetical' it may be, it is also a magnificent presentation
of the full force of desire in triumphant action; this is no game.
And through it we soon feel, and more fully as the speech develops, the force of actual experience that relates it to Mercutio:

And learn me how to lose a winning match,
Play'd for a pair of stainless maidenhoods.

(12–13)

But the obtrusive poeticalness is important in a more specific way:
for the speech does not only offer a general contrast of feeling with
Acts I and II, it has a direct relationship with an earlier passage of
obtrusive poetry: Juliet's steeds, galloping, waggoner, whip, and
night have all appeared before, in Mercutio's 'Queen Mab' speech
in Act I, scene iv:

O, then I see Queen Mab hath been with you.
She is the fairies' midwife, and she comes
In shape no bigger than an agate stone
On the fore-finger of an alderman,
Drawn with a team of little atomies
Athwart men's noses as they lie asleep;
Her waggon-spokes made of long spinners' legs . . .
Her whip, of cricket's bone; the lash, of film;
Her waggoner, a small grey-coated gnat,
Not half so big as a round little worm
Prick'd from the lazy finger of a maid.
Her chariot is an empty hazel-nut,
Made by the joiner squirrel or old grub,
Time out o' mind the fairies' coachmakers.

And in this state she gallops night by night
Through lovers' brains, and then they dream of love;
O'er courtiers' knees, that dream on curtsies straight;
O'er lawyers' fingers, who straight dream on fees;
O'er ladies' lips, who straight on kisses dream,
Which oft the angry Mab with blisters plagues,
Because their breaths with sweetmeats tainted are.

(I. iv. 53–76)

The emblems are the same, and their significance is similar: Phaeton's coach of day is driven into the night of Juliet's desire; Queen Mab's coach is driven through the night of dreams to fulfil the real ambitions of men and women, greed and lust. But the scale of the two waggons is radically different, in fact sheer opposite. Queen Mab is infinitely small, trivial, insignificant, malicious and contemptible (however gossamer-charming); Phaethon's chariot is the Sun, its region the whole sky, vast, and in its regular motion, irresistible. We *don't* resist Queen Mab, for although she may seem charmingly fanciful, she in fact represents everyman's common fantasy life; we *can't* resist the Sun-god (though the unimaginative may never feel his force). Both speeches are obviously set-pieces, designed to stand out from their context, as they do, and thus acquire a related significance as comments on the play. Their relationship is of very much the same kind as the successive emblem pictures of the countryside which I discussed in Act II of *Titus Andronicus*: radically *different* views of the *same* thing. In the case of Queen Mab, reduced to a minimum, as Mercutio sees it; and with Phaethon, in Juliet's view on her clandestine wedding night, at maximum extension, translated from the absurd to the magnificent. The dramatic pivot of this poetic irony, is Mercutio's death.

III

If this point is grasped, it enables me to call attention to several things of importance. First of all, the use of verse and prose is by no means a matter of variety for variety's sake; it is a highly

organized dramatic instrument. Liable, no doubt, to partial failure
by cause of its very self-consciousness; but the play does take
positive advantage of that, for it has, as I have said, a very formal
structure, and that is fulfilled by this use of language, which
therefore demonstrates effectively T. S. Eliot's contention that

> we should expect a dramatic poet like Shakespeare to write his
> finest poetry in his most dramatic scenes . . . what makes it most
> dramatic is what makes it most poetic.
>
> *(Selected Essays,* p. 52)

'Queen Mab' has been thought to be not perfectly this, because
not perfectly fitted into its dramatic context – the gossamer charm
being alien to Mercutio. But in fact the force of the speech, its
intense belittling of passionate experience, is a precise evocation
of his outlook; and both its eloquence and its irony are his.
'Gallop apace', because Juliet is recognized to be both imaginative
and passionate, is less often questioned. Yet actress just as much as
actor is liable to find such utterance something of a problem,
unless they are sustained by an element of stylization in the production as a whole. Mercutio's death is not an advertisement for
the more dramatic power of prose: its prosaic force works entirely
because of its context amidst verse. And Juliet's so poetical speech
is intensely dramatic in its capacity to bring out with maximum
force its contrast as well as its relationship to Queen Mab, to
prose, and Juliet's earlier childishness. The dramatic context
demands this complex revelation; and it is a mere truism to say
that only such poetry can achieve it. In Zeffirelli's production at
the Old Vic in the 1950's, in which the prose scenes of the play
were superlatively done, Juliet spoke this speech against a background of bells, bouncing up and down on her bed; the simple
point was effectively made, of course, but everything else was
missing. The words were quite inaudible, and she might well have
done no more than say 'God! I feel randy'.

Mercutio, then, has a very significant place in the play, and it is
worth remarking that this is entirely Shakespeare's creation. In
narrative and character generally he is fairly close to his source,
Arthur Brooke's verse-tale *The Tragicall Historye of Romeus and*

Juliet (1562); Mercutio is the sole major contribution, and looking at his function is an obvious way of grasping the significance of Shakespeare's recasting of the material. He is, among other things, reminiscent of Berowne in *Love's Labour's Lost*, and the connexion is suggestive. I have said that Mercutio's minimally stated, prosaic death makes a powerful impact in the courtly-comic world of love and acts as a catalyst projecting a freshly serious perception. A similar effect constitutes the final twist to *Love's Labour's Lost*: Mercadé's entrance in Act V, as a silent figure dressed in black, has a startling effect of invalidating the courtly games to which the play seems to have become committed for its finale. His name is one of the common forms used for the supposed author of the French 'Dance of Death', and whether that is coincidence or not, his presence projects the play suddenly into a radically different tone. But effective as it is, it comes too late in the play for any degree of elaboration; it has potentialities beyond the scope of comedy, and one may feel (without pressing the point too hard) that the sense of the nearness and oppositeness of a comic and a tragic sense of love is developed in *Romeo and Juliet* from the hint of earlier comedy. Hence the function here of a strong sense of comedy as well as of tragedy.

The play depends, then, very much on formal patterning, like that of a sonnet; but explored, criticized, and penetrated, so that the formal surface not only restrains but also reveals the inner experience. As part of this quality there is a constant stress on the nearness and oppositeness of comedy and tragedy, of triviality and seriousness, laughter and tears, minuteness and vastness, youth and age, and, of course, love and death. The play in fact develops round a series of paradoxes, as the opening chorus makes almost too plain:

> Two households, both alike in dignity,
> In fair Verona, where we lay our scene,
> From ancient grudge break to new mutiny,
> Where civil blood makes civil hands unclean.
> From forth the fatal loins of these two foes
> A pair of star-cross'd lovers take their life;
> Whose misadventur'd piteous overthrows

G

Doth with their death bury their parents' strife.
The fearful passage of their death-mark'd love . . .

(1–9)

It is a very formal statement, not very encouraging: 'star-cross'd
lovers' suggests a crude tragic theme of doom (which is present,
of course; as the theme of blood-feud reconciled in blood-match
is also present), but 'death-mark'd love', though it may only
mean the same thing, may also mean more. In Freudian terms,
which have been made all too familiar, it suggests a *kind* of love
which is in its nature death-marked. But Freudian speculation,
however suggestive, is not necessarily relevant.[1] It is necessary to
find out what Shakespeare makes this mean in the development of
the play: with the confidence which I have tried to engender that
this is not simply, or so much, an immature play, as a very highly
organized play about (among other things) immaturity.

IV

The first scene offers the maximum contrast to the clashing dis-
cords of the choric sonnet – from the high and mighty tragic
theme to an amusing but lumpish prose; lumpish, and slow. But
for all that it has, at its level, thematic relevance. The dialogue is
entirely moved by puns which start apparently at random (on coal
and colliers), and then moves through civil broil down the path of
all puns into bawdy (*Romeo and Juliet* is plausibly reported to be
Shakespeare's bawdiest play):

> therefore I will push Montague's men from the wall
> and thrust his maids to the wall.   (I. i. 17–19)

Already the quarrel and sex are juxtaposed; they are shortly
brought together (it is a climax of a kind) in a single word:

SAMPSON: Me they shall feel while I am able to stand; and
'tis known I am a pretty piece of flesh.
GREGORY: 'Tis well thou art not fish; if thou hadst, thou

---

1 That it is so here has been admirably demonstrated by M. M. Mahood in *Shakespeare's Wordplay*, 1957.

hadst been poor-John. Draw thy tool; here comes two of the house of Montagues.

SAMPSON: My naked weapon is out; quarrel, I will back thee.

(28-34)

Sampson's 'tool' and 'naked weapon' bring this dialogue to its simultaneous conclusion in sex and death. However coarse and light it is a variation on the theme proposed in the opening chorus, at the other end of the scale from the symbolic kiss with which Romeo and Juliet conclude this Act. That development prefigures the play, in its movement from the comic to the serious, and one function of this scene is therefore to set the play moving decisively in comic terms. I remarked that until Mercutio's death the tone is (in varied ways) predominantly comic; this does not mean, of course, that we do not know it is going to be a tragedy – the choruses, and periodic set speeches of foreboding, insist on that; it follows that the comic terms have to be clearly established.

From this point the scene accelerates, and both in numbers and pace the development is rapid; in utterance, it moves through a quicker prose into blank verse with Benvolio's

> Part, fools!
> Put up your swords; you know not what you do.
>
> (62-3)

An arresting line, which in its rhythmic assurance suggests Othello's

> Keep up your bright swords, for the dew will rust them.
>
> (I. ii. 59)

The 'brightness', 'dew', 'rust' are distinctively Othello's; by comparison, Benvolio is restrained. The crescendo continues through the entries of Tybalt, Capulet, Montague till a fully heroic verse emerges in the Prince's speech:

> Will they not hear? What, ho! you men, you beasts,
> That quench the fire of your pernicious rage
> With purple fountains issuing from your veins!
> On pain of torture, from those bloody hands
> Throw your mistempered weapons to the ground,
> And hear the sentence of your moved prince. (81-6)

The transition is complete from the lowest to the highest pitch, from dolts to princes. The Prince, in fact, is a civic authority, more than a mayor and corporation, but less than the full State of the history plays; the quarrel is no mere storm in a teacup, but it is not the Wars of the Roses either. It is necessary to recognize the restricted scope of the civil strife that is to be resolved in the deaths of Romeo and Juliet: its significance is local, almost domestic; and in this it reflects the restricted scope of the play's claim for their tragedy.

The Prince's image of blood – With purple fountains issuing from your veins – is confined here to death; if there are latent sexual implications they remain latent. The verse does not, here, focus death and love in one image, as the prose had. But the play veers soon to its other polarity, through a transition to a radical change of tone: Benvolio's blank verse arrives at a comfortable semi-couplet, Lady Montague caps this with a full couplet, on Romeo, and Benvolio embarks on the new theme in verse as high-flown as the Prince's, but quite different in imagery and far more lyrical in rhythm:

> BENVOLIO: While we were interchanging thrusts and blows,
> Came more and more, and fought on part and
> part,
> Till the Prince came, who parted either part.
> LADY M. O, where is Romeo? Saw you him to-day?
> Right glad I am he was not at this fray.
> BENVOLIO: Madam, an hour before the worshipp'd sun
> Peer'd forth the golden window of the east,
> A troubled mind drew me to walk abroad;
> Where, underneath the grove of sycamore
> That westward rooteth from this city side,
> So early walking did I see your son. (111–21)

The contrast with what has gone before is complete: we have moved from war to love, from discord to harmony; the separation of the two is therefore a different effect from the simultaneity of the chorus' portmanteau phrases, or the sex-death puns of the initial prose. Hate and love are given here as separate experiences.

The scene proceeds to one of Shakespeare's favourite expository devices (compare *The Merchant of Venice* and *Hamlet*): 'what's wrong with the hero?'. On Romeo's first entrance, the answer is: 'not much'. He is free to engage with Benvolio in a witty interchange in the tone of high comedy (as in Lyly's plays, or in *Love's Labour's Lost*). But this does repeat the prose pattern, and proceeds through broil to the hate–love complex; not, now, in bawdy puns, but in quibbling wit:

ROMEO: Here's much to do with hate, but more with love.
Why then, O brawling love! O loving hate!
O anything, of nothing first create!
O heavy lightness! serious vanity!
Mis-shapen chaos of well-seeming forms!
Feather of lead, bright smoke, cold fire, sick health!
Still-waking sleep, that is not what it is!
This love feel I, that feel no love in this.
Dost thou not laugh?
BENVOLIO: No, coz, I rather weep.
ROMEO: Good heart, at what?
BENVOLIO: At thy good heart's oppression.
                                                (173–84)

Benvolio's comment makes its effect: Romeo's offer to be witty about love and hate is felt to be out of tune, it reveals a pressure from within him, that the detachment is false. But here an aspect of the play that is peculiarly associated with Romeo (and exposed more directly later) emerges: through the comic mask the central theme became visible, and it was, for a moment, exposed to sensitive perception in Benvolio's last words which form a rhythmic climax to the passage and would, by themselves, form a closing cadence. But the exposure is immediately covered by Romeo's response, picking up Benvolio's 'oppression' and supplying, what was not required, a rhyme for it:

Why, such is love's transgression.   (185)

The serious tone is contained, and Romeo proceeds in couplets that rapidly restore the lightness to the dialogue; we are held back from a glimpse below the surface, and safely returned to comedy, and the scene closes in light exchanges about puppy love.

Comedy continues to predominate, almost without disturbance, in Act I, scene ii, the discussion of Capulet's plans for a party, and his messenger's encounter with Benvolio and Romeo. In fact, the only disturbance here is in the almost too *un*disturbing tone of Benvolio's diagnosis:

> Tut, man, one fire burns out another's burning,
> One pain is less'ned by another's anguish;
> Turn giddy, and be holp by backward turning;
> One desperate grief cures with another's languish.
> Take thou some new infection to thy eye,
> And the rank poison of the old will die.   (I. ii. 45–50)

The rhyming epigram (a quatrain and a couplet) affirms a peculiar blandness, seems to reduce the matter to the utmost triviality; yet the words so lightly contained in the verse precipitate suggestions that are ominous enough: 'giddy', 'desperate grief', 'new infection', 'rank poison'. The blandness of tone implies a kind of blindness, reduces the conception of love as a disease to mere cliché; placed here, the blindness is itself ominous, the whole epigram acting chorically, as a prelude (rather too obviously) to the introduction of Juliet, with her nurse and mother, in I. iii.

The comedy here is much richer: the nurse's utterance is something altogether new, both in this play and, in fact, in Shakespeare's output. Its nearest antecedent is the prose of I. i, but it goes far beyond that. Yet its characteristic is that it is close to prose, or rather to prosaic speech, developing its own rhythmic momentum (in *The Merchant of Venice* Shylock's utterance begins as prose and only gradually develops a verse rhythm retaining its idiosyncratic quality as speech):

>   nay, by th' rood,
> She could have run and waddled all about;
> For even the day before, she broke her brow;
> And then my husband – God be with his soul!
> 'A was a merry man – took up the child.
> 'Yea,' quoth he 'dost thou fall upon thy face?

Thou wilt fall backward when thou hast more wit,
Wilt thou not, Jule?' And, by my holidam,
The pretty wretch left crying, and said 'Ay'.
To see, now, how a jest shall come about!
I warrant, an I should live a thousand years,
I never should forget it: 'Wilt thou not, Jule?'

quoth he;
And, pretty fool, it stinted, and said 'Ay'.

(I. iii. 37–49)

This offers a very telling contrast to the hollow courtliness of
I. ii: earthy, sentimental, warm-blooded, bawdy, repetitious. At
all levels delightful, and most refreshing in its unselfconsciousness.
It is also, humanly speaking, shallow enough in its own way, and
this will be sharply exposed later; but here the judgement is withheld.

Juliet is introduced between her mother and the nurse and thus
has, from the start, a fuller humanity than Romeo has yet displayed; the long discussion of her age (not quite 14) stresses it as
the age of puberty, of suddenly emergent physical maturity (it is,
of course, sheer hypocrisy to pretend this is exceptionally young;
that was a Victorian illusion which they almost made true). Juliet,
then, is a child growing up; immature, obviously, but in a very
different way from Romeo who is evidently older; he is continually revealed as 'immature' in the sense of being less grown-up
than he seems (withdrawing, for instance, in courtly coupleting).
With Juliet, it is rather the other way up. There is a hint here of
the peculiar relationship between Othello and Desdemona: where
he retreats officiously into a denial of desire, she confronts her
father and the senators with a bold candour:

That I did love the Moor to live with him,
My downright violence and storm of fortunes
May trumpet to the world.   (I. iii. 248–50)

It is in fact common for Shakespeare's heroines to appear more
mature than their men – Portia, Rosalind, and Imogen all have
this quality.

Act I, scene iv, insists decisively on the lightest comic atmosphere: it is governed by Mercutio, preparing with the other masquers. The tone is cynical and reductive of any degree of romantic pretension, and it is this which is given emblematic development in the description of Queen Mab: the diminutive figure of lust – for sex, wealth, power, or whatever. A mockery of all serious values, but a slightly uncomfortable one. The comic image she presents is recognized as cynical, promiscuous, and even nasty:

> O'er ladies' lips, who straight on kisses dream,
> Which oft the angry Mab with blisters plagues.
>
> (I. iv. 74–5)

The image of venereal disease may seem strange in a speech about fairies, but that is largely because of the sentimental image of the fairy generated in the last century (by Mendelssohn for instance) out of *A Midsummer Night's Dream* – at the expense of distorting that play, let alone this speech. In any case, this crystallizes the tone of the speech, and of Mercutio. It is the fullest exposition of one comic development, the spirit of the sonneteer's courtly love seen as absurd; that it is not a final statement I have already shown when Juliet restates the emblems in 'Gallop apace . . .'. The romantic theme itself has yet to emerge from the various attendant comic tones – the rank bawdry of the servants, the warm earthiness of the Nurse, and the witty cynicism of Mercutio. It does so here, anticipated in a rather clumsy speech of foreboding by Romeo himself:

> my mind misgives
> Some consequence, yet hanging in the stars,
> Shall bitterly begin his fearful date
> With this night's revels . . .   (106–9)

v

We are thus brought to the full climax of Act I in Masque and Dance, the action equivalent to its formal love poetry; and we have also a staged enactment of the play's love–hate theme as Montague and Capulet dance into betrothal. The point is stressed by Tybalt's violent outburst, his repudiation of the harmonious dance. The opening movement of the play is recapitulated in a rapid development from bustling prose to lusty verse to the full dance and Romeo and Juliet encountering in a full-blown sonnet. The initial prose stresses the last of the play's themes, the contrast of age and youth, as Capulet reminisces with his aged cousin: they are outside the dance, lamenting (complacently enough) the inevitable onset of impotence (their dialogue suggests the physical worries of the French king in *All's Well That Ends Well*, but with less edge).

Seeing the Act in its fullness, with its functional contrasts of prose and several kinds of verse, we can see this climax in a very elaborate verse becomes musically almost inevitable. And the sense of ritual is dramatically right: what, out of context, would be empty courtliness, in its context is solemn celebration. In psychological terms, this sonnet represents the spell of mutual recognition; but thus formalized, the psychological moment is carried forward into full betrothal – the implication of such a recognition. To grasp the best of *Romeo and Juliet*, we have to grasp that this does work on the stage. So also does the breaking of the spell: the sonnet completed, Romeo's continuation in the same mode becomes a work of supererogation, and Juliet bluntly rejects the falsity:

ROMEO: Sin from my lips? O trespass sweetly urg'd!
         Give me my sin again.
JULIET: You kiss by th' book.

                                        (I. v. 107–8)

Just so. The formality which *was* right, is *now* wrong, once the pattern is completed in its final cadence; a recognition which is at once obvious, and very subtle. Critical awareness of true and false tones is promoted in this play with remarkable delicacy and assurance.

Thus Act I involves a very full and brilliantly varied establishment of themes completed here in action. It is very much a single movement with its own climax, and it is therefore followed by a choric sonnet which both concludes this and preludes Act II:

> Now old desire doth in his death-bed lie,
> And young affection gapes to be his heir.   (1–2)

The central theme has been often suggested, but is not yet fully explicit: Romeo has met his match, but the experience has not yet more than in hints broken the tidy confines of a sonnet to fulfil the violent suggestion of 'affection gapes'.

VI

The critical alertness demanded in Act I – involving a consciousness of sonnet as formal embodiment of valid feeling in distinction from sonneteering as mere attitudinizing – is still very marked in Act II. It opens with a brilliant display of Mercutio's bawdy wit, exposing the fatuity of lovers' rhymes, and follows that with the supreme instance of what has been mocked, the garden scene between Romeo and Juliet. It is a case of the parody coming *before* the thing parodied (as with Shylock's loss of daughter and ducats in *The Merchant of Venice*). A critical sense has been established to make us very aware of true and false values: what Mercutio mocked is here taking place. But as we see it, it is not – quite – the thing he mocked, though it seems to get very close to it. When Juliet plays on 'What's in a name', it could easily become mere verbal jiggery-pokery; it does not, for two reasons. Firstly, that the distinction between 'name' and 'thing' is a real problem, and felt to be so here, as the sexual roots which (Freudian-wise, as Professor Mahood has shown) promote the quibbling thrust continually through it:

> What's Montague? It is nor hand, nor foot,
> Nor arm, nor face, nor any other part
> Belonging to a man. O, be some other name!
>   (II. ii. 40–2)

The unnamed 'part' on which her fancy rests becomes clearer still as she mates it with the symbolic rose:

> What's in a name? That which we call a rose
> By any other name would smell as sweet.   (43–4)

Secondly, and arising from this, Juliet's speech goes through this emerging recognition to a climax in which the quibbling is finally shed:

> Romeo, doff thy name;
> And for thy name, which is no part of thee,
> Take all myself. (47–9)

It is, very forcibly, the thing and not the name which Juliet will offer; but that directness is something which Romeo does not achieve. The force, the life of the scene rests largely with Juliet: Romeo jumps walls with gay abandon, but his words have less assurance, and Juliet reproves him:

ROMEO: Lady, by yonder blessed moon I vow,
That tips with silver all these fruit-tree tops –
JULIET: O, swear not by the moon, th'inconstant moon,
That monthly changes in her circled orb,
Lest that thy love prove likewise variable.
ROMEO: What shall I swear by?
JULIET: Do not swear at all;
Or, if thou wilt, swear by thy gracious self,
Which is the god of my idolatry,
And I'll believe thee.
ROMEO: If my heart's dear love –
JULIET: Well, do not swear. (107–16)

Romeo is, as Juliet is not, fair game for Mercutio's mockery; his ineptitude is finally felt in the ambiguity of his question:

> O, wilt thou leave me so unsatisfied? (125)

The only 'satisfaction' he suggests is vows; Juliet has a franker thought:

What satisfaction canst thou have to-night?
ROMEO: Th'exchange of thy love's faithful vow for mine.
JULIET: I gave thee mine before thou didst request it;
And yet I would it were to give again.
ROMEO: Wouldst thou withdraw it? For what purpose, love?
JULIET: But to be frank, and give it thee again. (126–31)

Romeo is never frank; and Juliet is given the last word, before the nurse interrupts, with her magnificently erotic image:

> My bounty is as boundless as the sea,
> My love as deep: the more I give to thee,
> The more I have, for both are infinite.　　　(133–5)

Critical interaction proceeds to a new point in Act II, scene iv; it is again a very witty, and very bawdy parody of romantic love, and it is now in prose; for now the sense of the last scene criticizes this. Mercutio takes it for granted that Romeo has been to bed with Rosaline, and the assumption is doubly wide of the mark: it was not with Rosaline, and it was not to bed. The blunder is inherent in Mercutio's outlook, there are values entirely beyond his comprehension, as he makes plain:

> Why, is not this better now than groaning for love? Now art thou sociable, now art thou Romeo; now art thou what thou art by art as well as by nature; for this drivelling love is like a great natural that runs lolling up and down to hide his bauble in a hole.　　　　　　　　　　　　　　　　(II. iv. 85–9)

The rank bawdy is most welcome, as it brings romance back to earth; but this also serves to stress the actuality of experience outside Mercutio's range.

The comic sense is fully restored as the dominant tone here, with the addition of the nurse and Peter; but it is rich comedy, with a latent intelligence. It is carried over, brilliantly, into Act II, scene v, where the nurse's garrulity counterpoints Juliet's impatience, which is itself a prelude to the final brief scene of the wedding in the friary, which finally (the ceremony itself) takes place offstage. The betrothal was given maximum ceremonial as the climax to Act I; the wedding is reduced to an absolute minimum in the end of Act II.

VII

Act III, as I have already shown, is the pivotal centre of the play: the anticipated poetic climax – the consummation of their love – is there. But it is deferred for another climax which, despite the repeated foreboding, has not been precisely anticipated: the prose climax of Mercutio's death. And that it has not been anticipated marks it as an operation of chance, it has in its sharp prose the brusqueness of accident more effectively than the more fanciful mischance which later keeps Romeo from knowing of Juliet's potion. Its effect, now, is that when the consummation arrives it is distinctly 'death-mark'd': the deaths of Mercutio and Tybalt have already happened, that of Romeo's banishment is known to be about to happen. The sense of it is thus what Romeo *later* remarks at the point of his real death:

> How oft when men are at the point of death
> Have they been merry! Which their keepers call
> A lightning before death. (V. iii. 88–90)

This is, in fact, what their love had been; when Romeo says that, its peculiar power is the characteristic irony (overdone, so that some of its power is lost) that the death he alludes to – Juliet's – is unreal. She is in fact still alive and they 'could' go on from there. But, by then, such a suggestion is ludicrous – they could not go on anywhere, to anything. It has become an essential aspect of their love that it *must be* a lightning before death. The pressure of haste is a marked stress in Shakespeare's adaptation of the tale, and it is explicit in Juliet's early use of the lightning image (as well as, characteristically, parodied in Capulet's preparations for the second wedding):

> It is too rash, too unadvis'd, too sudden;
> Too like the lightning, which doth cease to be
> Ere one can say 'It lightens'. (II. ii. 118–20)

One cannot, by the end, conceive of their love otherwise than as a lightning before death, and this is one of the play's most characteristic diagnoses of the sonnet-love tradition: it is indeed the most serious aspect of the play as tragedy – that the sense of it as comedy (sonneteer's romance) demands death as its fulfilment.

This is the ultimate development from the sequence of events in Act III, which embeds (as it were) the love in death. But not simply, of course, as copulation excited by death. Hence Juliet's

'Gallop apace' is put *after* Mercutio's death, but *before* she has
heard of it. It is, as *we* see it, an experience of 'what might have
been'. In itself it is a magnificently full-bodied evocation of
sexual desire, enacting a series of paradoxes that are already more
or less familiar, as the emblems are familiar. But they are striking,
on examination, both for what they do and for what they do not
include. The focal image throughout is the day–night contrast,
and Juliet's desire for night becomes a cluster of powerfully
associated ideas: night, of course, is sex-time; it is blindness; it is
the 'madame' of a brothel:

> Come, civil night,
> Thou sober-suited matron, all in black,
> And learn me how to lose a winning match,
> Play'd for a pair of stainless maidenhoods.
>
> (III. ii. 10–13)

And, beyond that, follows the discovery that 'true love' can para-
doxically only be expressed in 'strange love':

> Hood my unmann'd blood, bating in my cheeks,
> With thy black mantle, till strange love, grown bold,
> Think true love acted simple modesty.   (14–16)

A paradox inherent in all sexual experience, that love is never 'nice
clean fun', and the concept of 'true love' as 'simple' is mere nonsense, since love and modesty have, when it comes to action, no
relationship whatever. The core of this is Juliet's discovery that in
most wanting her true love with Romeo she must experience the
wish to be a whore in the fullest sense:

> O, I have bought the mansion of a love,
> But not possess'd it; and though I am sold,
> Not yet enjoy'd.   (26–8)

But night has more than sex and the brothel: it is also the
raven's back:

> Come, gentle night, come, loving black-brow'd night,
> Give me my Romeo; and, when he shall die,
> Take him and cut him out in little stars . . .   (20–2)

This 'gentle night' is death; both in the seventeenth century sense as orgasm (hence the extraordinary image 'cut him out in little stars'), but also as literal death. There is no gap here between the expression of love and the expression of death:

> That all the world will be in love with night,
> And pay no worship to the garish sun.　　(24–5)

This remarkable complex of associations is superb: this *is* desire, recognized and focused as it must be at that point where love and lust are identical, or love is not love but 'simple modesty' (a nonentity). But there is a further aspect: it jumps the life to come – not the after-life, but the extension of life here; Juliet's speech is itself magnificently alive, but it leaps straight into death.

Thus, as I said, the speech is as remarkable for what it is not as for what it is: what it is not, is anything to do with fertility, or growth at all. In this it is markedly different from *Antony and Cleopatra*, where love is commonly *said* to be sterile; in fact, the Nile is essentially known for its fertility, Cleopatra has children, and she dies, not in orgasm, but as a nursing mother. There is none of this, anywhere that I can discover, in *Romeo and Juliet*; the sense of love here does not include that. Juliet is (several times) a bud that will flower and be killed by frost, never one that will grow seeds. I do not, of course, suggest that Romeo and Juliet 'ought' to be hoping 'all their troubles will be little ones', but the complete absence of fertility in the concept of love is as remarkable as it is apt: it leaves the love–death conjunction without division or alternative. Hence, a hundred lines later, we find Juliet, after she has heard of Romeo's banishment, saying:

> Come, cords; come, nurse; I'll to my wedding-bed;
> And death, not Romeo, take my maidenhead!　(136–7)

By IV. i Juliet's feeling has arrived at full-scale necrophilia:

> Or hide me nightly in a charnel house,
> O'er-cover'd quite with dead men's rattling bones,
> With reeky shanks and yellow chapless skulls;
> Or bid me go into a new-made grave,
> And hide me with a dead man in his shroud . . .
>
> 　　　　　　　　　　　　　(IV. i. 81–5)

In this one grasps how the final consummation must be in a tomb.

This point needs stressing, in order to focus the actual sense of the play, as against the common image of it as 'love's young dream'. It *is* that; but it also makes us know what that is: as Keats put it, 'half in love with easeful Death', except that 'easeful' is not a dominant stress in *Romeo and Juliet*. Admirers of Hemingway are apt to compare his novels with this play: and in both *A Farewell to Arms* and *For Whom the Bell Tolls* there is a similarity. In both there is a love affair of passionate intensity for which it is impossible to imagine a settled future, and in both the fantasy is completed by death. In *For Whom the Bell Tolls*, indeed, the hero's death is assured before he embarks on his love for Maria; yet when it comes at last it seems by no means so inevitable as had been claimed. In other words it is, after all, the quality of the imagined love, and not (as we are repeatedly assured) the facts of the military engagement, which guarantees his death. But Hemingway tries to pass this off without acknowledging its limitations, and it is just in this that the superiority of *Romeo and Juliet* is so obvious: for Shakespeare places their affair in a critical context, and establishes the equation of love and death as part of their youngness.

That it is paradoxical is obvious, and it becomes the centre of the play's general insistence on paradox. It is set against an extraordinary vitality in the play, a sense of life which is manifest in all the roles most alien to Romeo and Juliet themselves, that is to say the nurse, Mercutio, and the old Capulets. In all of these the stuff of life is earthy, bawdy, comic, certainly thoughtless, and impatient; and it has the conditions for continuance, the instinct of self-preservation and fertility. Mercutio dies; but his death is sheer accident, in no sense an inevitability of his nature. All of these have a warmth that is reassuring, but which is also utterly in contrast to the glory of Romeo and Juliet. The very vitality – manifested in Capulet's absurd hastiness – contributes powerfully to the disaster; and the play's characteristic perception is that this sense of Life is utterly alien to the romantic vision; and that each criticizes the other. The ecstatic love–death becomes unreal,

fantasy-type experience set against this; but this becomes tawdry
set against beauty's ensign and death's pale flag.

That is the final sense of Act III:

> NURSE: Romeo is banished; and all the world to nothing
> That he dares ne'er come back to challenge you;
> Or, if he do, it needs must be by stealth.
> Then, since the case so stands as now it doth,
> I think it best you married with the County.
> O, he's a lovely gentleman!
> Romeo's a dishclout to him; an eagle, madam,
> Hath not so green, so quick, so fair an eye
> As Paris hath. Beshrew my very heart,
> I think you are happy in this second match,
> For it excels your first; or, if it did not,
> Your first is dead, or 'twere as good he were
> As living here and you no use of him.
> JULIET: Speak'st thou from thy heart?
> NURSE: And from my soul too, else beshrew them both.

That this is true is what is to be grasped, as Juliet grasps it, to the
nurse's discomfiture:

> JULIET: Amen!
> NURSE: What?
> JULIET: Well, thou hast comforted me marvellous much.
> Go in; and tell my lady I am gone,
> Having displeas'd my father, to Lawrence' cell
> To make confession, and to be absolv'd.
> NURSE: Marry, I will; and this is wisely done.

She exits, and the trap is sprung:

> JULIET: Ancient damnation! O most wicked fiend!
> Is it more sin to wish me thus forsworn,
> Or to dispraise my lord with that same tongue
> Which she hath prais'd him with above compare
> So many thousand times? Go, counsellor;
> Thou and my bosom henceforth shall be twain.
> I'll to the friar to know his remedy;
> If all else fail, myself have power to die.
>
> (III. v. 214–43)

H

The nurse never recovers much force in the play: after this the sense of blind vitality passes to old Capulet, and remains with him.

VIII

The latter part of the play is rather burdened by the load of plotting which has to be expounded, but it is by no means so cumbersome as it is commonly made to seem with elaborations of scenic devices, especially for the tomb. Act III is very long, but Acts IV and V are both short. Their function is to fulfil the formal structure of the play, and they do this by reversing the sense of Acts I and II: there, a mock-love was exposed, and displaced by a real one; here a mock-death is similarly followed by a real death. It is in the sense of a mock-death that Juliet comes to the sensual awareness of the charnel-house that I quoted, and in this context her longing becomes a passionate cry:

> Give me, give me! O, tell me not of fear!
> (IV. i. 121)

And as Mercutio was left behind in the second Act, mocking the mock-love and never perceiving the real, so now the Capulets are left wailing the mock-death (in seeming parody of *The Spanish Tragedy*), excluded from what follows; and on that, Peter and the musicians play an apt scherzo:

PETER: Musicians, O, musicians, 'Heart's ease', 'Heart's ease'! O, an you will have me live, play 'Heart's ease'.
MUSICIAN: Why 'Heart's ease'?
PETER: O, musicians, because my heart itself plays 'My heart is full of woe'. O, play me some merry dump to comfort me.   (IV. v. 100–4)

Peter's merry dump is a moment of mirth in tragedy, equivalent to the moments of sententious foreboding in the prevailing comedy of the opening Acts. The balance has been reversed, and the play is now predominantly tragic, with comic infiltrations that become increasingly macabre: from the Capulets' activity in Act IV, not knowing what they do, through Peter's musical interlude, to

Romeo's grotesque apothecary and the Friar's bungling ineptitude
in Act V.

The key speeches in the first part belonged to Mercutio and
Juliet; here they are Romeo's, bringing the action of death to an
erotic climax:

> How oft when men are at the point of death
> Have they been merry! Which their keepers call
> A lightning before death. O, how may I
> Call this a lightning? O my love! my wife!
> Death, that hath suck'd the honey of thy breath,
> Hath had no power yet upon thy beauty.
> Thou art not conquer'd; beauty's ensign yet
> Is crimson in thy lips and in thy cheeks,
> And death's pale flag is not advanced there.
>
>   (V. iii. 88–96)

Earlier, the hint of death emerged from images of desire; here the
hints of sexual fulfilment appear among the talk of death. Romeo
wants from Juliet

> A precious ring – a ring that I must use
> In dear employment.   (31–2)

He will 'lie with thee tonight':

>   Here, here will I remain
> With worms that are thy chambermaids.   (108–9)

He dies in a last embrace, which Juliet brings to consummation in
a final play on death and love (echoing, at an opposite extreme,
'my naked weapon is out'):

>   O happy dagger!
> This is thy sheath; there rust, and let me die.
>   (168–9)

Thus the mock-death is translated into the real one. But the
'real' death is not, perhaps, very real. It is far more obviously the
beautiful consummation of the unfulfilled love, and its place as
climax of the formal structure is very strongly felt: it is moving as
part of the formal dance to which I compared the play, rather than
as the shock of death in the living world, which Mercutio's was.

So the movement from this is very rapid to the highly formalized
ending in rhyming verse to make golden statues of the lovers:

> For never was a story of more woe
> Than this of Juliet and her Romeo.   (308–9)

The terms are apt: a formal tale is what is concluded. But within
it, there has been an extraordinarily full penetration of exploration.

The play is overall suspended between two major ceremonies:
the dance-betrothal of Act I, and the wedding-funeral of Act V.
Between them it projects a double climax in Act III, which is in
both parts entirely unceremonial: Mercutio's death, and Romeo
and Juliet's clandestine consummation (with rope ladder to the
balcony and so on it has the air of stolen love). What *is* real is
perceived between these opposite polarities of ceremony and un-
ceremoniousness; and both are contrasted with a persistent consciousness of a noisy, bustling, healthy, bawdy, shabby vitality
which is sustained throughout. This sense of contrasts is almost
endlessly multiplied (I have said nothing of, for instance, the
friar's 'philosophy') and focused in the persistent punning,
quibbling, and paradox-mongering in the verse. About all these
things it is, no doubt, over-emphatic – like *Titus*, it is an over-
loaded play; but brilliant in its controlled multiplicity. And the
final sense we may have of a hot-house atmosphere, a slightly
cloying over-sweetness, is no accident, for it is just that with
which it is concerned: a highly perceptive exploration of the love-
death embrace of the sonneteering tradition, which regards both
its superiority and its inferiority to the world of common day.

Richard II

[1595]

I

There are a few untidy patches in the text of *Richard II* which give rise to argument about the unity of the play, the possibility that it is a revision of an earlier play, and so on. None of this is very impressive,[1] certainly not enough to question Shakespeare's authorship of, and responsibility for, the play as it stands. The only scenes one might wish away are V. ii and V. iii, the feebly protracted concerns of the Duke of York and his family; but these do not suggest another play, or another hand, so much as Shakespeare writing at very low pressure. The date generally accepted for it is 1595, which is plausible enough but by no means certain. It leaves us in doubt whether *Romeo and Juliet* is the earlier or later play, which is perhaps not very serious: the important point is that they were written close together in time, an association marked in the extent of rhymed passages, and even lyrical forms, in both plays. Together they constitute, as it were, a second round in Shakespeare's tragic output: *Romeo and Juliet*, like *Titus Andronicus*, is in a sense a 'classical' tragedy and clearly conceived in five Acts; whereas *Richard II*, like *Richard III*, is a 'tragical history' and more flexibly constructed in successive movements separated by brief scenes for the queen, but not answering to the Folio Act divisions. The first movement is continuous to the death of Gaunt in II. i; the second contains the whole of Boling-

---

1 The textual confusions at I. iii. 129–38 and II. ii. 98–122 seem to me insignificant. Failure to provide an exit for Gaunt during I. i, and the odd Quarto direction at the end of V. iii, '*Manet sir Pierce Exton, &*', when Exton cannot be on the stage, may be no more than relics of changes of mind during composition.

broke's rebellion and ends with Richard's surrender in III. iii;[1]
the fourth Act, encompassing the abdication, may reasonably be
taken as a complete unit, and Act V covers Richard's imprison-
ment and murder. In this, the structure resembles *Richard III*'s
development; but it is a much less formal ordering than *Titus* or
Romeo are given. One may reasonably suppose that Shakespeare
understood a difference of genre between the two pairs of plays.

Richard II had a chequered career with the censor during its first
hundred years: it is probable that it was performed entire in the
theatre from the beginning; but when the first Quarto was
printed in 1597, Richard's uncrowning of himself in Act IV was
omitted (the censorship for books was then, as now, quite
separate from the control of plays). The successful deposition of a
lawful monarch was dangerous matter, and Essex had the play
performed on the 7th February 1601, the day before his abortive
rebellion. In the Restoration, Tate produced the usual 'improved'
version, but even that was found too dangerous in 1680, when it
was twice banned. The play was popular in the early eighteenth
century, but became less so later; it was in the early nineteenth
century that modern attitudes to it took shape. With this play,
however, it was not Kean who set the pattern: reviewing his
performance in 1815, Hazlitt complained that 'Kean . . . made
[Richard II] a character of *passion*, that is, of feeling combined
with energy; whereas it is a character of *pathos*, that is to say, of
feeling combined with weakness.'[2] Kean's performance sounds
refreshing to me; but if he was as consistent as Hazlitt suggests, he
must have had difficulty with some of Richard's elegiac speeches
in III. ii. On the other hand, modern preconceptions about it
seem to derive from trying to impose Hazlitt's view consistently
on the whole play. Harold Child[3] commented on Benson's performance of 1900: 'He realised the force of the poet-king's
imagination, and gave him, in his weakness and his strength, a

---

1 For a slightly different division into four parts, see P. Ure's Introduction to *Richard
II*, 1956, p. lxii; the differences can largely be attributed to the fact that the structure
is designed to be continuous so that the parts overlap.
2 *A View of the English Stage*, *The Complete Works of William Hazlitt*, ed. P. P. Howe,
1930, vol. V, p. 223.
3 In *Richard II*, ed. J. Dover Wilson, Cambridge, 1939, p. lxxxviii.

flower-like beauty which appealed irresistably for sympathy.'
Benson's Richard would seem to have stepped straight out of a
Pre-Raphaelite painting, but this is the figure that has been with
us ever since: a petulant, effeminate Richard, swooping gracefully
to the bare earth, but looking embarrassed every time – and these
are several[1] – that someone remarks how like his father the Black
Prince he looks.

The other preconception we have to consider in clearing the
ground for a fresh consideration of the play derives from the
political interests of the 1930s, which radically revised current
attitudes to the history plays, and recognized their vitality as
political-morality – the progeny of *Kynge Johan, Gorboduc,* and *The
Mirror for Magistrates.* The relevance of this is obvious in the
censorship trouble at both ends of the seventeenth century; and
the deposition scene emerged at last as more than a demonstration
of Richard's narcissism ('Let it command a mirror hither
straight . . .'). Even Gaunt's too-familiar death-bed speech could
now be seen to have more relevance to the play than a local outburst of poetic patriotism. But the play, as play, did not really
benefit greatly, for the combination of political discussion-play
with wilting flower-king precluded any possibility of tragedy.
E. M. W. Tillyard[2] substituted the idea of it as the first part of a
tetralogous epic, not to be regarded as an autonomous play so
much as the prelude to *Henry IV*. Tillyard recognized that it was
radically different in style from its successors, but tried to explain
away this objection on the grounds that this play is a deliberate
re-creation of the medieval scene, a dramatic realization of manu-
script illuminations (the flower-king again) as a prelude to the
emerging 'modern' world of *Henry IV*.

This seems to me quite unacceptable. The politics of the play
were clearly contemporaneous; the jousting was Elizabethan; and
the figure of Richard is far more significant to the play than a mere
image of medieval man. Furthermore, if the play is a prelude to
Henry IV it seems to need a prelude itself: for Hall's pattern of

---

1 e.g. II. i. 176–7, III. iii. 68–70.
2 *Shakespeare's History Plays*, 1944, pp. 234–63.

history (on which, as Tillyard showed, Shakespeare strings his plays) depends from the murder of Woodstock, before this play begins: there are important references to it (in I. ii and later) but they are somewhat obscure, seeming to rely on the audience's foreknowledge rather than to aim at exposition. The subsequent development of Hall's pattern is certainly invoked in prophetic speeches towards the end of the play, but these again do not seem designed to pre-figure further plays so much as to conclude the themes of this one. I do not mean to imply that the *Henry IV* plays were written as if *Richard II* did not exist, but simply that its relation to them is much looser than Tillyard suggested; it can and should be treated as an independent play.

II

The conception of Richard as a wilting poet is completely out of place in Act I, which opens in terms of high rhetorical splendour:

> Old John of Gaunt, time-honoured Lancaster,
> Hast thou according to thy oath and band
> Brought hither Henry Herford thy bold son . . .
>   (I. i. 1–3)

This pitch is sustained throughout the court scenes, i and iii. It is, of course, possible to make Richard bleat these lines in feeble imitation of royal utterance, but only in defiance of the strong rhetorical rhythm they obviously have. That this is often done points to a general contempt for Shakespeare's use of words in his early plays: but the controlled variety of utterance which I have noted should give us more confidence in accepting his rhythms here, and we shall find the same variations of tone in this play as in its predecessors. Richard, here, is every inch a king: his reply to the first greetings of Bolingbroke and Mowbray suggests authority:

> We thank you both, yet one but flatters us,
> As well appeareth by the cause you come,
> Namely, to appeal each other of high treason. (25–7)

The logic is questionable, but that does not diminish the shrewd-ness and confidence of the royal pomp; and these qualities are still apparent in Richard's speech at the end of the scene:

> We were not born to sue, but to command.   (196)

And the commands he then issues are obeyed.

The main substance of the scene is in the vaunting speeches of Bolingbroke and Mowbray which seem to me rather strange. They accuse each other, indeed, of high treason, but mostly only in the form of abuse: the only real charges are Bolingbroke's, of Mowbray's misappropriation of cash, and his responsibility for the murder of Gloucester (Woodstock), and these Mowbray answers with some dignity (124–51). It is true that in both defences the king is implicated, but very obscurely, and the point is not taken up. Richard's response – and it is Gaunt's too – is to treat the matter as a personal quarrel, taking virtually no notice of the charges themselves:

> Wrath-kindled gentlemen, be rul'd by me . . .
> Forget, forgive, conclude and be agreed.   (152, 156)

There is no suggestion that Richard is 'huddling it aside' because he is implicated. The complexities of historical detail are sub-merged in the general stress on wrath-kindled gentlemen, the threat they offer to civil peace, and Richard's efforts to calm them:

> Let's purge this choler without letting blood.   (153)

The main development is of the choleric utterance, and the imagery of blood. The first is stressed in Richard's comment be-fore Bolingbroke and Mowbray appear:

> High-stomach'd are they both and full of ire,
> In rage, deaf as the sea, hasty as fire.   (18–19)

The tone is Marlowan, the heroic note of Tamburlaine, which is clearly heard in Mowbray's

> . . . I would allow him odds,
> And meet him were I tied to run afoot
> Even to the frozen ridges of the Alps.   (62–4)

And Richard remarks of Bolingbroke:

> How high a pitch his resolution soars!   (109)

It does indeed, in the startling image with which Bolingbroke follows up his charges:

> That he did plot the Duke of Gloucester's death,
> Suggest his soon-believing adversaries,
> And consequently, like a traitor coward,
> Sluic'd out his innocent soul through streams of blood,
> Which blood, like sacrificing Abel's, cries
> Even from the tongueless caverns of the earth
> To me for justice and rough chastisement.   (100–6)

The streams of blood may seem to take us straight into the world of *Titus Andronicus*, and so does much else in this scene. But, in fact, though there is far more blood on the stage in *Titus*, there is more in the poetry of *Richard II*. Blood in this scene refers to the choleric humour, the nobility of high blood, and the tie of kinship, as well as the spilt blood of fratricide (or civil war). This is developed more formally in scene ii, and extended later when the sun itself becomes bloody. But here it is associated with the significant reference to Abel's murder, the offence against God himself. Biblical allusion is at least as prominent here as Ovidian in *Titus Andronicus*, and it serves a similar interpretative function. Judas, Pilate, and Christ himself are all invoked in later scenes, and the play ends with a return to the guilt of Cain, in Bolingbroke's curse on Exton:

> With Cain go wander thorough shades of night,
> And never show thy head by day nor light.
>   (V. vi. 43–4)

The crimes of men in this play are very directly related to the divine scheme of things; and the problem of man as anointed king develops into a tragic dilemma which neither Richard nor Bolingbroke can solve. The Marlowan afflatus in the verse of this Act sets the play on a very high heroic plane indeed; when, later, a more flexible and human utterance emerges, it is not so much a maturing of Shakespeare's way of writing as the assertion of a

humanity that cannot fulfil the divine image. In this respect
Richard II differs from *Richard III*, for no character here seeks
independence by repudiating the divine order, though there are
several points at which the play itself (apparently supremely
orthodox) could be accused of blasphemy.

The consistent impress of this opening scene, then, is of the
heroic pitch of choler; the soaring resolution of the contestants
(in renaissance, not medieval, form) and the supreme status of the
king who rules them under, but only just under, God. All these
things are related to the blood image, in the significant circumstances of the first murder. The historical–political situation is
given, but, as it seems to me, suppressed for the time being to
permit the establishing of a blood tragedy, and of a Richard who
is a King. Similarly, his badness as a ruler and his weakness as a
man are held back for subsequent revelation: no hint of either has
been given yet.

III

The blood image is fully defined in scene ii, where Gaunt and the
Duchess of Gloucester develop a series of formal emblems in a
manner which might reasonably be called 'choric': the scene has
something of the air of a prologue postponed till the initial
tableau has been presented. But the hieratic tone is varied by
reference to the violent actions of men, in a fashion reminiscent of
Act I of *Titus*: Gloucester is said to have been 'hack'd down' by
'butcher Mowbray'. The apparent concern of the scene is with
Gloucester's murder and his widow's desire for revenge; but the
handling of this is again rather odd, as though the audience
already knew of it, rather than had to be told. On the other hand,
it is very explicit in elaboration of the blood relationship in which
the central figures are involved:

> Edward's seven sons, whereof thyself art one,
> Were as seven vials of his sacred blood,
> Or seven fair branches springing from one root.
> Some of those seven are dried by nature's course,

> Some of those branches by the Destinies cut;
> But Thomas my dear lord, my life, my Gloucester,
> One vial full of Edward's sacred blood,
> One flourishing branch of his most royal root,
> Is crack'd, and all the precious liquor spilt,
> Is hack'd down, and his summer leaves all faded,
> By envy's hand, and murder's bloody axe. (I. ii. 11–21)

The Duchess sustains her double emblem, of tree and blood vessels, at great length: it is at once a compulsion to unity, and to revenge; an emblem of family unity, and of what distinguishes princes from lesser men:

> That which in mean men we intitle patience
> Is pale cold cowardice in noble breasts.   (33–4)

Gaunt, like Marcus Andronicus, resists the impulsion to human revenge: 'God's is the quarrel'; and instead of descending into bestial insanity, he proceeds to elaborate the divine order and the rule of law:

>   for God's substitute,
> His deputy anointed in His sight,
> Hath caus'd his death; the which if wrongfully,
> Let heaven revenge, for I may never lift
> An angry arm against His minister.   (37–41)

Gaunt implies, once more, Richard's guilt, but sets the actions of men against the divine appointment of kings, and thus establishes the dilemma of the play. The Duchess sustains her plea for revenge, but never against Richard:

> Be Mowbray's sins so heavy in his bosom
> That they may break his foaming courser's back . . .
>   (50–1)

The spirited courser recurs as an image of spirited humanity: Shakespeare had presented it at length in *Venus and Adonis* in the stallion who can nothing lack 'Save a proud rider on so proud a back' (l. 300), and he reverts to it at key points in this play. Richard, in III. iii, comes down to the base court 'like glist'ring Phaeton, Wanting the manage of unruly jades'; and in the last

Act there is a strange interlude with the groom, discussing the
faithlessness of Roan Barbary:

RICHARD: Rode he on Barbary? Tell me, gentle friend,
            How went he under him?
GROOM: So proudly as if he disdain'd the ground.
RICHARD: So proud that Bolingbroke was on his back!
            That jade hath eat bread from my royal hand;
            This hand hath made him proud with clapping
            him.
            Would he not stumble? would he not fall down,
            Since pride must have a fall, and break the neck
            Of that proud man that did usurp his back?
                                              (V. v. 81–9)

Richard is divorced from both his divine anointment and his
animal spirits in the end, the links in the chain of being broken at
both ends, God and Roan Barbary seeming equally indifferent.

Here in I. ii, the old Duchess, deprived of her passionate hope of
revenge, loses the will to live and waits bloodless with her com-
panion Grief for death to visit her

            empty lodgings and unfurnish'd walls,
        Unpeopled offices, untrodden stones . . .
                                              (I. ii. 68–9)

The scene establishes, then, an elaborate and vivid sequence of
emblems: the living tree, rooted in the earth but associated with
the vials of human blood; the threatening figures of Envy and
Murder, and the noble spiritedness of violent action, contrasted
with the bloodless figure of Grief pouring watery tears on un-
trodden stones. All these recur in pointed echoes till they are re-
assembled at the end of the play. They serve here to interpret the
heroic terms of the opening scene, the conflict of an anointed King
with high-blooded subjects. That is established *first*; other facets
develop subsequently: of a criminal Richard we have had hints
(no more); of a weak man, so far none at all.

IV

I. iii sustains the heroic pitch: the full panoply of royalty in the
elaborate staging of the joust. It proceeds in much the same tone
as scene i until the sudden anticlimax of Richard's intervention:
the audience's disappointment is as intense as the combatants', for
we are deprived of a promised spectacle. But the effect of this is
not to affirm Richard's uncertainty so much as to shift the play to a
more sophisticated plane than armed combat. Richard's speech
links the emblems already noted to a stress only implicit before,
but now explicit, on the realm of England. The tree and blood
collocation reappears as:

> our kingdom's earth should not be soil'd
> With that dear blood which it hath fostered.
>
> (I. iii. 125–6)

Bolingbroke and Mowbray threaten civil war with their

> eagle-winged pride
> Of sky-aspiring and ambitious thoughts.   (129–30)

Their 'greatness' will 'make us wade even in our kindred's blood'.
The independence of the eagle is contrasted with the organic
structure of earth–tree–sky: an opposition of the will of man to
the order of nature and the divine will. The sentence of banishment provokes contrasting reactions: Bolingbroke's stoical
acceptance –

> That sun that warms you here, shall shine on me (145)

– includes a sense of organic unity preserved, and is set against
Mowbray's sense of tragic deprivation in being cut off from his
roots, his source of life:

> What is thy sentence then but speechless death . . .
> Then thus I turn me from my country's light,
> To dwell in solemn shades of endless night.
>
> (172, 176–7)

Gaunt has a similar vision:

> My oil-dried lamp and time-bewasted light
> Shall be extinct with age and endless night.   (221–2)

The crushing of ambitious pride provokes for them, as lack of revenge did for the Duchess, death and endless night, and Bolingbroke's reflections on the soul wandering in the air:

> Banish'd this frail sepulchre of our flesh,
> As now our flesh is banish'd from this land. (196–7)

The place of man in the organic structure of nature and heavens is felt to be curiously insecure.

The insecurity is brought to bear on Richard himself: he has acted with divine right, and his clemency in reducing Bolingbroke's sentence by four years may also seem divine; but it provokes the response:

> Four lagging winters and four wanton springs
> End in a word: such is the breath of kings. (214–15)

The irony is completed ten lines later:

> RICHARD: Why, uncle, thou hast many years to live.
> GAUNT: But not a minute, king, that thou canst give . . .
> Thy word is current with him for my death,
> But dead, thy kingdom cannot buy my breath.
> (225–32)

Richard's authority is still unquestioned, but he is brought sharply within the confines of mortality; Bolingbroke, on the other hand, appropriates the organic images to himself:

> Then, England's ground, farewell; sweet soil, adieu,
> My mother and my nurse that bears me yet! (306–7)

Out of this he can achieve the final development into excruciating patriotism that establishes him clearly as a growing branch:

> Where'er I wander boast of this I can,
> Though banish'd, yet a true-born Englishman.
> (308–9)

These opening scenes have developed a series of related conflicts: of human self-sufficient pride against dependence on a superior will; of the force of individual will against a determined pattern; of violence against the process of continuous growth.

All these characteristic themes are imaginatively realized in the
splendour of the staging and the utterance, and unified in the all-
pervading blood imagery. All this has been applied (by both
Richard and Bolingbroke) to political questions of order or chaos
in government; but so far the highly formal rhetoric, and the
formalized verse patterns, have resisted any considerable shift of
attention from the cosmic scale.

v

The next two scenes (I. iv and II. i) provide a series of shocks, reinforced by abrupt changes of tone. The heroic, the grandiose,
and the universal is suddenly presented in a different light.
Aumerle's account of his farewell to Bolingbroke has an offensive
levity:

> I brought high Herford, if you call him so,
> But to the next highway, and there I left him.
>
> (I. iv. 3–4)

Richard does not immediately imitate this tone (nor reprove it),
but he does turn to questions of political expediency: Bolingbroke's wooing of the people – 'What reverence he did throw
away on slaves' – and from the suspicion that Bolingbroke will
end in rebellion he turns to the economic problems of the Irish
war:

> We are inforc'd to farm our royal realm . . .
>   If that come short,
> Our substitutes at home shall have blank charters,
> Whereto, when they shall know what men are rich,
> They shall subscribe them for large sums of gold.
>
> (45–50)

The climax of this movement comes with Bushy's announcement
of Gaunt's illness:

> RICHARD: Now put it, God, in the physician's mind
>   To help him to his grave immediately!
>   The lining of his coffers shall make coats
>   To deck our soldiers for these Irish wars.

Come, gentlemen, let's all go visit him,
Pray God we may make haste and come too late!
(59–64)

The offensive levity of Aumerle and the plain falsity of Richard's economics are conflated in this blasphemous wit. The puissant and glorious Monarch is presented suddenly as a cold politician with atheistic tendencies. The figure of the Machiavel is remotely discernible here; but without the ambitious mastery of Richard III or Marlowe's Guise, it is merely distasteful. The more so, because this emerges as Richard's personality, cheap however witty; but still confident, he is not yet hesitant or weak.

The material for this scene is largely drawn from the anonymous *Woodstock*,[1] and the comparison serves to indicate differences in Shakespeare's stress. *Woodstock* is very largely concerned with economics: it goes into great detail with statistics showing the 'farming' and 'blank-chartering' in action round the country. Shakespeare suppresses a great deal, and brings in what he does use only incidentally, by no means as a central issue in his play. Further, his Richard is a radically different figure, even here: in *Woodstock*, the king is a 'rude boy' who derives his nasty schemes from his flatterers; and he wants the money chiefly for lavish spending:

At Westminster shalt see my sumptuous hall,
My royal tables richly furnished
Where every day I feast ten thousand men:
To furnish out which feast I daily spend
Thirty fat oxen and three hundred sheep,
With fish and fowl in numbers numberless.

(III. i. 83–8)

(The statistical tendency is clear enough.) This Richard is a feeble-minded luxur: Shakespeare's king has at least the ability to evolve his own nasty schemes, and he wants the cash to supply his Irish wars. He is, in short, still a king in action as well as name; the nastiness that is personal is also political, in him it springs from

---

1 *Woodstock: A Moral History*, ed. A. P. Rossiter, 1946, pp. 47–53. The relationship with Shakespeare's play is fully discussed in Rossiter's Introduction.

I

the problems of government. We have as yet no sign of feebleness.

The ideas and responses suggested by setting this scene against its predecessors are worked out in II. i (I have suggested that the Act division is misplaced here). Gaunt's famous prophetic speech sets

> This royal throne of kings, this scept'red isle
> (II. i. 40)

modulating through a long series of images to

> Is now leas'd out – I die pronouncing it –
> Like to a tenement or pelting farm.   (59–60)

Richard's entry is preluded by York's warning,

> deal mildly with his youth,
> For young hot colts being rag'd do rage the more
> (69–70)

which introduces a further discovery of his private character, whose limitations are clearly indicated in the contrast between the queen's greeting:

> How fares our noble uncle, Lancaster?   (71)

and his own:

> What comfort, man? how is't with aged Gaunt?   (72)

It is very poetical with aged Gaunt, as Richard (not yet a poet-king, or in the least flower-like) remarks:

> Can sick men play so nicely with their names?   (84)

Gaunt proceeds nevertheless to utter his criticism:

> A thousand flatterers sit within thy crown,
> Whose compass is no bigger than thy head . . .
> O, had thy grandsire with a prophet's eye
> Seen how his son's son should destroy his sons . . .

through to:

> Landlord of England art thou now, not king. (100–13)

Richard's temper blazes as York had anticipated:

> A lunatic lean-witted fool,
> Presuming on an ague's privilege. (115–16)

York is right: Richard is a hot colt, and his tone is obviously inappropriate. But Gaunt is not altogether right: Richard is still a king:

> Now by my seat's right royal majesty,
> Wert thou not brother to great Edward's son,
> This tongue that runs so roundly in thy head
> Should run thy head from thy unreverent shoulders.
>
> (120–3)

It is therefore Richard himself who leads Gaunt back to his major theme, the blood and plant emblems:

> O, spare me not, my brother Edward's son,
> For that I was his father Edward's son;
> That blood already, like the pelican,
> Hast thou tapp'd out and drunkenly carous'd:
> My brother Gloucester, plain well-meaning soul,
> Whom fair befall in heaven 'mongst happy souls,
> May be a president and witness good
> That thou respect'st not spilling Edward's blood.
> Join with the present sickness that I have,
> And thy unkindness be like crooked age,
> To crop at once a too long withered flower. (124–34)

That is the climax of Gaunt's scene; the sequel is the specific crime that upsets the unstable equilibrium of the realm: Richard's illegal seizure of Gaunt's property (still for the purpose of fighting in Ireland), which sets York off again on Edward's sons, comparing Richard to his father:

> His face thou hast, for even so look'd he,
> Accomplish'd with the number of thy hours.
>
> (176–7)

York prophesies rebellion; but Richard goes no further in offence than to stick to his point, makes York regent, and exits to make merry with his queen.

The first movement ends with Northumberland's news of Bolingbroke's imminent landing, and the plotting of rebellion. It has proceeded from the majestic royalty of I. i, through a series of discoveries to this final indication of disaster. In this it resembles, structurally, the first Act of *Titus Andronicus*, with its succession of prepared revelations; and as in *Titus* the emergence of human qualities that betray the royal image is revealed in striking contrasts of tone. It is the gap between the two which constitutes the tragic foundation of the play. On the one hand, Richard as king fulfils, in utterance and appearance, the panoply of royalty, the theme of blood as linking man and man, spilt in destruction, related to the family tree of Edward's progeny which grows out of the fertile soil of England. On the other, within this grandiose framework, Richard is a hot colt, whose misrule provokes rebellion. In the heroic frame, Richard is King, Bolingbroke a sky-aspiring rebel, whose doom in blood and guilt is evident; in the second, Richard is a bad governor whose downfall in rebellion is foretold, and Bolingbroke the necessary substitute. This distinction is lost entirely if it is assumed that the rhetoric of the opening scenes is merely a conventional dramatic mode without a specific function in this play, or if the actor attempts to reveal Richard's faults before Shakespeare exposes them in I. iv. The blood tragedy, in its largest terms, is established first; the political in a narrow sense, only secondarily. Whereas *Woodstock* sees the affairs of man in terms of a purely social environment, Shakespeare sets these against a cosmic continuum, represented by 'England' and symbolized by the generative soil. Economics is so much less Shakespeare's concern than *Woodstock*'s that it hardly becomes a major stress at all; it is used only to establish a particular local effect. The splendour of man is fulfilment as king, the sun shining on his kingdom; his tragedy is in his humanity, that he is beneath the sun, no less mortal than his subjects.

VI

This is the sense that can allow the play to develop a personal tragedy, of a man caught in an impossible predicament, whose sufferings are only marginally related to his faults (in contrast to Richard III). The queen foresees this in her chorus-like speeches in II. ii, opening the second movement of the play:

> Why I should welcome such a guest as grief,
> Save bidding farewell to so sweet a guest
> As my sweet Richard. Yet again methinks
> Some unborn sorrow ripe in Fortune's womb
> Is coming towards me . . .   (II. ii. 7–11)

The image of pregnant Fortune (representing, like the Duchess of York's 'Destinies', a fatalism that is distinct from divine justice) recurs in the queen's response to news of rebellion:

> So, Greene, thou art the midwife to my woe,
> And Bolingbroke my sorrow's dismal heir;
> Now hath my soul brought forth her prodigy,
> And I, a gasping new-deliver'd mother,
> Have woe to woe, sorrow to sorrow join'd.   (62–6)

The queen is now the labouring mother – she and Fortune together give birth to the future.

This I take to be a choric prelude to the second movement of the play, which runs right through to III. iii: its main concern is the narrative of rebellion from its inception here (anticipated, of course, in II. i) to its climax in the meeting of Richard and Bolingbroke at 'Barkloughly' (a confusing error for Harlech, derived from a misprint in Holinshed). That final scene is one of the finest and most characteristic in the play, but its predecessors are less interesting, rehearsing necessary material at a noticeably lower pitch than what goes before and after; though they do develop the celebrated (and at times embarrassing) lyrical laments by Richard which pick up the tone his queen has established in II. ii.

There are, however, some particular aspects of this sequence which call for comment. Richard himself is withheld for a considerable time (until III. ii), so that it is Bolingbroke who dominates here, for an obvious reason: he has now to be developed as a central figure, where before he was only one against several, and Richard dominated alone. The rebellion itself is remarkable for the lack of any struggle: it is a triumphal march by Bolingbroke. The only sense of struggle in this part appears in the indecisions of York, which are dramatically very effective,[1] as he balances right against right and can discover no firm basis for decision but simply drifts sadly on the current of necessity.

The absence of struggle is very evident: the queen, Bushy and Greene, York, the Welsh captain, and finally Richard himself all assume defeat. Throughout this sequence we are never given to feel that anything can be done: the result is foretold, and as inevitable as night following day. Fortune is giving birth, and no mere man can intervene. But the birth is still monstrous: that is what is stressed in the interesting brief scene between Salisbury and the Welsh captain, II. iv:

> CAPTAIN: 'Tis thought the king is dead; we will not stay.
> The bay-trees in our country are all wither'd,
> And meteors fright the fixed stars of heaven,
> The pale-fac'd moon looks bloody on the earth,
> And lean-look'd prophets whisper fearful change . . .
> These signs forerun the death or fall of kings.
> Farewell: our countrymen are gone and fled,
> As well assured Richard their king is dead.
> SALISBURY: Ah, Richard! with the eyes of heavy mind
> I see thy glory like a shooting star
> Fall to the base earth from the firmament.
> Thy sun sets weeping in the lowly west,
> Witnessing storms to come, woe, and unrest.
>
> (II. iv. 7–22)

The stars presage disaster, but in a rather curious way: the fixed stars are frightened by meteors, and Richard is a shooting star: his glory has no resting place in the heavens, but must blaze out and fall. It is again an image of man's brief candle set against the unmoved and unmoving continuum. But it should also be noted that Richard must *have* a glory to fall to the base earth: unless the

---

1 His speech, II. ii. 98–121, has worried editors because it continually infringes metrical regularity: but its broken rhythm, and ultimate collapse into prose, is admirably expressive of his frantic hithering and thithering.

opening scenes have been given their full weight, this image becomes absurd.

The emblem patterns established earlier are recapitulated here, and made more clearly to represent the tragic sense. In Act III Bolingbroke emerges as a reasonable and competent man; but the weakness of his position is hinted even in his words to Bushy and Greene:

> yet, to wash your blood
> From off my hands, here in the view of men
> I will unfold some causes of your deaths.
>
> (III. i. 5–7)

The image of Pilate lies behind these words, another competent but unattractive governor. Bolingbroke is shown as in every way fit to govern, and the hypocrisies which his position compels him to are scarcely obtruded at all.[1] Richard, in Act III, is more obviously than before unfit to rule. But though that judgement is established, we are made to feel that it is almost irrelevant: Bolingbroke cannot escape the taint of blood, nor Richard lose the mark of glory. And when Richard's sun 'sets weeping in the lowly west', the 'pale-fac'd moon' will inevitably 'look bloody on the earth'.

The sun, blood, and washing meet together in Richard's famous lines:

> So when this thief, this traitor, Bolingbroke,
> Who all this while hath revell'd in the night,
> Whilst we were wand'ring with the Antipodes,
> Shall see us rising in our throne the east,
> His treasons will sit blushing in his face,
> Not able to endure the sight of day,
> But self-affrighted tremble at his sin.
> Not all the water in the rough rude sea
> Can wash the balm off from an anointed king;
> The breath of worldly men cannot depose
> The deputy elected by the Lord.   (III. ii. 47–57)

---

1 See Brents Stirling: 'Bolingbroke's "Decision" ', *Shakespeare Quarterly*, 2, 1951, pp. 27–34.

That can be true, and yet Bolingbroke triumph. Hence Richard's well-known speeches in this Act, all in the elegiac mode of 'For God's sake let us sit upon the ground And tell sad stories of the death of kings', enact fully the glorious sun setting in the west. In them we may feel simultaneously, what we have not seen before, the weakness of the man oscillating between extremes of hope and despair as the news comes in, demanding a courage that he does not possess. The man who speaks these lines does command our attention as well as the lines he speaks; 'as well as', but not 'instead of'. This double attention sustains the counterpoint between the two levels of the play which I noted: glory and blood-guilt on the one hand, and the men as men on the other.

Richard is already identified with the sun: an even loftier claim is hinted when he suspects his favourites of treachery:

> Three Judases, each one thrice worse than Judas! (132)

which picks up the hint of Bolingbroke as Pilate. The more we are allowed to see Richard's deficiencies as man, the more powerfully his glory is imagined. Its climax comes in III. iii. The emblems of Act I are rehearsed once more, this time by Bolingbroke himself:

> If not, I'll use the advantage of my power
> And lay the summer's dust with showers of blood
> Rain'd from the wounds of slaughtered Englishmen –
> The which, how far off from the mind of Bolingbroke
> It is such crimson tempest should bedrench
> The fresh green lap of fair King Richard's land,
> My stooping duty tenderly shall show.   (III. iii. 42–8)

Bolingbroke the man is also felt in this speech: echoing the heroic vaunt of his utterance in Act I, albeit now overlaid with diplomatic disclaimers. He repeats the same ambiguous pattern a few lines later:

> Methinks King Richard and myself should meet
> With no less terror than the elements
> Of fire and water, when the thund'ring shock
> At meeting tears the cloudy cheeks of heaven.
> Be he the fire, I'll be the yielding water.   (54–8)

The water that opposes fire in a thundering shock is no more
'yielding' in spirit than Bolingbroke himself; he is having it both
ways, as he does about Richard (with more overt irony) when the
king appears on the upper stage:

> See, see, King Richard doth himself appear,
> As doth the blushing discontented sun
> From out the fiery portal of the East,
> When he perceives the envious clouds are bent
> To dim his glory and to stain the track
> Of his bright passage to the occident.   (62–7)

York notes that the outward appearance fulfils the image:

> Yet looks he like a king. Behold, his eye,
> As bright as is the eagle's, lightens forth
> Controlling majesty.   (68–70)

His words, too, have controlling majesty, as he uses Bolingbroke's
emblems to judge him without any ambiguity:

> He is come to open
> The purple testament of bleeding war.
> But ere the crown he looks for live in peace,
> Ten thousand bloody crowns of mothers' sons
> Shall ill become the flower of England's face,
> Change the complexion of her maid-pale peace
> To scarlet indignation and bedew
> Her pastures' grass with faithful English blood.
>   (93–100)

The climax of this movement is achieved in action as emblematic as the verse: Richard's descent into the base court:

> Down, down I come, like glist'ring Phaeton,
> Wanting the manage of unruly jades.   (178–9)

where his tears and sighs will be storms that make a dearth in this
revolting land. We have already felt the fact of Richard's weakness, and he acknowledges it in his words to Bolingbroke:

> They well deserve to have
> That know the strong'st and surest way to get.

and,

> For do we must what force will have us do.
>
> (200–1, 207)

But if the personal quality of the men is dilated to dominate the whole scene, it destroys it. This descent of the king is a disaster of real magnitude, not in the least a fiction of Richard's 'poetic imagination'; and Bolingbroke states it as clearly as Richard.

In that scene, the play's central stress is firmly re-established, with a new complexity. For we have got to see not just the simple situation of Act I – the royal greatness versus sky-aspiring lords; nor just that complicated by the crimes of the sacred majesty; but now both these things set against the personal qualities of Richard and Bolingbroke, weakness and strength. That is to say there are now three distinct scales of value, each yielding different judgements: first, the divine order, in which Richard is king, Bolingbroke a rebellious angel; second, the political order, in which Richard is a bad king, Bolingbroke a competent rebel; third, the personal order, in which Richard is a weak man, Bolingbroke a strong one. These are, I suggest, three separate and distinct things which are held simultaneously before us: to speak of Richard's 'character' in a single sense is to simplify grossly. It involves turning those aspects of his speech and action which represent the sacred majesty into a mere reflex of the weak man, and calling it just his poetic imagination (as if the whole of this aspect of the play were a sort of *Secret Life of Walter Mitty*), which is nonsense; the more obviously so because this is fully sustained in the speech and action of others. Richard's imagination is no more 'poetic' than Bolingbroke's.

The fact is that the emergence of Richard as a person, though important, is awkward, in that it is liable to cloud the issue. It must not be suppressed, but it must be kept under restraint or the cosmic theme will collapse, as it tends to do on the modern stage. This becomes a special problem in Act IV, where the double vision is both the special brilliance of the de-coronation scene, and the cause of its partial failure.

VII

These two major scenes are distanced from each other by the Queen's interlude with her gardeners, of which the function is very obviously choric. The tears and growing earth emblems are given a final extension in the lecture demonstration on good husbandry. The scene is embarrassing nowadays, and can never have been very lively; but if the rhetorical structure was allowed its full development, this brief commentary would seem more in place than it does in productions struggling to invest the play with a false naturalism. The scene is important to revive the political theme, which has been obscured by the more personal stress in IV. iii. England the sea-walled garden continues to grow in spite of weeping queens, but needs a gardener; it needs in fact the speciality, not of majesty, but of rule. In Richard's fall his queen imagines a second loss of Eden:

> What Eve, what serpent, hath suggested thee
> To make a second fall of cursed man?
>
> (III. iv. 75–6)

The allusion ties in with the Biblical reference of the play; but the gardener's retort is bluntly matter-of-fact:

> King Richard he is in the mighty hold
> Of Bolingbroke. Their fortunes both are weigh'd;
> In your lord's scale is nothing but himself,
> And some few vanities that make him light.   (83–6)

The need for Bolingbroke is plainly stated, and the inevitability of Richard's fall. To this view, the whole edifice of rhetorical and imaginative splendour has no validity; the play is momentarily stripped of all its larger forms. But only for a moment: if government needs Bolingbroke, Bolingbroke needs majesty, as the opening of Act IV plainly demonstrates.

The first part consists of a quarrel over responsibility for Gloucester's murder. The crime which should be the central item of the indictment against Richard only leads to a vulgar brawl from which we can never learn who really was guilty. The situation of

I. i is recapitulated, but without the splendour; and Bolingbroke now has less power to control the squabbling lords than Richard had then. He tries to restore the tone by announcing the repeal of Mowbray; but the gesture is nullified by Carlisle's news of his death. The fates, obscurely here but clearly in a moment, are spoiling Bolingbroke's triumph.

The second part of the scene follows York's announcement that Richard will abdicate. Bolingbroke ascends the throne without ceremony, which produces a startling peripeteia in Carlisle's prompt and magnificent attack. Richard's crime has just been dissolved in doubt and argument; Bolingbroke's is before us, the stage setting the emblem of usurpation as he sits on Richard's throne. The scene is set for Carlisle's denunciation:

> The blood of English shall manure the ground,
> And future ages groan for this foul act.
>
> (IV. i. 137–8)

The heroic memory of Mowbray fighting crusades

> For Jesu Christ in glorious Christian field,
> Streaming the ensign of the Christian cross
> Against black Pagans, Turks, and Saracens   (93–5)

is transposed into

> Peace shall go sleep with Turks and infidels.   (139)

And, finally, Carlisle translates the established blood emblems into the supreme sacrifice:

> Disorder, horror, fear, and mutiny,
> Shall here inhabit, and this land be call'd
> The field of Golgotha and dead men's skulls.
>
> (142–4)

The name of Christ echoes through the rest of the scene. Richard takes it up on his entry:

> So Judas did to Christ. But he, in twelve,
> Found truth in all but one; I, in twelve thousand, none.
>
> (170–1)

Against this image, Bolingbroke's rational intention ('so we shall proceed without suspicion') becomes ironical; and Richard does not spare him. This, I take it, is the effect of the famous speech in which Richard goes through the coronation rites in reverse:

> With mine own tears I wash away my balm,
> With mine own hands I give away my crown,
> With mine own tongue deny my sacred state,
> With mine own breath release all duteous oaths.
>
> (207–10)

The image of Christ leads us to this ritual solemnity; and at the same time Bolingbroke on the throne is in a conspicuously false position. Richard presses home his advantage:

> Though some of you, with Pilate, wash your hands,
> Showing an outward pity – yet you Pilates
> Have here deliver'd me to my sour cross,
> And water cannot wash away your sin.   (239–42)

Bolingbroke has no reply: Shakespeare interpolates the cruder figure of Northumberland to resist the imaginative power with blunt insensitivity; Northumberland who can (in V. i) dispose of guilt with a brusqueness in marked contrast to Bolingbroke:

> My guilt be on my head, and there an end.
>
> (V. i. 69)

Northumberland's bluntness, however, cannot dispose of the power that Richard has invoked, and Bolingbroke has to restrain him:

> Urge it no more, my Lord Northumberland.   (271)

This preludes the 'mirror scene', which is too often underestimated. Richard has been descanting on the proposition that, deprived of the throne to which he was born, he has no identity:

> No, not that name was given me at the font.   (256)

He develops this theme into the mirror-image:

> That it may show me what a face I have
> Since it is bankrupt of his majesty.   (266–7)

What he sees when the looking-glass is brought derives its numerals from Holinshed, but its verbal form from Marlowe's *Faustus*:[1]

> Was this face the face
> That every day under his household roof
> Did keep ten thousand men? (281–3)

The echo of Faustus, the man who was thrust forever from the sight of Christ, is curious here; and more remarkable since there are two other echoes of Faustus within the previous twenty lines:

> O that I were a mockery king of snow,
> Standing before the sun of Bolingbroke,
> To melt myself away in water-drops (260–2)

and,

> Fiend, thou torments me ere I come to hell. (270)

The words are addressed to Northumberland, but their force is strange: Richard has represented himself as Christ; but he is now the damned Faustus on his way to hell, seeking oblivion. So that when he speaks of

> the unseen grief
> That swells with silence in the tortur'd soul (297–8)

he is expressly referring to his own guilt; a guilt which is reflected on Bolingbroke, who, seated on the throne, is another 'mirror' of Richard's predicament:

> Mark, silent king, the moral of this sport –
> How soon my sorrow hath destroy'd my face. (290–1)

Bolingbroke's silent figure adds to its emblematic connotations that of 'silence in the tortur'd soul'. Their guilts reflect each other: men who, like Marlowe's heroes, presume to the sweet fruition of an earthly crown, and are damned for it. The peculiar twist here is that Richard was born to it; but his sense of damnation is no less strong than his divinity. Bolingbroke's immediate

---

1 See Ure's note on line 283.

implication in all this is too often overlooked, because his silent presence, so impressive on the stage, is invisible to the reader.

The problem that drove Richard to look in the glass is by no means a purely fanciful one. To Tudor orthodoxy, the *man* who was *king* was an exceptional mortal, possessed of peculiar virtú, and by this fitted for his role so that he could fill no lesser one. Richard 'looks like a king' but is not one. Shakespeare does not here (it is different in *Henry IV*) make a simple distinction between the man and the office: the office is the necessary concomitant of the man.

Richard has involved Bolingbroke in this emblematic reflection of greatness and guilt; he leaves him with impressive scorn:

> Then give me leave to go.
> BOLINGBROKE: Whither?
> RICHARD: Whither you will, so I were from your
>   sights.   (313–15)

It is Richard who is dominant here, not as a weeping Narcissus, but as a man conscious of moral victory. Our final impression cannot be of his weakness alone. The question in fact is, how far should we (freed from traditional prejudice) feel his weakness in this scene? I am somewhat uncertain. By concentrating on the imaginative power of the emblem-images, I have seen a tragic splendour, as I think it should be seen, moving between man and divine appointment, heaven and hell. The other view of the scene derives from noting that it is Richard who says all this, that it is his romantic vision of himself. It is, however, obviously more than this: it was Carlisle, not Richard, who invoked the figure of Christ on the field of Golgotha, and the only challenge to these terms comes from Northumberland who rather serves to test the strength of the imaginative power than to countervale it. A hint of criticism can be heard in Bolingbroke's shrewd retort –

> The shadow of your sorrow hath destroy'd
> The shadow of your face –   (292–3)

but Richard's come-back is strong enough to embarrass Bolingbroke more than himself. The abruptness with which Bolingbroke turns from Richard's exit to announce his own coronation is ambiguous in effect: one may take it as the reticence of guilt, or as efficiency released from patient endurance of a long and embarrassing exhibition. Efficiency predominates in Bolingbroke's performance in the opening of Act V; but the burden of guilt returns to him at the end of the play.

One cannot simplify this: we are to feel simultaneously the force of all Richard's utterance, and yet to see the weakness implicit in the fact that *he* is uttering it. It is partly the dilemma evident in all these early plays, of a form of poetic statement derived from narrative verse, where it would be unequivocal (Richard not seeming weak unless the narrator called him so) becoming equivocal by the mere fact of being delivered by an actor on the stage. But here, I think, Shakespeare is partly taking advantage of that ambiguity: Richard's character is the least important aspect of the scene, but it is allowed to be felt; and the same is (even more ambiguously) true of Bolingbroke. The resultant complexity of effect is impressive, but somewhat distracting, because it is not handled with the assurance of Shakespeare's later technique (when, for instance, Othello speaks of his own splendour, the double sense is far more sharply defined).

VIII

In Act IV the major themes of the play reach their climax in the formal interchange of guilty majesty with a staging as emblematic as the verse. It proves, in a sense, more climactic than it should be, with an Act still to go. Act V proceeds, obviously enough, to Richard's death and Bolingbroke's mounting burden of guilt, and is provided with a prelude from the queen. But the major conflict being over, there is nothing left but to develop our awareness of the two *men*, and that is not done with much conviction. The one significant development is Richard's brilliant (but specifically not magnificent) soliloquy in prison on the relation of man to the space and time of the world and the universe:

> A generation of still-breeding thoughts,
> And these same thoughts people this little world,

In humours like the people of this world;
For no thought is contented. (V. v. 8–11)

He runs over the 'thoughts' of the play: divine thoughts which
tend to set 'the word itself Against the word' (13–14); thoughts
tending to ambition, which do plot

Unlikely wonders: how these vain weak nails
May tear a passage thorough the flinty ribs
Of this hard world, my ragged prison walls. (19–21)

And so on – the themes of the play reduced from their splendour
to a reflection of the diminutive absurdity of Man, who

With nothing shall be pleas'd, till he be eas'd
With being nothing. (40–1)

This great speech takes us a long way from the politico-
historical aspects of the play, to comment on the insubstantial
pageant. These reflections spring from the tragic experience of
the play: the Marlowan pitch of the opening (and of subsequent
scenes), important though it is, never had Marlowe's persuasive-
ness; so that in the end it comes to no more than vain weak nails
tearing a passage through flinty ribs. A futile gesture, however
heroic, emphasized in the odd little scene with the groom when
Richard learns that Roan Barbary will prostitute himself to
jauncing Bolingbroke. Deserted by God before, Richard is finally
deprived of ambitious spirits as well; but he has still the energy to
make a dramatic last stand against his murderers: it is no mere
dreamer we are to remember at the end.

Richard's scenes contain about all that is good in Act V. The
York scenes – ii and iii – are curiously inept (though not in such a
way as to suggest earlier composition, and certainly not another
author). There remains only the final acknowledgement of guilt in
Bolingbroke's last speech, tying in these dominant emblem
figures:

With Cain go wander thorough shades of night,
And never show thy head by day nor light.
Lords, I protest my soul is full of woe
That blood should sprinkle me to make me grow . . .

K

I'll make a voyage to the Holy Land,
To wash this blood off from my guilty hand.

(V. vi. 43–50)

IX

The play emerges, I think, in a somewhat different form from the way it has usually been presented. Many of the speeches on which I have laid my main stress have proved unpopular with critics, precisely because they *are* stressed: that is to say, the main structure of the play is rhetorical, and it calls for boldly rhetorical performance, both in stage arrangement, and in speech. As in *Richard III*, this rhetorical structure supports a view of the divine order which is here, more than in the earlier play, seen as splendid, but none the less making demands of men which cannot be fulfilled. In *Richard III* this produced a counter-figure in Richard himself, fulfilling the human will in defiance of law and order. In *Richard II*, it produces no such protest, but a complex ambivalence in the counter-theme of the irrelevance of the rhetorical vision to human abilities, and the need for mere politic competence in affairs; the need for Bolingbroke, and even for Northumberland.

In many respects, the play still resembles the form of *Titus Andronicus*: a blood tragedy (and as it is Shakespeare's most splendidly rhetorical play, so also it is the one most preoccupied with blood) evolving its own commentary in recurrent emblems in the verse, echoed in emblematic staging. It is like *Titus*, too, in its presentation of character through successive discoveries: the callousness of 'sweet Richard' revealed in I. iv is similar to the vulgarity of 'gentle Lavinia' in II. iii. But in other respects it is very different. Like *Richard III*, it is involved in political history, and the emblems are planted in England as the fecund source of the plants that grow out of human blood, and the tree with its lopped branches. This produces a more complex play than either *Titus Andronicus* or *Richard III*, but with the complexity goes some loss of clarity in construction, and some consequent obscurity or confusion. At the same time, just as in the contemporary *Romeo and Juliet*, a more significant concern with man as man (neither angel, devil, nor beast) is, however erratically, emerging. Richard II is a person with whom our sympathies can be engaged, as Titus was not, nor Richard III. Criticism has sometimes suggested that a more mature dramatic style can be seen evolving in this play; and the criterion of maturity implied seems to be a closer approximation to natural speech. But the contrast here, I have suggested, is functional; and contrasting modes of utterance, rhetorical or natural, continue to function in Shakespeare's plays to the very end of his career. If we value here the natural to the exclusion of the rhetorical, we lose entirely the framework in which Richard the man is set. When that happens, sympathy runs out of the control of detachment, and the play's greatness is swallowed up in the petite imaginings of a poet-king.

I have tried to show how much more it is than that: we lose all its quality if we devote ourselves solely to subtilizing on Richard's character. But equally I would not wish to leave the impression that that is small, or that it is not an advance on *Titus Andronicus*. The reflections of Richard's soliloquy in prison lead in time to:

> The fault, dear Brutus, is not in our stars,
> But in ourselves, that we are underlings.

Ourselves, what men are as men, gains an increasing proportion of attention; but it never occupies a play of Shakespeare's on its own: the more abstract structure, and thematic emblems, the rhetorical detachment, all these retain a significant place in his work.

Julius Caesar
[1599]

I

There is a gap of three years between *Richard II* and *Julius Caesar*, during which (as far as we know) Shakespeare wrote no tragedies. It hardly seems time enough to fuss about, but in Shakespeare's prodigious output it is relatively long; there is no comparable gap before or after until by about 1609 he turned all his work to tragicomedy. The interim is filled by histories – the two parts of *Henry IV*, and *Henry V* – and by comedies – *The Merchant of Venice*, *Much Ado about Nothing*, and possibly *All's Well that Ends Well*.[1] That these later histories were not, like *Richard III* or *Richard II*, conceived as tragedies is not of course remarkable: the events they relate, and the Tudor version of history they enact, require them otherwise. But neither they, nor the comedies contemporary with them, are altogether like earlier plays of similar kinds. *The Merchant* juxtaposes an extremely romantic theme, of Portia and Belmont, with its opposite in Shylock's cruel operations of profit and loss on the Rialto; its conclusion is firmly in favour of comedy, but only after a reckoning with realities far harsher than afflicted any earlier comedy. *Much Ado* is far less certain in tone, but it offers a pattern of tragi-comedy which demands serious attention to the tragic elements. *Henry IV* part I is gay enough in its comic elements, but Falstaff's role in the last Act

---

1 G. K. Hunter in *All's Well That Ends Well*, 1959, dates the play considerably later; I am inclined to prefer Chambers' suggestion of 1599, roughly contemporary with *Julius Caesar*.

is to parody the heroic idea of Honour on which the political morality of the play is built. Hence it is not altogether surprising that part 2 displays a far more general scepticism about human values and behaviour; its main lines echo the first play, but the tone contrasts: the new rebellion is put down by cunning, not honour, and Falstaff's erring humanity is less enchanting as an exposure of senile desire and public corruption. *Henry V* is generally supposed to fulfil its function as heroic climax to the series well enough, and perhaps it does; but there is much about it which seems odd: the gap between the splendours of Harfleur and the realities of ordinary soldiers is made very apparent, and Henry's journeyings between the two do not leave him uncriticized; it is even possible to wonder whether the rhetoric of 'Once more unto the breach' is not as well (or as cynically) judged as Antony's 'Friends, Romans, countrymen'.

The critical light on Henry may not be quite so acute as that, but it is certain that in these plays the linguistic contrasts explored in *Titus Andronicus* have become sharper and more extreme. The well-known increase in the proportion of prose witnesses a new attention to natural speech, to the language, and therefore the behaviour, of men as men; and much of the verse grows more immediately out of prose speech, as with Juliet's nurse, or, even more remarkably, with Shylock's utterance.

But prose, in the context of a verse play, is not merely closer to natural speech, it is also reductive; the view of men as men presented has much earthy warmth, but it is not wholly benevolent: the Nurse is also 'ancient damnation'; Falstaff is the Lord of Misrule in serious as well as comic senses, and Shylock is unequivocally evil. Henry V is a brilliant king, and a devout man, but he is far more remote from the divine hierarchy than Richard II. The symbolic and the natural in man no longer echo one another, but rather seem to conflict, and there seems to be a growing scepticism about the validity of the symbolic structures. The king in *All's Well* is merely an ageing man, afraid of ill-health and impotence.

The same scepticism appears in the ideas of these plays: politics and economics are no longer judged by a concept of divine ordination, but far more by an empirical inquiry into what really happens: what men do, not what they ought to do, as Bacon said of Machiavelli. The competence of Bolingbroke, and the crude self-sufficiency of Northumberland in *Richard II* give way to the cynical adroitness of Prince John in *Henry IV*, part 2. The frivolous mismanagements of Richard yield to the far more disturbing logic of usury in *The Merchant*. The Tudor dream was fading, and the obtruding sense of reality was decidedly less splendid. It became correspondingly more difficult to fulfil a tragic pattern, for in tragedy the idea of splendour must ultimately dominate all that can be thrown against it. The bestiality and evil of *Titus* or of *Richard III* work in a context of heroic and divine possibility; a framework of orderly affirmation sustains the plays, they are rhetorical in structure as well as language. So is *Julius Caesar*; but here rhetoric is brought more sharply in question than ever, and though it unquestionably has a rhetorical structure still, that too is much less easily accepted.

II

There is more certain evidence for dating *Julius Caesar* than for most of Shakespeare's plays. It was not in Meres' list in 1598, but in the Autumn of 1599 Thomas Platter, the Swiss traveller, described a performance of it at the Globe; and there are several literary allusions to it in the next two years. Even if these points are not individually conclusive, we should expect to date it around 1599, for such a date makes sense of what seems to me its peculiar kind of unsatisfactoriness. For all its brilliance, and its success, it has an uncertainty of tone, structure, and total statement which seems to me in some ways like the uncertainty of *All's Well*; although (witness its popularity) *Julius Caesar* 'comes off' in a sense in which *All's Well* does not, its basic equilibrium is not really much greater.

Yet if we should not expect to date it before the end of the 1590s, we should also not expect it to be much later; for behind the 'new' elements which I have been indicating there is a familiar shape to be recognized, a Senecan shape, of revenge tragedy. The play is firmly based on the Greatness of Caesar, and

the ritual crime of his murder, which is preceded by an elaborate
display of portents, storms, and portentous rhetoric; Antony
fills the role of faithful (and not very hesitant) revenger; Caesar's
ghost sustains the portentous atmosphere, and the revenge is
finally accomplished.

All this suggests a form and significance for the play remote from
the portrait gallery of 'characters' which every schoolboy knows,
and seemingly equally remote from the concern with men as men
which I have been postulating. Hence it is important to stress first
that it *is* the play's structure, establishing a simple pattern elaborated by a stress on supernatural forces and blood imagery very
like what we have already seen in *Richard II*. Antony's speech over
Caesar's body seems to roll *Titus*, *The Spanish Tragedy*, and
Richard II all up in one:

> O, pardon me, thou bleeding piece of earth,
> That I am meek and gentle with these butchers.
> Thou art the ruins of the noblest man
> That ever lived in the tide of times.
> Woe to the hand that shed this costly blood!
> Over thy wounds now do I prophesy
> (Which like dumb mouths do ope their ruby lips,
> To beg the voice and utterance of my tongue),
> A curse shall light upon the limbs of men;
> Domestic fury and fierce civil strife
> Shall cumber all the parts of Italy;
> Blood and destruction shall be so in use,
> And dreadful objects so familiar,
> That mothers shall but smile when they behold
> Their infants quartered with the hands of war,
> All pity chok'd with custom of fell deeds;
> And Caesar's spirit, ranging for revenge,
> With Ate by his side come hot from hell,
> Shall in these confines with a monarch's voice
> Cry havoc and let slip the dogs of war,
> That this foul deed shall smell above the earth
> With carrion men, groaning for burial. (III. i. 254–75)

In general form, this speech is close to the prophetic handling of
sap and blood images in the first two Acts of *Richard II*; in ornate

detail it goes further back, with the ruby lips of the bleeding
wounds, to Marcus' speech at the end of Act II of *Titus*; and
Caesar's Senecan spirit with Ate by his side substitutes the
classical figures of *The Spanish Tragedy* for the biblical Cain that
haunted Richard. For a famous, but rather curious, moment
towards the end the 'monarch's voice' seems close to Henry V
with 'Cry havoc and let slip the dogs of war'; Antony's rallying
cry is unexpected before he returns to carrion men groaning for
burial, but it is not here that his rhetoric is called in question.
What he utters here is, very powerfully, an emblematic summary
of the play. In this it is an extension of the tremendous elaboration
of cosmic disturbance in the storm which shatters Roman peace
in Act II.

But here there is a strong point of difference from earlier plays:
the emblematic commentary on *Titus* was not questioned; that on
Richard II hardly could be, since the supernatural powers invoked
were so explicitly biblical. But here belief in cosmic portents
(although apparently confirmed by the whole play – the storm
precedes Caesar's death, and the ghost Brutus's) is frequently described as mere superstition, and Caesar's scepticism is debated:

> But it is doubtful yet
> Whether Caesar will come forth to-day or no;
> For he is superstitious grown of late,
> Quite from the main opinion he held once
> Of fantasy, of dreams, and ceremonies.
> It may be these apparent prodigies,
> The unaccustom'd terror of this night,
> And the persuasion of his augurers,
> May hold him from the Capitol to-day.
>
> (II. i. 193–201)

If Shakespeare did not make this up, he certainly amplified it, for
it is not in Plutarch. It produces an odd effect, for Caesar's credulity, identified with his ageing megalomania, discredits all
credulity, discredits in fact the structure of portents on which I
have said the play is constructed; or at least questions it, for the
result is ambivalent. This ambivalence casts a similarly indefinite
shadow on the play in other ways: the great Caesar is also absurd

in his Marlowan self-assertion; Antony, with all his devotion and skill, is offensive; a similar irony reveals in Cassius (but only occasionally) a crude jealousy, and it calls Brutus' high-mindedness into question. The play seems to have equal and opposite tendencies towards the nobility of tragedy on the one hand, and a world of dust and ashes on the other. There is also a perplexing hovering on the edge of comedy which is sometimes explicit (as, for instance, with Casca's description of Caesar in comic prose in I. ii), but sometimes not at all clear: there are many passages which seem at least to invite a sense of the ridiculous without being decisively 'meant' to be funny.

This sense of absurdity is involved in the gap I have indicated between the play's portentous magniloquence, and its insistent concern with men as men; its interest in demagogy, and in 'characters'. But this is not quite such a simple matter as it has been made out. Certain differences from earlier plays are obvious: even the most formal speeches here do not reach the conclusive ending in couplets, and the utterance has very often a decidedly 'naturalistic' tone close to prose, as well as sometimes actually being prose. In this way the stress is laid more directly than in earlier plays on how men actually behave. We are made to feel this very clearly in the first scene between the tribunes and the populace, a trivial dialogue mostly in prose, with only one adventure in rhetoric, the lament for Pompey.

Thus far we are certainly directed to men as men; and the same insistent naturalism emerges in the carefully interposed glimpses of Brutus' home life: we are to feel that these men are like ourselves at least as much as that, being Roman, they are very different. Roman society lacked a divine sanction, or at least it seemed to the Christian tradition to have done so; it was therefore a fit ground in which to explore the political behaviour of men empirically, freed from the assumption of a providence shaping their ends. To push this attitude too far in considering English history or politics was ideologically dangerous, and this may account for the succession of Roman plays which succeeded the earlier spate of English history plays: *Julius Caesar*, Jonson's *Sejanus* and *Catiline*, Chapman's *Caesar and Pompey*, *Coriolanus*, all have a common interest in politics as an autonomous activity. The political interest in *Titus Andronicus* cast the Roman empery in a mould only marginally different from Tudor despotism; but in *Julius Caesar* the danger of monarchy is the basis of the conflict.

In this way the character interest subserves a function in the play; but when (for instance) T. S. Dorsch devotes nearly all of his critical discussion[1] of the play to an analysis of characters we soon become aware not only that this is old familiar ground, but that it is distorting it fatally. 'The character of Decius Brutus is clearly established in half a dozen speeches' (lvii) provokes me to retort that Decius Brutus has no defined character at all, he has only a function; actors of widely different characteristics can play him equally satisfactorily: he may be fat or thin, honest or dishonest, what you will: what he *does*, in the play, is to bring out Caesar's proneness to flattery. But this kind of attention is no less absurd when applied to major figures:

> We have good-humouredly accepted arrogance of this kind in recent English leaders who have served us conspicuously; why not in Shakespeare's Caesar? . . . Casca's account of the scene in the market-place, with its scarcely veiled hostility to Caesar, must not, for what it can tell us of Caesar's character, be taken any more seriously than Cassius's tirade.　　　(xxxi–xxxii)

This proposes a kind of historical inquiry into the character of Caesar, using the play as a document from which to make deductions – and discounting anything that casts doubt on the image of a 'noble' Caesar (or Churchill). But this is a play: words cannot be judged in the same way as in a historical document; though the motives of the speaker may qualify the judgement on his words, they cannot simply be 'rejected' unless we cut the play. We are not trying Caesar in a court of law where some witnesses will be deemed 'unreliable': all the figures and all their utterances are part of the structure which we are to regard.

It becomes clear, I think, that the central issue of the play is not 'what is the character of Caesar' – the more obviously because he

---

1 *Julius Caesar*, 1955, pp. xxvi–lx.

is dead half-way through. The stress on men as men is vitally important as modifying the structure of pattern and emblem evident in earlier plays: modifying, not replacing. Caesar's arrogance and weakness are part of an insistent naturalism set against another order governed by storm and blood. The relationship between them can only be understood in the process of the play.

III

Act I, scene i, opens with men at their cheapest, the opposite of the pomp and ceremony of the opening scene of *Richard II*: a street scene, with politicians, and a crowd. It starts on a note of contempt for the crowd, and moves immediately into comic prose, clownish quibbling by the cobbler on his trade. The (rather crude) imputation of clownishness to the crowd is taken up in the rhetoric which the tribune then addresses to them:

> O you hard hearts, you cruel men of Rome,
> Knew you not Pompey? Many a time and oft
> Have you climb'd up to walls and battlements,
> To towers and windows, yea, to chimney-tops,
> Your infants in your arms, and there have sat
> The livelong day, with patient expectation,
> To see great Pompey pass the streets of Rome:
> And when you saw his chariot but appear,
> Have you not made an universal shout,
> That Tiber trembled underneath her banks
> To hear the replication of your sounds
> Made in her concave shores?   (I. i. 36–47)

This rhetoric is simple in itself, but rather more complex in its context. In itself it gives us the splendour and pomp of the greatness of Rome, made unequivocal in

> To hear the replication of your sounds
> Made in her concave shores.

But simultaneously we are forced to see that all this echoing splendour comes from the voices of the same clowns who are

being abused by this splendid utterance. They are just 'the vulgar',
'growing feathers pluck'd from Caesar's wing' so that he will

> fly an ordinary pitch,
> Who else would soar above the view of men
> And keep us all in servile fearfulness.   (73–5)

The rhetoric, in fact, was being used, to serve a political end:
crowds are easily swayed, and Caesar is a soaring bird whose
wings (men) must be clipped or all men will be slaves. But men
thus easily clipped are slaves already; and the flight which Caesar
can make on 'wings' such as these is inevitably shaky. This attitude to the mob is familiar in Shakespeare from the Cade scenes of
Henry VI, the crowd scene in *Sir Thomas More*, and later (and far
more elaborately and subtly) in *Coriolanus*.

So we have simultaneously here: the splendour and greatness of
Rome, the unstable foundations of that greatness in the clownish
crowd, the political manoeuvring of the tribunes, and the
dangerousness of great men. This is the preparation for Caesar's
entry:

CAESAR: Calphurnia.
CASCA: Peace, ho! Caesar speaks.
CAESAR: ✦   Calphurnia.
                                                    (I. ii. 1)

This is on the verge of comedy: the great man does nothing but
address his wife beside him, but his lightest word is magnified by
the megaphone of sycophants. What follows has all to do with
superstition: Calphurnia is to be cured of sterility by the touch of
the athlete (Antony) in the Lupercalia. But a moment later, the
warning of a soothsayer – 'Beware the ides of March' – is dis-
regarded: 'He is a dreamer. Let us leave him. Pass.' The difference
is merely the stupid one, of welcome or unwelcome superstitions,
and there is nothing in the least god-like in Caesar's judgement.
This is pomposity, not pomp; the presumption of greatness in
Caesar is reduced at his first appearance to a minimum: there is
not much of it apparent to us but the actor's stage presence.

Thus the stage is set for Cassius to develop the hint of rottenness, of instability in all this display; and to do it in a very different utterance. He and Brutus speak verse indeed, but a verse which is as flexible as prose, and thus far removed from either the complacent commonplace of Caesar or the inflated rhetoric of the tribunes. And when the rhetoric is echoed here it becomes overtly ironic:

> I have heard,
> Where many of the best respect in Rome
> (Except immortal Caesar) . . .   (57-9)

Cassius' attempt to persuade Brutus to sedition finds little immediate response, until the shouts of acclaim off-stage bring back the awareness of crowd and soaring Caesar:

BRUTUS: What means this shouting? I do fear the people
                Choose Caesar for their king.
CASSIUS: Ay, do you fear it?
                                      (78-9)

This makes an initial climax to an argument which has been, so far, little more than shadow-boxing. Both speakers declare themselves more openly, and doing so develop a more rhetorical rhythm. Brutus states his main theme:

> For let the gods so speed me as I love
> The name of honour more than I fear death. (87-8)

Cassius' response is to build on the theme of 'honour' ('honour is the subject of my story') his splendid account of Caesar's inability to swim the Tiber in flood:

> And this man
> Is now become a God, and Cassius is
> A wretched creature . . .   (114-16)

Cassius' utterance gains rhythmic warmth as his jealousy takes charge: it is obvious that the figure who becomes ridiculous here is not Caesar, but Cassius. The 'honour' that Brutus spoke of was not this kind of thing at all. But the concept of honour does involve this (as with Hotspur in *Henry IV*): the 'great man' is sup-

posed to be all-round great – *mens sana in corpore sano.* Hence
Cassius does make a point at a certain level:

> Ay, and that tongue of his, that bade the Romans
> Mark him and write his speeches in their books,
> Alas, it cried, 'Give me some drink, Titinius,'
> As a sick girl.   (124–7)

The gibe is fair, the more so as it takes the form of a parody of
rhetoric, 'that tongue of his'. But the irony is brought back on to
the parodist: for Cassius' denunciation has been gathering its own
afflatus, and he ends with just such a rhetorical flourish as he has
mocked in Caesar:

> Ye gods, it doth amaze me
> A man of such a feeble temper should
> So get the start of the majestic world,
> And bear the palm alone.   (127–30)

Brutus is significantly silent about all this, and comments again on
the shouts off-stage – and Cassius completes his peroration with a
superbly grotesque image:

> Why, man, he doth bestride the narrow world
> Like a Colossus, and we petty men
> Walk under his huge legs, and peep about
> To find ourselves dishonourable graves.   (133–6)

The movement from the Marlowan 'Like a Colossus' to the
physical particularity of 'huge legs' makes the overall effect of
this scene: the contrast between an abstract concept of greatness
and the concrete object, man. Cassius' words continually confuse
the two, or bring them, as here, into ironic juxtaposition. Brutus
keeps them rigidly distinct: his honour is nothing to do with
swimming matches; and his final comment in an oddly constricted
utterance makes a clear discrimination, refusing to comment on
Cassius' rhetoric, or his confusion of values, and confining himself to an admission of alarm

> Under these hard conditions as this time
> Is like to lay upon us.   (172–3)

So that there is a nice irony in Cassius' reply:

> I am glad
> That my weak words have struck but thus much show
> Of fire from Brutus.   (173-5)

The fact is that most of them have been tacitly rejected; the limitations of Cassius' attitude, as of the rhetoric to which it impels him, are impressed upon us.

Caesar's re-entry develops these contrasting modes of valuation – the grandiose and the physical – in a manner which insists on a slightly grotesque form of comedy:

CAESAR: Antonius.
ANTONY: Caesar?
CAESAR: Let me have men about me that are fat,
          Sleek-headed men, and such as sleep a-nights.
          Yond Cassius has a lean and hungry look;
          He thinks too much: such men are dangerous.
                                                  (188-92)

The final comment is shrewd enough, whatever its implications for the entourage of a dictator (it is addressed to the athlete Antony); but the comic effect is gained first. Antony reminds us of the other standard of judgement:

> He is a noble Roman . . .   (194)

and Caesar reverts to the comic:

> Would he were fatter!   (195)

But when he goes on 'I fear him not', the juxtaposition of 'fear' with crude physical valuation recalls Cassius' reference to the sick girl. What follows is a further shrewd analysis of Cassius (such as Brutus did *not* provide):

> Such men as he be never at heart's ease
> Whiles they behold a greater than themselves.
>   (205-6)

This is obviously a truth, and for the moment we can accept that assertion of Caesar's greatness without being immediately con-

cerned that it is Caesar himself who utters it; but for the moment
only – the point is immediately re-affirmed:

> I rather tell thee what is to be fear'd
> Than what I fear; for always I am Caesar.
> Come on my right hand, for this ear is deaf,
> And tell me truly what thou think'st of him.
>
> (208–11)

The grotesque conceit of 'always I am Caesar' is again juxtaposed
with the physical image 'this ear is deaf' (which, again, is not in
Plutarch). Caroline Spurgeon found a lack of any dominant image
pattern in this play: but there seems to me a very insistent one
here in this continual juxtaposition of heroic valuation with crude
physical characteristics – strength in swimming, sick girl, huge
legs, fat men, deaf ear: these are merely men, playing out a noble
action ('immortal Caesar') which is also a grotesque (almost
Falstaffian) comedy: an uncomfortable reflection.

The comic element, latent from the first, has gradually been
thrust through the noble Romans: it takes over entirely in Casca's
prose account of the scene which has been off-stage, culminating
in the supreme physical failing, Caesar's epileptic fit and its relation to his unfavourable reception by the crowd.

These opening scenes, then, direct our attention on to the
political business of men, with the stress on valuation: what *is*
human greatness? And the effect is ambivalent. We recognize
nobility as something which is there, but we see also the sham, the
mere bullying bodies, the ludicrous. The dual vision is insisted on
in the structure, keeping the big ceremonial scene offstage and
finally relating it in comic prose; and in the utterance, rhetorical or
prosaic verse; heroic idea or physical image. These are comments
on men as men which are general in their application as well as
specific, and it is clearly limiting their relevance to refer them only
to the 'characters' of, say, Caesar and Cassius. In *Titus Andronicus*
the contrast of Imperial splendour and human bestiality ('his
limbs are lopp'd') was a generic one; the development is both
more subtle and infinitely more complex here, but it is not wholly
unlike in kind. But whereas in *Titus* the ceremony of Imperial

election was staged, while the ritual murder took place off-stage, here that situation is reversed, and the ritual murder is to be the play's central scene.

IV

There is a further structural likeness to *Titus* to be noted before I drop a parallel which may easily be overpressed. In that play the second Act is unified by the pastoral emblems of the hunt; what I take to be the second movement here (I. iii to II. iv: no interval is implied between the Acts and the division seems to be arbitrary) is entirely dominated by the great storm. The stress is shifted to forces outside men. But whereas the overall movement in the first scenes seemed clear, I have less confidence in this second movement. However obviously ironic Caesar's repudiation of the soothsayer might be, we have generally been led firmly towards a critical and sceptical outlook which inevitably complicates our response to the storm. If it is to be taken simply as an image of the civil strife of Rome, it is bound to seem overdone. If, on the other hand, it symbolizes a natural or supernatural order beyond human control, the difficulty is to credit it. I do not, of course, mean that such a symbol cannot be used for dramatic purposes unless we literally believe in it; by no means; but where the play itself so clearly invokes scepticism the suspension of disbelief is more difficult. The required ambivalence is easier to recognize than to imagine.

The storm, of course, is naturally as well as supernaturally terrifying: pedestrians are killed in the streets of Rome. It is insisted on in the original stage directions (*Thunder and Lightning; Thunder still; Thunder and Lightning*, and so on) and continually in the dialogue, whether as an expression of fear, courage, superstition, or scepticism. The only intermission is provided by the scene in Brutus' orchard where the contrasting calm is very effective. And that serves to emphasize the symbolic significance of the storm. Brutus stands and talks outside the world of Rome, the human whirligig of storm, and his orchard, like a May garden, is similarly withdrawn; a position of physical and mental calm

L

from which he can view the tempest as a distant firework display in the city.

But the idyllic withdrawal is not of course possible; or at least is not possible without a complete surrender of power and responsibility. Within the dialogue of the conspirators the storm image is replaced by its equivalent in the little world of man, the image of blood. Brutus strains the security of his position by continually forcing distinctions on the blood-lust of others:

> No, not an oath . . .   (II. i. 114)

> Swear priests and cowards, and men cautelous,
> Old feeble carrions, and such suffering souls
> That welcome wrongs; unto bad causes swear
> Such creatures as men doubt; but do not stain
> The even virtue of our enterprise,
> Nor th' insuppressive mettle of our spirits,
> To think that or our cause or our performance
> Did need an oath; when every drop of blood
> That every Roman bears, and nobly bears,
> Is guilty of a several bastardy,
> If he do break the smallest particle
> Of any promise that hath pass'd from him. (129–40)

The concept of honour which is thus rooted in blood has manifest dangers, for blood cannot be dissociated from its other senses (as we feel here). This is even more striking a few lines later:

> Let's be sacrificers, but not butchers, Caius.
> We all stand up against the spirit of Caesar,
> And in the spirit of men there is no blood.
> O, that we then could come by Caesar's spirit,
> And not dismember Caesar! But, alas,
> Caesar must bleed for it. And, gentle friends,
> Let's kill him boldly, but not wrathfully;
> Let's carve him as a dish fit for the gods,
> Not hew him as a carcass fit for hounds. (166–74)

One could fairly say that the whole tragic conception of the play is concentrated in that last astonishing image. Brutus is trying to sustain the distinction I noted in I. ii, between spirits and bodies, magnanimity and mere physical domination; and as Cassius walks boldly in the storm while Brutus worries apart in his orchard, so Brutus wants to kill a spirit without a drop of blood while Cassius is content (or realistic enough) to be a butcher. Like Titus before him and Othello after, Brutus would justify a murder by ritualistic dedication: 'Let's be sacrificers, but not butchers.' Thus there is something preposterous about 'carve him as a dish fit for the gods', which is surely not a failure in the symbolic organization, but a positive indictment of the fatuous distinction. Men *are* bodies, Caesar's blood *must* flow, and Brutus must leave the orchard to be destroyed in the storm. Brutus' much vaunted nobility comes in question here: in one sense it is real enough – we do not doubt his moral superiority to Cassius; but it is quite unreal in another sense, for its valuation of men, ignoring their brute nature, is inevitably false. Brutus' utterance stands in direct contrast to Cassius' tale of the swimming match; but it reveals a confusion of values no less radical.

Thus the correspondence is established between the distinguishable aspects of this part of the play: between the symbolic storm and the orchard, between the contrasting images of flesh and spirit, and between Brutus' conspiracy and Cassius's. And they are all linked by an uncertainty of outlook: the storm is portentous of a force superior to man, or else it is a vulgar superstition to regard it as a portent at all, it is 'just a storm'; and the conspiracy is either a necessary and inevitable action (an 'enterprise'), or else it is a vulgar deed of jealous underlings. The ambivalence persists, and it is the vitally interesting thing about the play; but it is not altogether satisfactory. It seems, as I have suggested, over-insisted on, and therefore a trifle absurd when our attention is so often directed away from symbols on to men as they are, a naturalism which appears here in the brief glimpses of Brutus' domestic life (so different from Caesar's just afterwards). The storm is part of the intricate structure of the play as I see it, but it is also outgrowing that, generalizing and simplifying into the obvious Senecan pattern that I propounded initially. In later plays, *Pericles* or *The Tempest*, the storm symbol is virtually the extent of our knowledge of a tragic experience for which we have little dramatic equivalent; but here we are concerned with the dramatic equivalent, and the symbol seems less than the thing, not more (as the storm which opens Act II of Othello seems excessive for its symbolic function). The emblem patterns of *Titus* or of *Richard II* grew into their own structures; but here the emblems and the action do not co-exist so easily, the symbols need to grow out of the action more organically, as the image of grotesque flesh in Act I does. The difference, of course, is that although in *Richard II* a distinction is established between divine order and human competence, there they do not become radical alternatives, whereas here they are set in conflict as modes of thought. The same is, I think, true of *Hamlet*, and creates acute problems there; but the system of belief involved in a Christian cosmology is more readily established than one in Roman augury which is distanced from the start.

Likeness and difference from *Hamlet* can be seen in the handling of dawn at the end of this scene compared with Horatio's famous lines concluding the opening of the later play. Here there is a slightly comic maladroitness in the debate between the conspirators as to where the dawn *is*: it neatly suggests their lack of direction at the same time as moving the play on to the day that follows the night of storm; but it is more than a little absurd. So also is the emblem of the Roman matrons' nobility when Portia displays her self-inflicted wound: this may represent the physical brutality of the society, and does contrast oddly (but not at all clearly) with Brutus' wish not to shed blood, but chiefly it seems to be a striking incident in Plutarch for which Shakespeare has not discovered a sufficiently explicit relevance.

Act II, scene ii, returns to the storm and the portents, with Calphurnia's dreams and her fears, and Caesar's reiterated 'Caesar shall go forth' which is variously courageous and idiotic. In the last scene Brutus was struggling for coherence of values amid the conspirators on whom the comment was clear, not because Brutus ever made it, but precisely because he did not, because of the difference between his utterance and theirs. Here Caesar also, in a different way, is concerned with value:

Caesar should be a beast without a heart
If he should stay at home to-day for fear.

(II. ii. 42–3)

Caesar is a lion with a heart – in Calphurnia's dream 'an hundred spouts did run pure blood' – and this directly negates Brutus' ambition to destroy a spirit without blood. The lion is the king of beasts; but with Caesar we do not forget that he *is* a beast, an animal of blood. So, when we reach Caesar's clearest statement of *his* value – 'The cause is in my will: I will not come' (71) – we recognize this 'will' as being, however splendid, 'blood-ruled' in the Elizabethan sense. Value is, and is not, here. Just as Brutus' values are false because men are *not* spirits, but *men*, filled with blood; so Caesar's value is only an outgrowth of the blood-ruled beast, and there follows immediately a demonstration of his will succumbing to flattery.

The dramatic core of this is clearly concerned with value: should men be regarded as noble, or as beastly? Different men and different values are juxtaposed such that none can clearly triumph: we are in a way brought close to the debates on 'will' and 'value' in *Troilus and Cressida*, where a similarly dusty answer is returned, with clearer definition. The obvious comment on Caesar is in the Trojan debate on Helen:

TROILUS: What's aught but as 'tis valued?
HECTOR: But value dwells not in particular will.

(II. ii. 52–3)

There the image of the ageing flirt Helen makes the point very clear: here we have an ageing, blustering Caesar, not so clearly valueless, but his value cannot lie in his 'particular will'. That irony is enforced here in a way which is not repeated in *Troilus*, by the structure that is larger than any man, the world of storms, of dreams, and predicted spouts of blood.

v

This irony is used to superb effect to establish the climax of Caesar's murder in Act III, scene i. His 'will' has brought him forth, and he parades it with preposterous pride against the appeals of the conspirators; his Marlowan rhetoric mounts against their pleas:

> I could be well mov'd, if I were as you;
> If I could pray to move, prayers would move me;
> But I am constant as the northern star,
> Of whose true-fix'd and resting quality
> There is no fellow in the firmament.
> The skies are painted with unnumber'd sparks,
> They are all fire, and every one doth shine;
> But there's but one in all doth hold his place.
> So in the world: 'tis furnish'd well with men,
> And men are flesh and blood, and apprehensive;
> Yet in the number I do know but one
> That unassailable holds on his rank,
> Unshak'd of motion; and that I am he,
> Let me a little show it . . .   (III. i. 58–71)

The climax of Caesar's hyperbole —

> Hence! Wilt thou lift up Olympus?   (74)

forms the cue for the murder: Caesar is, after all, a man of flesh and blood. The Marlowan hero of sky-aspiring pride has reached a point of parody, and is destroyed.

Brutus and his fellows make an impressive emblem of blood as they wash their hands and swords in Caesar's wounds – an emblem which is as ambiguous as Calphurnia's dream: she saw it as destruction, while Decius persuaded Caesar it implied 'great Rome shall suck Reviving blood' (II. ii. 87–8). So here, the conspirators offer their bloodstains as the revivifying of Rome:

> BRUTUS: How many times shall Caesar bleed in sport,
> That now on Pompey's basis lies along,
> No worthier than the dust!
> CASSIUS: So oft as that shall be,
> So often shall the knot of us be call'd
> The men that gave their country liberty.
>   (III. i. 114–18)

Whereas for Antony

> this foul deed shall smell above the earth
> With carrion men, groaning for burial.   (274-5)

Antony, of course, carries his point – carrion is all that follows
this deed, this mighty enterprise; but only because Antony is a
more competent politician than Brutus.

The key to the subsequent development is in the crowd scenes
which follow: the root of these values, as the first Act made clear,
whether of Caesar's greatness or of Brutus' rectitude, lies in the
men who make up the Commonwealth: and in that the fundamental irony asserts itself, the futility of either becomes uncom-
fortably plain. A simpler irony has already been stressed, in the
news that one emperor will replace another, that Antony intends
to replace Caesar with Octavius. Now Brutus and Antony successively face the crowd. Both offer, as they must, rhetoric; but
there is a marked difference between them. Brutus' rhetoric,
significantly in prose, is relatively simple. But his reasonableness
is made ironic in his success, as the crowd shouts out:

> Live, Brutus! live! live!
> Bring him with triumph home unto his house.
> Give him a statue with his ancestors.
> Let him be Caesar. Caesar's better parts
> Shall be crown'd in Brutus.   (III. ii. 49-53)

That is the 'value' of Brutus' high-minded effort to resist monarchy. The point is rammed home when Antony trumps Brutus'
ace; his change to verse marks the growing emotional charge, but
it marks too the shift from Brutus' cool reasoning to Antony's
blatant emotional trickery. His repulsive 'Friends, Romans,
countrymen' speech is an exhibition of the destruction of reason
by rhetoric; the continuous play on 'Brutus is an honourable man'
becomes unbearable in its insistence – to us – on its truth, at the
same time that it is used to enforce – on the crowd – the belief that
it is not true.

Once again the crowd is used to point the irony. Antony concludes:

> I speak not to disprove what Brutus spoke,
> But here I am to speak what I do know . . .
> O judgement, thou art fled to brutish beasts,
> And men have lost their reason.   (102–7)

Which is true, but not as Antony means it. The plebeians shout back:

> Methinks there is much reason in his sayings.
> If thou consider rightly of the matter,
> Caesar has had great wrong.   (110–12)

The inanity of this discredits it.

The rest of the scene is progressively more repulsive, following out the process initiated here. Antony wheedles the crowd into hearing Caesar's will, the blood is up, roused by words beyond the recall of words, and all Brutus' reasonable intents are lost. A final emblem is provided in the brutal little farce of the lynching of Cinna the poet:

> CINNA: I am not Cinna the conspirator.
> PLEBEIANS: It is no matter, his name's Cinna.
> (III. iii. 32–3)

Brutus' 'honour' can have no more growth in reality than Caesar's 'greatness': both end in farcical bestiality, for both are rooted in the mindless instability of the mob.

VI

This part of the play ends, then, like the first with prose comedy; but this scene has a sharper and a far more brutal edge than Casca's account of Caesar's fit. The general movement of the play is away from the noble image towards the ignobility of man. This is continued in Act IV in the unpleasant scenes between Antony, Octavius, and Lepidus, as well as less obviously but even more damagingly, in the quarrel scene between Cassius and Brutus, which implicates even Brutus' personal honour. His anger emerges in a rhetorical recounting of the honourable murder of

Caesar, which keeps echoing Caesar's own utterance, as well as lapsing into Cassius's:

CASSIUS:	O ye gods, ye gods! Must I endure all this?
BRUTUS:	All this? ay, more: fret till your proud heart break;
	Go show your slaves how choleric you are,
	And make your bondmen tremble. Must I budge?
	Must I observe you? Must I stand and crouch
	Under your testy humour? By the gods,
	You shall digest the venom of your spleen,
	Though it do split you; for, from this day forth,
	I'll use you for my mirth, yea, for my laughter,
	When you are waspish.
CASSIUS:	Is it come to this?
BRUTUS:	You say you are a better soldier:
	Let it appear so; make your vaunting true,
	And it shall please me well. For mine own part,
	I shall be glad to learn of noble men.

(IV. iii. 41–54)

Brutus' rage is expressed in physical images like Cassius' in Act I, and he arrives at a patent physical jealousy. Before long he has reached out to gods, thunderbolts, and high Olympus. The mother–child images in which their reconciliation is effected are hardly impressive, any more than the farcical little scene with the poet just afterwards. But these may be as much weaknesses in Shakespeare's writing as in his creatures. And there is another side to this: compared with Cassius' petty dishonesty, Brutus' anger can fairly approach the heroic tone, and the subsequent demonstrations of his stoicism on hearing of Portia's death seem to reinforce this reconstructing of the heroic figure. But in the images, and the echoes of absurdity, and in our knowledge of the insufficiency of honour there are curious undercurrents: the play is being turned into heroic tragedy, but the process is rather clumsy, and in the diminishing echoes of critical attitudes, apparently unwilling. It is difficult to respond to this rhetoric when rhetoric, and the ideas of value, honour, and so on which it conveys, have been so carefully exposed earlier.

None the less, this seems to be what the play demands. Caesar's ghost drives Brutus to the recognition

> O Julius Caesar, thou art mighty yet!
> Thy spirit walks abroad, and turns our swords
> In our own proper entrails.   (V. iii. 94–6)

But all this is slightly confused as a new and simpler set of values emerge to endorse the tragic conclusion. It is true that it is not altogether simple: Cassius dies by error, and there is emblematic amplification of the error:

> MESSALA: Mistrust of good success hath done this deed.
>   O hateful Error, Melancholy's child,
>   Why dost thou show to the apt thoughts of men
>   The things that are not?   (V. iii. 66–9)

Such an end is apt enough for Cassius, but it seems to put even him into a framework of heroic error, so that Brutus can speak a noble epitaph over him and Titinius:

> Are yet two Romans living such as these?
> The last of all the Romans, fare thee well!   (98–9)

They are not the last of course, for Brutus' death is yet to come. The idea of the noble Roman dominates unchallenged at the end, even in Cassius. Brutus' suicide is overdone, as everyone coyly declines to kill him, but it is certainly not deliberate farce, and Antony can affirm Brutus' value without question:

> This was the noblest Roman of them all.
> All the conspirators save only he
> Did that they did in envy of great Caesar;
> He only, in a general honest thought
> And common good to all, made one of them.
> His life was gentle, and the elements
> So mix'd in him, that Nature might stand up
> And say to all the world, 'This was a man!'
>   (V. v. 68–75)

This is, of course, magnificent; and it goes without question in the text. But in our minds questions must arise, if not at once while under its immediate spell, then shortly afterwards. The play has indeed been concerned with noble Romans, but we have been taught by it to see that nobility ambivalently; and even more have we learnt to question 'great Caesar'.

In other words, Brutus' tragedy, of noble error, in which Cassius has fat enough to participate, has been a part of the play; but never till now was it the whole. The questioning of values, the contrasting of the blood-free spirit of man with the grotesque image of his clumsy body, the inclination to see Roman nobility as comically or farcically degraded – all these things have been strong in the play, but they find no place in this noble finale. It is inevitable, I think, that their absence should be felt as a criticism of the end. The parts of the play have not grown consistently into a whole, and it is therefore a fragile tragic value that is built up here, one which cannot survive criticism.

Hence my suggestion of a likeness to *All's Well*: a process of probing and questioning of value joined to a final assertion of rectitude, where the two do not stand in a clear relation. *All's Well* has a false and cheap happy ending; and in a sense the end of *Julius Caesar*, though far more powerful, is equally 'happy': it is reassuring – all's well, when such a glow of assured values can be accepted. But the play as I have seen it implied something less reassuring, something more like *Troilus and Cressida* where no tragedy is allowed and the end shows life simply going on, Troilus to more futile wars, and Pandarus groaning at his diseases. Here again *Julius Caesar* is like *All's Well*, in its stress on physical decrepitude; but *Julius Caesar* is not venereal, the canker'd rose is not involved as yet. That is part of the profounder disturbance in *Hamlet*. And in *Hamlet* there is something of the same problem, of a tragic ending not fully responsive to the play; but it is a far more complex situation. In *Hamlet* there is also a conflict of different dramatic worlds: a Senecan play of Ghost and Revenge, and a sceptical one which gives such things no credence. This duality I remarked in *Julius Caesar*, and in the end the ghost has the better of it. Considering how long it has been read as a gallery of characters and played as a political commentary in modern dress, it is worth reiterating that there is at least as much blood, both on the stage and in the words, in this play as in *Titus Andronicus*.

In short, I find a quality in the play which exceeds its simple framework, and is not reconciled with it. Splendid as it is, Antony's last speech is a tour-de-force, the use of rhetorical poetry to overwhelm our doubts. And it is ironical that this should occur in a play which almost more than any other sharpens its audience's critical awareness of language, and especially of the power of rhetoric to deceive: for *Julius Caesar* is a brilliantly written play, a climax to the developing sensitivity to varying modes of utterance with which Shakespeare experimented in his earliest work.

Hamlet
[1600—1]

I

I have remarked that the weight of preconception about Shakespeare lies heavily upon us: with *Hamlet* the weight is almost crushing. The greatest effort of forgetting has to be made, and yet we have to know what we are forgetting, or else the vague shadows of Coleridge and Bradley, for instance, and even of Ernest Jones, will continue to oppress us; it is necessary to know what they said, what we want to retain of it, and *why* the rest should be rejected. I am not proposing a full inquiry on these lines, only to sketch its outline as hinting at some of the bearings we must take in arriving at a view of the play.

Hamlet has always been a haunted man; but for the seventeenth and eighteenth centuries he was haunted by a ghost, and one can hardly say that of his more recent history, when the ghost (though rarely altogether banished from the stage) has become so much of an embarrassment. The scene chosen to illustrate the play in Rowe's edition of 1709 is supposed to represent Betterton's performance: it shows the prince's second encounter with his father, in his mother's bedchamber. Garrick still made much of that, but his greatest concentration seems to have been on the first encounter, in Act I. The ghost himself was already producing laughter in the seventeen thirties, but the *confrontation* remained central. Garrick, at any rate in his later years, sustained the first meeting with the aid of a mechanical wig, and however well that consorts with the Gothick taste of the mid-century, the elaboration suggests that the scene no longer fully justified its prominence. Henry Mackenzie, author of *The Man of Feeling*, wrote (in 1780) of a Hamlet more haunted by himself than by his father, and this has been the dominant theme ever since. The great Hamlets, on the stage as well as in criticism, have for a hundred and fifty years been haunted from within far more than from without.

It is really only of historical interest to go back so far: Coleridge, for us, is the most clearly recognizable starting point.[1] His central observation about the play, and the one most justly remembered, is: 'Hence great, enormous, intellectual activity, and a consequent proportionate aversion to real action.'[2] The idea that thinking, in itself, is inimical to action amounted to a profound assumption of romantic psychology, and in far more vulgar forms it became popular currency later in the century. In Hamlet was found the exemplum of one of the oddest fallacies of that (and subsequent) periods. The man of action (railway engineer or empire builder) became sharply divided from the intellectual man, and a mighty slanging match began which is dying, but dying hard, even now. The human race was divided into bloody intellectuals and moronic toughs; or the University world into absent-minded professors and those who rowed boats – it was considered a most extraordinary feat to be both. *Hamlet's* popularity, on this showing, is composed of one half of the audience enjoying a demonstration of the futility of the intellectual, while the other half responds with ardent sympathy to the way this sensitive intellectual gets knocked about in the public school of life.

Coleridge did not, of course, envisage any such nonsense as that. But it is notorious how deeply anti-intellectualism has penetrated the traditions of English thought, and that it is still pervasive in public life, still influential in attitudes to education. Such vulgarity has kept Coleridge's fallacy alive. Its origin was linked to Rousseau's theories, and so to Wordsworth's attitude to 'the

1 Schlegel and Coleridge both lectured on the play in 1808; the report of Coleridge's remarks is later, but the argument as to whether they depend on a plagiarism he denied seems to me utterly sterile.
2 From a transcript of Coleridge's notebook in S. T. Coleridge: *Shakespearean Criticism*, ed. T. M. Raysor, second edition (*Everyman's Library*) 1960, vol. 1, p. 34.

meddling intellect'. Its results have been very varied, but involve a general assumption that Hamlet *was* a potent intellectual, a philosopher who should have remained in the University of Wittenberg, which seems to rest on three forms of evidence: the stress on Hamlet as a student; his expressed 'philosophy', largely found in the 'To be or not to be' soliloquy; and finally two or three carefully selected lines from the play.

Student life certainly looms larger here than elsewhere in Shakespeare, but its image is not represented by Hamlet alone. He, Horatio, Rosencrantz, and Guildenstern had all been at Wittenberg; Laertes returns to the University of Paris. Horatio displays no aversion to action, nor is he supposed to be thoughtless. Rosencrantz and Guildenstern are certainly not offered as intellectuals. Polonius inquires into Laertes' drinking and whoring, and we hear about his duelling. No one, anywhere, refers to their intellectual studies at all. The idea of the student offered in the play is remote indeed from that of one whose will is paralysed by thought.

The conviction has, nevertheless, somehow grown up that Hamlet offers us profound philosophical thinking, although this is not the opinion of philosophers. The point is important, and has been admirably dealt with by D. G. James in *The Dream of Learning*. James contrasts Bacon and Shakespeare: Bacon *thinks* (though he may not be a great philosopher if compared with Descartes); so does Shakespeare, but in a different mode. 'To be or not to be', which challenges the central values of life (why we don't commit suicide) does it by an interconnected series of concrete images, associated by a suggested thought process ('thus . . . thus . . .'); but regarded primarily as *thought*, it is the nearest thing to incoherent. It is not, in fact, philosophical exploration, it is imaginative exploration; reasonable and intelligent certainly, but not philosophy. Against that one may urge that Hamlet does use the language of reason, his syntactical formulae assert an intellectual activity; that we are, in other words, given to understand that he is (as a person in the play) meditating. In that sense it may be legitimate to call him a philosophical character; but it is a very limited sense which has been grossly exaggerated.

Lastly, there are the specific references in the text, and they are curiously few. Hamlet twice attributes failure in action to 'thought' or 'thinking', and a third allusion has been adduced since Coleridge's day by semantic ingenuity. The first, from the 'To be or not to be' soliloquy, is:

> And thus the native hue of resolution
> Is sicklied o'er with the pale cast of thought.
>
> (III. i. 84-5)

But this 'pale cast' is not the scholar's pasty complexion derived from too much midnight oil, and 'thought' is not philosophical ratiocination. 'Thought' here (as elsewhere in the play) carries strong suggestions of melancholy, and it relates directly to the thoughts of something after death that go before it. Hence the 'pale cast' is simultaneously melancholy and cowardice. The thoughts are specific ones on consequences, and not the generalizing tendency towards abstraction which Coleridge postulated.[1] It is the same with the last soliloquy, with words that are often cited as direct evidence for Coleridge's idea – 'thinking too precisely on th'event' (IV. iv. 41). Coleridge claimed that thinking is in its nature indefinite: Hamlet says 'precisely'. That is, as before, that it is thinking of the consequences which induces cowardice:

> A thought which, quarter'd, hath but one part wisdom
> And ever three parts coward . . .   (IV. iv. 42-3)

There is no fifth quarter for the inactive intellectual. The third case is from the same context as the first:

> Thus conscience does make cowards of us all.
>
> (III. i. 83)

It has been argued, by Bradley as well as others, that 'conscience' here means (as it could at the time) 'consciousness', the process of thinking, and not the moral quality at all. But elsewhere in *Hamlet* the word occurs several times, and the moral quality is at least

---

1 See *Shakespearean Criticism*, vol. 2, p. 224: 'His mind, unseated from its healthy balance, is for ever occupied with the world within him, and abstracted from external things. . . . It is the nature of thought to be indefinite, while definiteness belongs to reality.'

part of its meaning in each case; in one, it is the whole of it, when
Hamlet says of Claudius:

                                    is't not perfect conscience
            To quit him with this arm?   (V. ii. 67–8)

I am inclined to think that we have no business to exclude the
moral sense from the earlier context either, but a more precise
account of this line will have to wait for a full analysis of the 'To
be or not to be' soliloquy later.

My contention is, then, that Coleridge was interpreting *Hamlet*
in the context of romantic thought, quite properly; but more, that
he was *distorting* the play, and that the image which derives from
his account is quite misleading. The inactive intellectual is not the
heart of Hamlet's mystery. Bradley, in fact, did not suppose that it
was. He accepted Coleridge's notion as an account of something
which happened to Hamlet, but not as a generalization about
human behaviour, even as he had observed it in Universities.[1]
What had previously been thought of as cause was therefore de-
moted to symptom, and under it Bradley sub-imposed a new
cause: a profound moral shock which withdrew him into a world
of inactive imagining. The shock in question was not, of course,
his father's death, but his mother's marriage: 'It was the moral
shock of the sudden ghastly disclosure of his mother's true
nature.' Bradley's Hamlet discovered that Ellen Terry and Fanny
Hill were sisters under the skin.

It is worth recalling that it was only in the late eighteenth
century that the 'problem' of *Hamlet* came to be thought of as
primarily a psychological one; we should not be surprised to
realize that it was in the beginning of the twentieth century that
this was transposed into sexual psychology, and specifically the
shocking recognition of female sexuality. *If* the psychological
stress is the right one, we must always measure it by the best
understanding of contemporary psychology. That is what Coleridge did for his age, and Bradley (immediately pre-Freud) for
his; and that is what Ernest Jones, Freud's friend and biographer,
did for the 1920s. The explanation offered, of course, was the

---

1 *Shakespearean Tragedy*, pp. 115–16.
M

Oedipus complex. Hamlet's behaviour has puzzled people for a long time; the puzzle hinges on why Hamlet can't get on with it and kill Claudius; Shakespeare doesn't provide us with an answer, only a problem. Hence T. S. Eliot concluded that *Hamlet* is an artistic failure. Shakespeare could not himself understand what he wanted to portray, which was emotion in excess of the object, the disgust Hamlet felt at his Mother's behaviour. Bradley, Eliot, and Jones are all in fact extensions of the same view of the play.

Jones contended that Shakespeare portrayed what he had, very keenly, observed; he didn't 'explain' it, because he couldn't; Freud could. Hamlet's problem is psychological: he wants to murder his uncle–father, to be cruel to his mother, to abuse his girl-friend; and all this emerges in hysteria and sex-disgust. Why? The Oedipus complex works with a wonderful neatness: Hamlet (like the rest of us) responds to his father as simultaneously a benevolent patriarch and the hated rival in love for his mother. So he has always wanted and not wanted to murder his father. Claudius *does* murder him, *and* marries his mother – and thus doubly projects himself into Hamlet's psychological conflict: he becomes Hamlet's father, but solely in the hated sense, so Hamlet can now separate the father figures, the dead one becomes wholly benevolent while the living is now wholly the hated rival; but simultaneously Claudius becomes identified as the figure who has acted *both* Hamlet's repressed desires: killed his father and slept with his mother. So Claudius becomes identified with both Hamlet's father and Hamlet's self: a new conflict develops in Hamlet's psyche overlaying the old, and the result is an intolerable strain which leads to paralysis of the will, hysteric self-disgust, sex-disgust, uncontrollable outbursts. And all this eludes his efforts at self-probing because it is repressed within his subconscious mind.

This is superbly neat: it takes full account of the evidently neurotic basis for Hamlet's behaviour, the oscillation between an impressive sanity and an hysterical lack of control. But there are two basic objections, neither of which seemed important to Jones. Firstly: these things are in the play; so is much else: what is that doing there? And, more particularly, what is the relevance of all

the bearings Hamlet does give us for his behaviour? Jones waves
them all away – they are false explanations, or mere self-deception.
He has a good deal of waving to do, but many critics have done
no less. He is not looking at a play at all, as he knew, but at a man,
yet the apologia seems to me confused. It is true that a psychological explanation of Hamlet is interesting in itself, but it is not
true that such a one as this is relevant to a critical account of the
play. This kind of commentary has really two phases: first, deduce
a 'character' out of the play; then re-fit the play round that
character on the blatant assumption that that is all that matters.
But, manifestly, *Hamlet* the play offers a judgement on life in
general, not just on the man; and it is not an attractive one. But if
that is the case, then (as Jones saw) the Oedipus complex was
Shakespeare's, and the play was a brilliant, but not quite complete,
self-analysis.

That will not do, because there are other dramatic documents
suggesting a similar outlook: Marston's plays, Tourneur's, and so
on. Jones seems to have been unaware of this, or he would have
had to postulate a peculiar prevalence for the Oedipus complex
circa 1600. His dealings with Shakespeare's biography (Mary
Fitton, Pembroke, Essex, the death of Shakespeare's father in
1601, and so on) seem to me maladroit. The only escape would be
to postulate that everyone in 1601 felt Elizabeth as a mother figure,
Essex as a father, and so that Essex's execution projected a na-
tional Oedipus complex into disastrous activity. That is a reduc-
tion to absurdity; Jones' book is far from absurd, and I have not
discussed it at length in order to be facetious about it. The problem it raised was one of critical relevance; of the relevance of the
whole tradition of character criticism. If psychology were properly
the central concern of Shakespearean criticism, then Jones'
would still be the right approach. But it is not, even with *Hamlet*.
Yet we have, of course, to be circumspect; we must not throw the
baby out with the bathwater, and Hamlet's soul is quite a big baby.

My other objection to Jones' discussion has also, but more
recently, become a central problem of critical relevance. In
reality, he is not much interested in the play as such. Here and
there a good phrase illuminates his theme (such as when Hamlet

calls Claudius his mother by mistake); but mostly the words are irrelevant. What he is interested in is the pattern of relationships between Hamlet, Claudius, Gertrude, and the ghost, and their repetition in Laertes, Ophelia, and Polonius, and even further in Fortinbras and his uncle. That pattern, he suggests, belongs to an original myth which he takes to involve equally the Orestes affair. This is fascinating, over-simplified, and I doubt whether an analysis of Saxo Grammaticus (our earliest account of Hamlet) would bear it out. It certainly has very little to do with Shakespeare: my concern is with a poetic drama made out of a relatively sophisticated form of the myth (in Belleforest, via a lost play); Jones was concerned with the myth as he could discern it behind the poetic drama. It seems to me that here the proper concerns of anthropology and criticism lead in opposite directions; one can be interested in both, but they should not be confused, any more than should those of psychology and criticism. Relevance depends on how the particular concerns of the play are established, and on what those concerns turn out to be. Both the 'how' and the 'what' seems to me closely related to the modes analysed in earlier plays, and it is from this particular direction that I want to approach this one, seeing the development of words and action towards a whole which is neither a drama nor a poem simply, but a poetic drama. The inevitable disclaimer, that what I offer is very limited and partial, is more needed here than elsewhere only because this is the fullest and the most complex of all the plays I have discussed. And because it is far better known, which is why it has been more than usually necessary to try to relieve the pressures of traditional preconceptions.

II

The opening of the play was brilliantly analysed by Coleridge,[1] and T. S. Eliot further developed his suggestions.[2] It is characterized by the kind of vitality, of liveliness of situation and speech,

---

1 *Shakespearean Criticism*, vol. 1, pp. 18–20.
2 In 'Poetry and Drama', 1951, reprinted in *On Poetry and Poets*, 1957; see pp. 75–7.

which is felt throughout the play in positive contrast to many of
the attitudes and themes expressed (a vitality which makes it,
when performed straight, always 'good theatre', and thus contributes a great deal to its sustained popularity). The first words are
prose, rapidly spoken, by 'ordinary' (and unimportant) men – a
long way from sick-mindedness. In other words it is normality
which is first given us. But out of this normality the abnormal and
the ominous is very quickly developed:

> 'Tis now struck twelve; get thee to bed, Francisco. (7)

That only tells us (in prose) that we are at midnight; but it strikes
an immediate response:

> For this relief much thanks. 'Tis bitter cold,
> And I am sick at heart. (8–9)

This is not verse, but it is nearly so: a rhythm is taking charge and
the suggestions move out beyond the prose norm. 'Struck twelve'
moves through 'bitter cold' into the very different hint of 'sick at
heart'. Midnight is developing connotations of fear and un-
naturalness. The entry of Horatio and Marcellus re-affirms the
assurance of normality and humanity: 'Friends' – 'honest soldier'
lead naturally to:

> Welcome, Horatio; welcome, good Marcellus. (20)

But the reassuring cadence is immediately followed by:

> What, has this thing appear'd again to-night? (21)

The ominousness reappears, now in regular blank verse, in the
vaguely sinister suggestion of 'this thing'. Hereafter (for a while)
the blank verse works counter to the ominousness:

> Horatio says 'tis but our fantasy,
> And will not let belief take hold of him
> Touching this dreaded sight, twice seen of us. (23–5)

On the one hand, the 'thing' is growing into 'fantasy', 'dreaded
sight', and subsequently 'apparition'; but on the other hand the
tone is reasonable, calm. But it is no longer simple prose: when
Horatio interjects 'Tush, tush, 'twill not appear' the prose brusque-

ness cuts across what has already become felt as the measured
affirmation of blank verse. That develops a rapidly stronger emphasis, building up a rhetorical tone, of mighty consequences
involved; when Horatio agrees to hear the tale, an heroic verse is
fully established:

> Last night of all,
> When yond same star that's westward from the pole
> Had made his course t'illume that part of heaven
> Where now it burns, Marcellus and myself,
> The bell then beating one –   (35–9)

The ominous significance of what is involved is fully established;
at the same time its immediacy is sensibly diminished: the staccato
prose that settled into more steady blank verse has opened out
now into the sustained narration of epic simile. But equally the
human fear of darkness (midnight – not a mouse stirring) has
grown into a suggestion of mighty consequence: a 'fantasy' whose
reach is greater than 'normality', a nightmare that is *real*.

At this point, when ominousness is at its fullest expression, but
simultaneously removed from immediacy of anticipation, the
Ghost enters –

> Peace, break thee off; look where it comes again.   (40)

Hence the shock, and the significance, of this eruption, are as
great as possible.

One sense of the term 'poetic drama' is very apparent here: that
this opening is intensely dramatic in the theatrical sense is very
obvious; that its use of language lies outside the capacity of prose
drama is equally obvious. We have here (in 40 lines) prose, prose-
like blank verse, and blank verse which is radically unlike prose.
And these variations of tone are not fortuitous or clumsy (still
less are they intrusions of older styles which Shakespeare hadn't
grown out of): they grow rhythmically in and out of each other,
developing levels and suggestions in the drama which begins
(already) to relate the actions of persons on a stage to a structure
whose dimensions are of the kind one normally calls 'poetic'.
And by the possession of this poetic order it becomes, as T. S.
Eliot pointed out, the more and not the less dramatic.

The same oscillation of tones develops further in the rest of the scene. Prose exclamations at the ghost lead into Horatio's questioning:

> What art thou that usurp'st this time of night
> Together with that fair and warlike form
> In which the majesty of buried Denmark
> Did sometimes march?   (46–9)

Everything there is important: the tone is once more heroic, but no longer leisurely; and within it copious specific suggestions are planted. 'usurp' and 'night' are set against 'fair *and* warlike form', 'the majesty of *buried* Denmark'. All this tends to identify the ominous event more clearly in a specific situation, but also in a valuation of the world: 'usurp' and 'night' are set against 'fair' which is strikingly associated with 'warlike' in the majesty of Denmark. *Fair and Warlike Majesty* is the initial value against which the destructive disturbance in the play stands; and it is to that we are returned in the last speech of the play, Fortinbras's

> Bear Hamlet like a soldier to the stage;
> For he was likely, had he been put on,
> To have prov'd most royal . . .   (V. ii. 388–90)

That, then, is a main bearing to be grasped, to be related to the sense of men as they do act and speak (apparent in the prose interchanges of the scene) and also to a terrible distortion of this order in which other values or ways of regarding value will confront us than the 'normality' of these soldiers. The usurpation of order is heralded in Horatio's movement of speech from the decisive endorsement of the soldier's sanity:

> Before my God, I might not this believe
> Without the sensible and true avouch
> Of mine own eyes.   (I. i. 56–8)

The authority of legal language on oath leads on to:

> But, in the gross and scope of mine opinion,
> This bodes some strange eruption to our state. (68–9)

The scene settles down to a rather different tone at about this point, but still with significant shifts. The *authority* of the ghost is

decisively settled (for the audience) and nevermore to be shaken;
so is its ominousness. The question now promulgated is the precise nature of what it forbodes; but at first indirectly. An earlier
pattern is repeated after Horatio's decisive conclusion:

> MARCELLUS: Good now, sit down, and tell me, he that
> knows . . .   (70)

We are settling down to calm narrative again, but the thing to be
explained is not, at first, the ghost, but another boding of strange
eruption: the watch that nightly toils, the daily cast of cannon,
and so on. The list is considerable and impressively uttered: the
state is disturbed without the ghost. The cue is taken, of course,
for Horatio's exposition of the political strain between Denmark
and Norway – in itself calmly uttered, serious, but only a political
affair. As soon as Bernardo explicitly links *this* boded eruption to
the ghost, the tone begins to change again: Horatio's response is
to recall *Julius Caesar* – not Caesar's ghost, but the portents before
the murder, and the terms are very striking:

> In the most high and palmy state of Rome,
> A little ere the mightiest Julius fell,
> The graves stood tenantless, and the sheeted dead
> Did squeak and gibber in the Roman streets. (113–16)

The contrast of diction between 'high and palmy state' and 'squeak
and gibber' bodes something far more profoundly nasty than
anything envisaged before. This eruption of death destroying all
order and human dignity, and associated with civil disturbance
(not war with neighbours) moves us a stage further into the experience of the play – and it also gives the ghost a cue for re-
appearing. Its horror is now felt more immediately than before:

> I'll cross it, though it blast me. Stay, illusion. (127)

Crossing it, Horatio offers three successive reasons to it for walking, of which only one is the war with Norway. It does not
answer; the significance is left in oracular form. One major
'explanation' has been offered, accepted, challenged (by poetic and
dramatic implication, not explicit statement), and in the end we

have a sense of equivocation: of explanations which are both right and wrong, but which do not 'explain'. A pattern of relationship between experience and explanation which becomes characteristic of the whole play.

The rest of the scene moves into another tone again, picking up suggestions of what we heard before. The departure of the ghost at cockcrow is discussed, at first as confirming popular belief, but it grows (of course) to more than that:

> It faded on the crowing of the cock.
> Some say that ever 'gainst that season comes
> Wherein our Saviour's birth is celebrated,
> This bird of dawning singeth all night long;
> And then, they say, no spirit dare stir abroad,
> The nights are wholesome . . .   (157–62)

'This bird of dawning' associated with Christian salvation makes as powerful as possible the contrast of day and night, normality and abnormality, good and evil which has been continuously present to us, and becomes abundantly clear in 'The nights are wholesome' emphasizing the unwholesomeness of *this* kind of night (as well as adding good and bad health to the complex connotations of order and disorder developed in the scene).

Night and day are being established as emblems in a manner made familiar by the earlier plays. Horatio completes this in his famous formal reference to

> the morn, in russet mantle clad,
> Walks o'er the dew of yon high eastward hill.
>   (166–7)

This, again, is no chance reversion to outworn rhetorical manners, but a final picking up of the epic pitch of

> When yond same star that's westward from the pole . . .

so that the movement of time is felt overall, involving all that 'night' has come to mean and moving the stage action on to a contrasting scene – of daylight, normality, the court in active splendour.

III

Normality, in contrast with the last scene, is a very strongly made impression at the opening of scene ii. The tone of Claudius' first, very long, speech insists on confidence and orderliness – but with (as Ophelia would say) a difference. He deals with his marriage and its quick following on the late king's death, and deals with it very reasonably; a reasonableness which persists in his utterances throughout the scene, but which is not (of course) beyond criticism. The logic-chopping conceits proliferate – 'a defeated joy', 'With mirth in funeral, and with dirge in marriage' – and are carried smoothly to their conclusion. But the criticism is, for the moment, withheld: if we are inclined to make one, we are distracted by the capable (and tedious) arrangements for the embassy to Norway, which strongly emphasize the 'daylight' reasonableness of tone. This completes the exposition of the Norwegian affair, but at the same time it diminishes its ominousness: as an object correlative to the ghost's foreboding it becomes patently inadequate.

A still greater insistence on reasonableness, kindliness, and so on, is evident in Claudius' dealings with Laertes' request to return to Paris; but this leads round to the explosive point so long avoided:

> Take thy fair hour, Laertes; time be thine,
> And thy best graces spend it at thy will!
> But now, my cousin Hamlet, and my son –
> HAMLET: A little more than kin, and less than kind.
>
> (I. ii. 62–5)

Hamlet has, of course, been present all the time as a disturbing factor, his inky cloak negating the marriage feast and the daylight assurance of the court. A figure dressed in black on the Elizabethan stage had (apart from formal mourning) the emblematic significance of melancholy (like Jaques) and of death (like Mercade in *Love's Labour's Lost*), and here we must add the association of these with night: Hamlet's *appearance* obtrudes in I. ii like an emblem of I. i. This is immediately reinforced when he speaks: he denies the quality which Claudius has just shown – kindness – and proceeds to insist on the emblem suggestion:

> Not so, my lord; I am too much in the sun.
> QUEEN: Good Hamlet, cast thy nighted colour off. (67–8)

The ominousness returns, in a context where it cannot refer to Norway, must be more fundamental than that. And it already appears in a characteristic form of utterance, the mordant puns, the equivocation, crystallize the ambiguity which I noted in the oracular uncertainties of the ghost's significance in I. i.

The queen picks up Claudius' reasonable tone: but it does not pass now:

> Thou know'st 'tis common – all that lives must die,
> Passing through nature to eternity.
> HAMLET: Ay, madam, it is common.   (72–4)

But that only preludes the bigger bang to come:

> QUEEN: If it be,
> Why seems it so particular with thee?
> HAMLET: Seems, madam! Nay, it is; I know not seems.
> (74–6)

This criticism reflects over the whole scene: the normal, reassuring tone is destroyed in Hamlet's destruction of 'seems':

> For they are actions that a man might play;
> But I have that within which passes show.   (84–5)

The response to this is another very long speech from Claudius. Like his first, it is eminently reasonable in tone and suggestion, if anything more so: his ground is (seemingly) less precarious, as his own marriage is not the immediate matter. But: Hamlet on 'seems' and 'is' lies between; the criticism has been made, and our response to Claudius has been directed. Hence, in its context, this speech is more vulnerable and must (to carry adequate weight) be correspondingly *more* reasonable. But a clash of tones so extreme is inevitably betrayed, and when Claudius says:

> 'Tis sweet and commendable in your nature, Hamlet,
> To give these mourning duties to your father . . . (87–8)

he is forcing on us a reversal of tone and value: Hamlet's words were not sweet or, in Claudius' sense, 'commendable' – they were harsh and rude. And the whole point of what he said was that it was not 'duties' he was performing.

Our response is therefore conflicting: we must be fully aware of the critical force bearing on this speech, as well as recognizing its reasonableness. Reasonableness is and is not good enough. The fragility of this assured common sense is emphasized in Hamlet's single line to Gertrude:

> I shall in all my best obey you, madam.

and in Claudius' response:

> Why, 'tis a loving and a fair reply.
> Be as ourself in Denmark. Madam, come;
> This gentle and unforc'd accord of Hamlet . . .
>
> (120–3)

'Gentle' and 'unforc'd' betray the tone: they describe exactly what the accord was not.

On this patently insecure position Claudius exits with high rhetoric on the cannon of celebration echoing in the heavens. The explosion which we get is powerful enough, in all conscience, but of a radically different kind:

> O, that this too too solid flesh would melt,
> Thaw, and resolve itself into a dew!
> Or that the Everlasting had not fix'd
> His canon 'gainst self-slaughter!   (129–32)

The possible complacency that Claudius would establish we have seen being undermined; but the totality of its destruction is still a shock. The varied tones and stresses of the play so far come to a conclusive point here: the opposition of daylight and midnight, of normality and tremendous abnormality, of plausible political explanation and insistent awareness that more is involved – all that comes to sharp focus in that first line. Hamlet's black midnight concerns, not politics, but fundamental human values, and what he offers is an intense negation dependent on 'flesh'. There is a kind of ambiguity here, or, at least, two distinct responses are conveyed: first, the impossibility of the melting which Hamlet is longing for; and second, the fact, seen as unpleasant, of the absolute dominance of human life *by* flesh. Both find continuous reference in the speech, but the main emphasis shifts from one to the other. 'Self-slaughter' (insisting on the sense of physical violence) comes first, leading to the defined negation of the uses of this world – 'How weary, stale, flat, and unprofitable'. That is a summary and final statement; its corollary moves into an almost pulpit-like utterance: ''tis an unweeded garden, That grows to seed.'

Here there is another vital point: this speech is possibly the most potent negation of life in English poetry; but it is a negative whose positive is made as concretely felt as itself. 'Grows to seed' is a process of fecundity, here the business of weeds, but involving a recognition of what ought to be, of the orderly garden growing and reproducing. But this 'grows' is only 'gross', the comely ranks of this garden are 'rank' in the other sense; and so we move back through the weariness and longing for death to the other stress in 'too too solid flesh' – the 'rank and gross'.

I said that this vehement and complex shock emerged coherently out of the poetic structure of the play: it is only when that general function is established that the speech moves into direct narrative reference, 'But two months dead', and so on. Thereafter the principal stress (there are, of course, others) is on solid flesh, 'Hyperion to a satyr' (goatish lust) —

> so loving to my mother,
> That he might not beteem the winds of heaven
> Visit her face too roughly . . .   (140–2)

becomes the very different

> Why, she would hang on him
> As if increase of appetite had grown
> By what it fed on.   (143–5)

The movement from his father's protective loving to his mother's self-feeding appetite is marked in the growing urgency of 'within a month' – 'A little month'; the image of complete seeming in

'*Like* Niobe, all tears' becoming 'most unrighteous tears', while appetite recurs as 'a beast that wants discourse of reason'. All references to forms of relationship – love, lust, grief – move into the echoing 'married with my uncle . . . She married', until the gathered suggestions finally explode in

> O, most wicked speed, to post
> With such dexterity to incestuous sheets! (156–7)

Here evil, politic dexterity and the extreme degree of sexual nausea are linked in the word 'incestuous'.

Thus the speech is a complete commentary on the scene from which it arose: the normality so elaborately displayed was composed of dexterity and incest. The dexterity was clear enough; incest here is a technicality, but possibly more forceful for that, and the presence of 'solid flesh' is recognizable. The process follows Hamlet's last speech: what 'seems' has been stripped away; this speech reveals what 'is'. In other words, we are aware *first* of a way of regarding life, rather than that this is how an odd character called Hamlet regards it. But that suggestion does develop in the latter part of the speech: the growing urgency of utterance becomes hysterical, and excess of statement goes with it. But even here the distinction is not easy to draw: there is a profound imbalance between the king's asexual love, and the queen's appetitive hanging and feeding. The positive is suspiciously unreal: the very thing remembered, supposedly for contrast with her later fall, about his mother, is nasty in comparison with his father. It is a question whether this is the play's, rather than Hamlet's, imbalance.

At any rate, the play's characteristic ambiguity emerges again: the clear analysis which we seem to have becomes equivocal in the suggestion of hysteria growing in its utterance. This is *a* view (and a fundamental one); but, there are others. As this tone is one that recurs, but that there are other tones we are immediately reminded in the sudden shift from the profoundly abnormal (melancholic) judgement to Hamlet's delighted recognition of Horatio, and for a moment to a wholly positive and normal behaviour and utterance. A vital glimpse of what Hamlet would be like if he were not melancholy, of what life would be like if it were not rank and gross.

The normality is asserted by:

> My lord, I came to see your father's funeral.
>
> HAMLET: I prithee do not mock me, fellow-student;
>
>   I think it was to see my mother's wedding.
>
> HORATIO: Indeed, my lord, it followed hard upon.
>
>   (176–9)

Horatio's comment endorses Hamlet's view of it, but it provokes another shift of tone, into the wit which (as often later) contains a sense of hysteria:

> Thrift, thrift, Horatio! The funeral bak'd-meats
>
> Did coldly furnish forth the marriage tables. (180–1)

A parody of Claudius' equivocation on mirth in funeral. It is followed by yet one more shift of tone, to the almost gnomic finality of positive judgement on his father:

> 'A was a man, take him for all in all,
>
> I shall not look upon his like again.   (187–8)

And so, finally, into the revelation of the ghost's walking to join Hamlet's ominous sense of the worthless life.

IV

We have seen already – in only two scenes – something of the sheer variety which I claimed as a characteristic of the play. Act I, scene iii, offers another aspect of it: a relaxing of the tension so complete that it seems almost to be completely irrelevant. In fact it is not, but its relevance is of a remote kind. Laertes giving good advice to Ophelia ends in commonplace 'sentences'; Polonius talks in this manner all the time. Yet it sustains the play in three ways. First, this establishing of formal morality is one aspect of the play's concern with values; second, it supplies us with information of Hamlet's affair with Ophelia; and third, the complacent assurance stands in sharp contrast to Hamlet's delineation of a world within. Polonius' 'to thine own self be true' might be

acceptable anywhere but in this play, where 'self' has already become too ambiguous a thing, and *how* to be true to *what* emerges
as a profound problem.

Further, the contrast between Laertes' speech and Polonius' is
important. Laertes makes a sound point, on the limits of Hamlet's
freedom:

> He may not, as unvalued persons do,
> Carve for himself.   (I. iii. 19–20)

Laertes may be mistaken, but the reasonable honesty of his concern sets off Polonius' remarks as something altogether cheaper,
suggesting that Hamlet is just consciously toying with Ophelia
and will thoughtlessly desert her with a bastard. We have seen a
Hamlet of varied tones and behaviour, but seen enough to know
that *this* is outside his range. With Polonius, of course, there is
always an edge of the comic dotard (too often played as much
more than an edge); but it is not altogether pleasant, this elder
statesman, comic Machiavel, whose behaviour is governed by a
cheap cynicism.

Laertes' speech, however, was serious and important; and seems
all the more so for the sense that Polonius parodies it. It hinged on
the orthodox analysis of degree, like Ulysses' far fuller exposition
in *Troilus and Cressida*; and as in *Troilus*, the ultimate effect of the
play tends to make degree seem hardly relevant. The sense of
human disaster, of the collapse of civilization, which we have
encountered in Hamlet's first soliloquy, clearly challenges confidence in such an idea; but the force and vitality of language in
Laertes' utterance insist that it is one mode of judgement to be
taken seriously. Which Polonius' is not; though it is a form of
silliness which can have dreadful consequences.

The return to tension is rapidly established by a recapitulation
of the opening of scene i: a prose interchange associating cold
and midnight, growing rapidly into blank verse, and as it does so
moving away from the sense of immediate urgency. Here, in fact,
into what seems a more complete digression than the narrative
leisure of Marcellus before: Hamlet's lecture on Danish drunken-
ness (the cannon we heard of is shot off now, at midnight) which

leads him into the gnomic vein, lecturing on the vicious mole of nature in particular man. The play's concern with moral issues is evident here as well as its characteristic digressiveness. But this digression was cut in both the bad Quarto and the Folio, and therefore presumably on the stage in Shakespeare's time, not unreasonably; although this echo of Laertes' orthodoxy in Hamlet's own speech is significant. The digressive note is interrupted, as before, by the ghost, whose entry provokes Hamlet into the splendours of heroic verse again: 'thy canoniz'd bones', the sepulchre's 'ponderous and marble jaws', and then, against this rhetorical elaboration is set the very different 'I do not set my life at a pin's fee', which itself in turn gives way to Horatio's involved image of self-destruction in the roaring sea. Thus Hamlet's action in following the ghost is simultaneously heroic, and dangerous. Dangerous here in simple senses that are not very important, but the destructive sea is an image which recurs later at the play's heart in 'a sea of troubles'.

Hamlet's scene with the ghost develops the fullest sense of horrid impressiveness in the ghost's utterance, combined with immediate feeling in Hamlet's interjections. In this mode it echoes and entirely confirms Hamlet's vision of the state of life around him:

> Let not the royal bed of Denmark be
> A couch for luxury and damned incest.
>
> (I. v. 82–3)

But this is a statement of a very different kind from Hamlet's soliloquy earlier: the ghost exists in a plane whose bearings Hamlet gives:

> O all you host of heaven! O earth! What else?
> And shall I couple hell? (92–3)

The ghost's speech all leads to this heaven–hell antithesis, in his hints of eternal torture and his stress on

> sent to my account
> With all my imperfections on my head. (78–9)

This is very different from Hamlet's appalling nausea in his soliloquy born solely of experience on earth, and making no reference

N

to the supernatural. The play can be said to be developing more than one dramatic frame simultaneously: the rhetorical 'high style' drama of ghost, heaven, and hell where events are significant in an established and absolute scale of values, and where (we must suppose) order can be restored by a simple punitive action, killing Claudius; and on the other hand the very vivid presence of a mortal world where ideas of heaven and hell explain nothing, where the revulsion from lust is a recognition of fundamental human bestiality which no simple action will 'solve'. The distinction of these worlds of dramatic experience becomes glaringly plain later when Hamlet, who has seen and accepted his father's ghost, speaks of

> The undiscover'd country, from whose bourn
> No traveller returns . . .   (III. i. 79–80)

and can move on from that speech again to refusing to kill Claudius because he is praying.

Now these may be contradictions (as they have often been called), in which case the play is a chaos of contradictions, and best explained as a very imperfect revision of an old play in which heaven, hell, and ghost are 'old play', Hamlet's soliloquies 'new material', very ineptly grafted in. That is quickly answered: critically one can distinguish the kind but not the quality of the one from the other, and both are obviously Shakespearean. Modern minds may find one more immediately congenial – we do not believe in hell – but that is a very different matter.

If, therefore, we cannot simply regard all this as massive confusion and careless contradiction, we must see these two polarities as co-existing in a structure whose nature is to include such apparently irreconcilable elements. It is precisely this which it seems to me is suggested by my analysis of the shifting tones and kinds of utterance. Here it is necessary to insist again that this is poetic drama, not a play in verse; as in music (the analogy is very crude) a symphony is not a sonata orchestrated. The fact of an orchestra – its scope and range – makes a fundamental difference; so does the fact of poetry in *Hamlet*. I tried to show how at the opening the prose grows into prosaic blank verse, then into middle style and emerges in full-blown epic mode until the ghost blasts it. Now one can see this as a process akin to orchestration, and the response we make to each mode of utterance is as distinct as that to different solos or combinations of instruments. So that, as I remarked, a recurrence of midnight prose in I. iv revives in us that theme, and the same crescendo to heroic verse is rapidly achieved, more rapidly because it is a recapitulation of an already established progression. So we see, and are reminded of, several superimposed kinds of experience: that of the very ordinariness of exchanging a few words of greeting on a job of work; that of commonplace reflection on the significance of events and life in general; that of a supernatural chain of value; and that of a response to events and life in general which is far from commonplace, but at the same time is not concerned with the supernatural. And each of these is varied in its presentation, so that we get (for instance) such different aspects of normal judgement as Claudius' remonstration with Hamlet, Laertes' speech to Ophelia, or Hamlet's discussion of vicious moles in nature. These normalities are bordered on the one hand by Hamlet's reflection on the worthless grossness of life, or, on another, by Polonius' half-comic cynicism about human sensuality.

But this is not just a collocation of variety without any central focus. I tried to show in I. i an accretion of images of night and disaster which stands in opposition to day and normality; but also that the 'daylight' of I. ii is never a healthy thing. It is discoloured by Claudius' politic equivocation and by Hamlet's benighted presence. The attitudes to normality presented are patently inadequate (in, say, Claudius or Polonius), and the two polarities of poetic experience – the ghost, and Hamlet's soliloquy – both deal with death in their respective terms. The ghost as a matter of heaven and hell, crime and punishment; Hamlet as the repudiation of degrading life, that is suicide. Equally, the attitudes to life are very different: the ghost is judging a particular action which is redeemable by punishment (the *ethic* of a metaphysic of heaven and hell); Hamlet is judging a state of being where redemption is irrelevant because the state is felt to be universal.

Hence we are involved in a very complex poetic drama whose

concerns are with the values of life and of death, and whose tragic impetus derives from a strong sense of the failure and degradation of life. In one sense, perhaps, what Wilson Knight called it,[1] a play in which the mark of death is branded on every aspect of living. But yet, simultaneously, this play of death (and its near relation, disease) is characterized by an extraordinary vitality of language, and a controlled variety of verse and action beyond even Shakespeare's norm. This kind of writing we found in parts even in *Titus Andronicus*, more in *Richard II*, and more still in *Julius Caesar*. At the same time, this criticism of accepted values emerges in 2 *Henry IV*, *All's Well that Ends Well*, and again, partly, in *Julius Caesar*; and it is marked in these plays by the same sexual focus, and even by the same disturbing hint of fundamental imbalance that I suggested in Hamlet's comments on his mother's first marriage, where the proposition that sexuality *can* be vile merges indistinguishably into the concrete suggestion that *all* sex *is* vile. The evolution of a poetic drama that I have been tracing selectively through the early tragedies leads coherently into the kind of structure I have suggested in *Hamlet* – the difference being in *Hamlet's* evidently far greater range, and, perhaps, depth as well. It is obvious that this is the most ambitious of them all; and its reference is not contained by Hamlet's 'character', nor even by what is 'rotten in the state of Denmark' (i.e. England), but by the inter-relations of individual human experience (which Hamlet's speeches and behaviour often give us), general human nature (which Hamlet's speeches often give us), social behaviour, cosmic interpretation, and so on. It is a range which is very impressively achieved; but the ambitiousness does, no doubt, partly overstrain the form.

It follows from what I have said that to throw all the play into an analysis of Hamlet's psychology would be absurd; and also that all Hamlet's utterances lead us to understandings and questionings outside himself. But at the same time one vital aspect of this exploration of human experience does involve what it is to be *a* man. That, I have said, is vividly conveyed, at times,

---

1 See 'The Embassy of Death: an Essay on *Hamlet*', in *The Wheel of Fire*, 1930.

by Hamlet's utterance and behaviour – for instance in the hysteric wit which is one aspect of the play's response to life, and is also the means by which Hamlet moves us from one world to another, as in his whirling words to Horatio and the others after he's talked to the ghost. The 'character' of Hamlet is felt at various moments, very importantly, as *part* of the whole play; it partakes of some of the play's complexity. We become familiar with a figure who is at once noble and irresponsible, sensitive and cruel – and, significantly, such a figure is coherent – as a response to the world of the play. But we are not invited to probe into the psychological springs of this so much as into the nature of human life which will thus distract and all but ruin a fine man. The inner and outer bearings are well summarized by:

> The *time* is out of joint. O cursed spite,
> That ever *I* was born to set it right!   (I. v. 189–90)

This can be reduced to purely psychological questions, only if *all* the problems of living are thought to be psychological – and the trend, from the late eighteenth century towards Freud, was to suppose just that. It clearly was not Shakespeare's view; nor, I suggest, should it be ours.

V

This summary of critical approach to the play arises, I hope clearly, from my analysis of Act I, and should enable me to move much more rapidly through the remaining Acts. The difficulty of this in *Hamlet* is simply the multiplicity and variety of what takes place.

Act II, scene i, takes us back again into other levels. Polonius' scene with Reynaldo is apparently another digression, planning to spy on Laertes; its relevance soon becomes clear when we reach Claudius with Rosencrantz and Guildenstern, arranging to spy on Hamlet. But that we should have this sense of digression is important: the pattern is repeated shortly afterwards in the scene with the players which is very remote from the main action, but again becomes relevant in Hamlet's soliloquy comparing theatrical

seeming with his 'being'. This sequence of digression made relevant later (the graveyard scene is another obvious case) has an odd
effect: it contributes of course to the sense of variety, but it also
insists on our looking at things other than the action (because
while they are going on there seems to be nothing else to look at).
In other words we are forced to look outwards from the tragic
figure to the world in which he is placed, and we tend to see it first
at its most acceptable, last in a devastatingly critical light. Polonius' plan to spy on Laertes is very amusing, and his equivocal
values —

<blockquote>

	Drabbing – you may go so far.
REYNALDO:	My lord, that would dishonour him.
POLONIUS:	Faith, no; as you may season it in the charge.
	You must not put another scandal on him,
	That he is open to incontinency . . .

</blockquote>

(II. i. 26–30)

Incontinency, no; drabbing, yes: it is a distinction without a
difference. But all this is largely comic: it is a different thing when
Hamlet in III. i tells Ophelia to 'Get thee to a nunnery', meaning a
convent and/or a brothel. Similarly, the comic spying becomes
less amusing in II. ii when Claudius sets *his* spies on to Hamlet;
and it is not amusing at all when Hamlet confronts them and
charges them with spying. Just as we learnt to criticize Claudius'
diplomacy in Act I, so we learn here to criticize this statecraft
whatever its motives. The world that seems at first normal,
amiable, almost inoffensive, turns inside out, and human relationships which depend on spying are seen as intolerable, destroying
all confidence and security, and provoking the reflection that
'this goodly frame, the earth, seems to me a sterile promontory',
and this marvellous piece of work, a man, nothing but the 'quintessence of dust'.

The sterile promontory involves, of course, a bawdy allusion
to the sex theme which has also developed at different levels
closely involved with the spying matter (which forms a thread on
which Act II is strung). Ophelia describes an insane Hamlet who
is in one way the typical Elizabethan love-lorn lunatic – as
Polonius takes it. Claudius doubts the explanation, and Hamlet

blasts it in III. i where again we are taken to a more fundamental disturbance as he talks vilely to poor Ophelia.

So that this pattern of apparently digressive scenes of normal bits of life shifted by degrees into profoundly destructive criticism of their normality is constantly repeated, and has, I think, one further significance: it gives to the *play* a continual sense of not getting on with it, simultaneous with its continual sense of urgent action. And this odd effect of irrelevancies to the main development seems to be of a piece with the notorious tendency of Hamlet not to get on with *his* business (revenge), the 'delay' which has caused so much comment. The delay for which there are several explanations given in the play, none of them (as is so often observed) 'satisfactory' in terms of the character of a noble hero. I have suggested that this characteristic of (seeming) irrelevance and delay belongs to the play as a whole, and not just to Hamlet; the effect, as it seems to me, is to weaken the logic of cause and effect which is normally characteristic of this kind of tragic drama, as it was of *Richard II* and *Julius Caesar*. We are made to feel continually that each jolt forward in the action has a large measure of accident in it; and that is, of course, most acutely felt in the end of the play, when Osric is used to provoke Hamlet into a silly duel which turns very suddenly into the catastrophe.

The result is that we have a double sense about the development of the action: on the one hand it is a purposive dramatic chain of events leading from the murder to the revenge and the restoration of order (in the authority of Fortinbras); on the other hand it is a succession of muddles and accidents leading to an apparently unnecessary holocaust. The structural characteristic of apparent digressions which in fact become relevant emphasizes this, so do the contrasting worlds of value I pointed out in the verse of Act I. The heroic world assuming heaven and hell yields a purposive action, whereas the world of Hamlet's analysis of human worthlessness yields purposeless action, whose characteristics are irrelevance and chance. In Hamlet's verse this duality emerges as a poetic exploration of experience; it achieves direct conceptual statement once, significantly in prose, in the familiar speech from which I have already quoted:

I have of late – but wherefore I know not – lost all my mirth, forgone all custom of exercises; and indeed it goes so heavily with my disposition that this goodly frame, the earth, seems to me a sterile promontory; this most excellent canopy the air, look you, this brave o'er-hanging firmament, this majestical roof fretted with golden fire – why, it appeareth no other thing to me than a foul and pestilent congregation of vapours. What a piece of work is a man! How noble in reason! how in-finite in faculties! in form and moving, how express and admirable! in action, how like an angel! in apprehension, how like a god! the beauty of the world! the paragon of animals! And yet, to me, what is this quintessence of dust? Man de-lights not me – no, nor woman neither, though by your smiling you seem to say so.   (II. ii. 294–309)

This states, but does not *explore*, the ambivalence that I have been discussing, in terms simultaneously of traditional glorification and vilification, linked (via Montaigne, no doubt) to personal melan-cholia. Its psychological bearing is contained in the repeated 'seems to me'; how much, and how little, that is to be taken as of central importance one feels in this speech – as, I have insisted, the force of this ambivalence is found everywhere in the play and not alone in Hamlet's behaviour.

The affair with Ophelia has taken a clearer form in Hamlet's 'fishmonger' dialogue with Polonius:

For if the sun breed maggots in a dead dog, being a good kissing carrion – Have you a daughter?   (II. ii. 180–1)

It is touched on again when Polonius brings in the players, before the digressive sense takes charge again. Once more the sense is strong that, however indirectly, this does bear on the play. The Pyrrhus speech is given Hamlet's specific approval, and despite the commentators it is not really much more 'primitive' stylistic-ally than much else in the play: what it does, is to give us the sense of another play that this might have been – it is Hamlet delivering the speech he should utter if this were the ghost's drama simply. Hence the soliloquy which finally brings all this to bear directly on the play is a commentary on the Pyrrhus speech:

> Is it not monstrous that this player here,
> But in a fiction, in a dream of passion . . .   (544–5)

In a fiction, cause and effect relate directly, and an actor with a cue
for passion, weeps – 'Yet I . . . can say nothing'. The nature of
drama and the nature of life are different: drama, in this sense, is
so much clearer and cleaner than life. So, 'I should 'a fatted all the
region kites With this slave's offal' – which leads immediately into
a further recognition in this criticism of drama: the abuse of
Claudius becomes cheap and ends in a cry for vengeance, and the
inevitable reaction:

> Why, what an ass am I . . .
> Prompted to my revenge by heaven and hell,
> Must, like a whore, unpack my heart with words . . .
>   (578–81)

That juxtaposes very clearly the two values I have distinguished:
heaven and hell prompt to revenge; the destruction of that value
leaves you a world of whores, unpacking their hearts in words,
words, words. But the drama (the play within a play) *is* only
words, words, words: revenge motives do *not* lead to clean action
but only to the equal and opposite futility of cursing like a drab.
   In this it is clear why the revenge ethic, as such, is not questioned in the play, which is otherwise so ethically sensitive:
revenge is the tragic action of a supposedly established order of
being which *is* questioned. If life is like a play, then one revenges
and all is well; but it isn't, and one just curses; which is, after
all, all that a play does really – 'murder in sport'. So, as Hamlet's
speech veers away from the simple promptings of heaven and
hell, it becomes possible to contemplate an interim action – the
tenting of Claudius to the quick. Ghosts may be the devil, 'I'll
have grounds More relative than this.' The ghost – we know – is
not the devil; yet grounds more relative seem important, because
they lie in the play's other dimension which excludes the supernatural. So this speech does, in the end, seem to have real bearing,
as well as sustaining the strong sense of fatuity in juggling with
grounds which only means more failure to get on with it: it has

become clear why there can be *no* grounds relative enough to get Hamlet on with it.

This is succeeded, in III. i, by a further development of the Ophelia affair, the complicated spying arrangements, Polonius' enthusiastic confidence that Hamlet is only love-sick, set against the king's recognition that it is more complex than that – a recognition which leads to a sudden shift into a dealing with Claudius' conscience in an image of startling relevance to Hamlet's last speech, to Ophelia, and to the play's values altogether:

> The harlot's cheek, beautied with plast'ring art,
> Is not more ugly to the thing that helps it
> Than is my deed to my most painted word.   (III. i. 51–3)

Claudius, like Hamlet, sees himself as a whore – and all the beautiful normality of his painted world, just like Hamlet's promptings of heaven and hell, are only a gloss of art over the pox-ridden face of a prostitute.

VI

On this sudden revelation of depth behind the Claudius–Polonius–Ophelia scene, Hamlet returns with 'To be, or not to be' – and by now it really is the question in any sense you like to give the ambiguous phrase: life, revenge, action, faith, love – any of these is open to the question, to be or not to be.

Notoriously this speech is difficult of precise interpretation. Its context I have set as one of absolute question between the order of heaven and hell, or its opposite in the harlot's cheek. Thus, one reason for the form of Hamlet's opening words is to assert the generality and fundamental nature of the question: 'To be, or not to be' is deliberately unspecific. That generality is sustained throughout the speech: Hamlet never, here, makes specific reference to the actions of the play. This speech is a reflection on what those actions imply, not about themselves. We assume, of course, that the slings and arrows of outrageous fortune are in a measure Hamlet's fortune, and that enterprises of great pitch and moment may relate to his revenge: but the form

of language does not suggest a very close relation – and revenge is
rather oddly called an 'enterprise', which would apply more
naturally to, say, Raleigh's adventures in the Guianas.

So what is being explored here arises *from* the situation of the
play, but moves out from it to a commentary on life in general (in
no sense does it lead us inwards to a reflection on Hamlet's
character). In its nature it is a choric speech, like Marcus' in *Titus*,
Clarence's in *Richard III*, and other similar utterances which I have
noted. Hence the opening words are (I suppose) a literal translation of the familiar Latin question 'Esse aut non esse', more
usually Englished as 'Being or not being', and the opening of the
speech is delivered in the form of a philosophical disputation:

> To be, or not to be – that is the question;
>   (III. i. 56)

and the rest of the speech follows the general shape of a disputation, the rhetorical formula still practised in a withered form in
the modern school debate: Hamlet, the proposer, interpreting the
motion (Whether 'tis nobler in the mind . . .) and conducting the
argument to his own conclusions. It therefore follows that we do
not make the right comment by looking ahead and finding that
Hamlet speaks of whether there is a life after death, and say (with
Samuel Johnson) that *that* is the question; or (with Malone) that
Hamlet discusses suicide, and therefore that *that* is to be or not to
be; or (with Dowden) that Hamlet discusses action, and so it is
active revenge which is to be or not be. All these things (after-
life, suicide, action) are debated in the speech, all on the lines of
the opening formula, and all have a bearing on Hamlet's dramatic
affairs; but no one of them is immediately conveyed in the opening
phrase, any more than Hamlet's dramatic affairs are the *immediate*
matter of debate. Unless this is accepted, then so far from being a
great poetic speech, this is nothing but a contorted elliptical way
of saying something quite simple – an extreme example of words,
words, words.

Which is absurd. But further, I said before that it is not in fact a
philosophical speech either: the rhetorical structure is pursued in
concrete language and imagery in which the progression of

thought is that of experience rather than logic. So the next interpretative problem is the next lines:

> Whether 'tis nobler in the mind to suffer
> The slings and arrows of outrageous fortune,
> Or to take arms against a sea of troubles,
> And by opposing end them?   (57–60)

The first part is clear: nobility of mind equals stoic endurance of
the slings and arrows of Fortune, who is usually assumed to be
(because capricious) outrageous. It is the second part which has
given trouble: how do you take arms against a *sea* of troubles? Is
it simply a mixed metaphor, yielding nonsense? Numerous
emendations have been proposed; Dowden asserted that this was
quite unnecessary because 'sea' *merely* develops the metaphor of
battle – which seems to me to beg the question, not to solve it.
And, further, Hamlet moves on to discuss death, so that 'by
opposing end them' involves the ending of life, not apparently
someone else's but one's own. Does he mean suicide? Or does he
envisage the effect of killing Claudius to be his own death as well?
Clearly such a specific event is not what the words chiefly give us
(though it may be involved). So, *logically*, the lines make no sense.
But *poetically* the progression is far more coherent: 'nobler in the
mind to suffer' moves through the military activities of a specifically *outrageous* fortune (thus linking outrageous with action
against the nobility of suffering), and proceeds to invert that idea
to the nobility of taking arms – but where the odds are again outrageous because it is against a *sea* of troubles. Looked at in this
way, it is precisely the image of the sea which matters. To 'take
arms against' may be noble, but it will not simply settle the
matter (if it would there would be nothing to argue about) because the troubles are a *sea*. To take arms against the sea is a heroic
but futile action, the Canute trick. Hence the final ambiguity of
'And by opposing end them': the opposition is designed ('take
arms') to destroy the troubles; but its result is to destroy them in
a very different sense, by forcing them to destroy you. Hence 'To
die, to sleep – No more' follows coherently. It doesn't matter
whether killing Claudius involves Hamlet's death, in any case

taking arms against a sea of troubles ends inevitably in destruction (as it does in Act V).

That, of course, is a consummation devoutly to be wished, to end the heartache and the thousand natural shocks that flesh is heir to (the sea of troubles); *but* that the seeming dream of life may be nothing to the endless nightmare in death: it is that fear of a dream worse than waking reality (as dreams are) which makes calamity of so long life. In other words it is fear of after-death consciousness which makes us suffer calamity for so long, and not (we now feel) nobility of mind.

That moves us into the second part of the speech, where *nobility* of mind is not involved; where, in fact, a catalogue of familiar social evils (the oppressor's wrong, the law's delay, etc.) is set against the quietus to be achieved with a 'bare bodkin'. The whole question is so simple if reduced to a dreamless sleep, without involving nobility at all. Life comes down to the simplest labouring:

> Who would these fardels bear,
> To grunt and sweat under a weary life . . .   (76-7)

So we move back to the final response to 'Whether 'tis nobler in the mind to suffer' in very different terms:

> the dread of something after death . . .
> puzzles the will,
> And makes us rather bear those ills we have
> Than fly to others that we know not of.   (78-82)

This preludes the next crux of the speech:

> Thus conscience does make cowards of us all.   (83)

I referred before to my doubts about the word 'conscience'. It has been confidently glossed 'consciousness' by most recent commentators, though D. G. James among others has protested. That is, the line is read: 'consciousness of something after death [puzzles the will] and so makes us behave like cowards'

> And thus the native hue of resolution
> Is sicklied o'er with the pale cast of thought . . .   (84-5)

I think it is clear from that that the line could mean 'consciousness'; but as I read the speech it does not mean *only* that. Because, first, as I said before, the word 'conscience' is used elsewhere in the play in the modern sense, and just before this speech by the king ('how smart a lash that speech doth give my conscience') when he was touching on a theme that Hamlet is here greatly enlarging (that Hamlet did not hear the king is irrelevant: we did). Secondly, if that is all the word means, then the speech is very repetitive here, and in effect says the same thing three times in different words. Thirdly, in that reading, the important idea of the nobility of suffering seems to have disappeared altogether, and the final reappearance of 'action' becomes inconsequential.

So my tentative suggestion is that we assume that conscience must, at least in part, mean conscience. How? It is awkward, for the dread of something after death is easily seen as cowardice, not easily as conscience. But if one takes the speech whole, like an almost detachable poem (and it is framed as one, chorus-like) an interesting possibility arises. The question is whether it is *nobler* to suffer . . . or to take arms against a sea, a gesture as futile as it is heroic (i.e. the opposite of stoic: Hercules, not Seneca in the Elizabethan tradition; Hamlet elsewhere remarks on his unlikeness to Hercules), and being futile heroism, it can have only one end, death. Death is seen in this Herculean view as a consummation – but also as to be feared; hence it is noted that if it were *not* feared men would commit suicide (which is not Hercules at all). So that after all it is not nobility of mind which makes us suffer the slings and arrows (instead of opposing them), but rather dread which makes us bear those ills we have (instead of committing suicide): *thus* 'conscience' (nobility of mind, conscious virtue) which dictates not-suicide, is in fact making us cowards. Nobility of suffering is, in the result (men are judged by what they *do*) indistinguishable from cowardice. That is, the action dictated by conscience is the same as the action dictated by cowardice – no difference is visible.

This reading seems to me to have several merits: it accepts the evidently paradoxical form of the language; it unifies the speech, and sees in it a characteristic progression from reflection of two opposed nobilities towards the insinuation that there is no nobility at all, only a crowd of muddy-mettled rascals – and seeing the two things simultaneously, it resolves them into a paradox:

> Thus conscience does make cowards of us all

(just as, later, a king may go a journey through the guts of a beggar). The two worlds I have shown as co-existing in the play, co-exist here: the positive world of order, where action and in-action are judged by their nobility; and the negative chaotic world where they are just equally forms of cowardice. In the first there is a heaven and a hell and the ghost of a noble father; in the second, at best, an undiscovered country from whose bourn no traveller returns, an illusion, a dream – at worst, a nightmare. The first is manifested in military images (the soldier's virtue), 'to take arms'; the second in the common world of Mankind at its lowest, with an equivalent contrast of utterance:

> Who would these fardels bear,
> To grunt and sweat under a weary life.   (76–7)

So that there is here the play's ambivalence, with the usual slight imbalance, that we finish the speech aware of both nobility and nullity, but rather more aware of the latter than the former. This is the central speech of the play; but it is not a speech *about* it; rather, it is a speech arising from the play, about life outside this action: a commentary, looking outwards. And it is the only one of Hamlet's soliloquies which has no explicit reference to the play's action (the first leads into the action; the second opens as a com-ment on the scene which precedes it, etc.). But, this does not seem irrelevant in the least: the reflections here are ones which the whole structure of the play has led us to. Hence its great im-portance: here, if anywhere, we have the core of *Hamlet* (the play – it tells us nothing at all about the man who speaks it). But it is the core, not the whole: the whole explores at large and in all its variety the state of being dependent on this ambivalent core.

VII

From that core we move out at once to the nerve ends, Hamlet's dialogue with Ophelia. He goes through the ceremony of ending their affair to the questioning of honesty and beauty, and so through 'Why wouldst thou be a breeder of sinners?' to 'Where's your father?' and finally 'God hath given you one face, and you make yourselves another [The harlot's cheek, beautied with plast'ring art] . . . To a nunnery, go.' (III. i. 88–149) There follows the complete contrast of Ophelia's description of Hamlet:

> O, what a noble mind is here o'erthrown!
> The courtier's, soldier's, scholar's, eye, tongue, sword;
> Th' expectancy and rose of the fair state . . .   (150–2)

The two Hamlets divide as the two values of the play divide: we have seen the one, hag-ridden, abusing Ophelia cheaply, the opposite of all that Ophelia describes. But the achievement here, of course, is that we have no difficulty in believing Ophelia: the mode of utterance, hysterical and always disturbing, found for the o'erthrown Hamlet contains the possibility, always, of a noble mind.

It is in that light that I see the brilliance of Hamlet's 'character': Shakespeare is able to make his behaviour and utterance oscillate between the two polarities, to give us a man who can move in both worlds of the play, the orderly and the chaotic, and yet be convincingly *one* man, experiencing this strain of two worlds of value. The play does not explore significantly how it is possible to be like this psychologically; it uses the observed possibility to make coherent and unified in a central figure the questions about human life which it does explore. The speech of the play tells us much about the values of life, and it constructs different kinds of drama and behaviour; it tells us very little of importance about psychology. That is why I dismissed Jones: the questions which the play deals with are not his questions. I said that Hamlet behaves like this and it is credible. But not everyone finds it so: the nineteenth century (and many recent productions) made Hamlet *see* Polonius (in hiding) before he said 'Where's your father?', so providing a very simple explanation for his rudeness after. Dover Wilson[1] saw that this weakened the point of the scene, but still thought that Hamlet must somehow *know* that Polonius was there, and so brought him on early in II. ii to over-hear the plotting – which seems to me no less crude than the business he was trying to replace. The plot exists, *we* know; Hamlet has already perceived that he lives in a world of spies, with the destruction of value which that entails; of that world this scene is a major development, and Hamlet's implied guess (at what we know to be the truth) sharply defines the point. He pro-ceeds to see Ophelia as far more evil than she is, and yet, which is why it is disturbing, he is not wholly wrong. It is the terms of Hamlet's commentary here which come out, in dreadfully parodied form, in Ophelia's mad scene later.

The credibility of Hamlet the man is, however, strained in other ways, most conspicuously after Claudius' soliloquy on Prayer. We have been through the climax of the spying motif in the play scene – everybody watching everybody else as the audience of a play which is itself the mirror of their own actions. This produces an equivalent climax of Hamlet's hysteria, grown very near indeed to madness. Ophelia called it 'Like sweet bells jangled, out of time and harsh'; the image recurs (as Wilson Knight noted) in Hamlet's cry for music after the King's exit, and it is finally expounded in his dialogue with Rosencrantz and Guildenstern:

> You would play upon me; you would seem to know my stops; you would pluck out the heart of my mystery . . .
>
> (III. ii. 354–5)

Scene iii effects a complete reversal of tone: the King, when Polonius leaves him alone, delivers a soliloquy representing a desperate attempt to move into the world of heaven and hell from his normal one of dexterous politics and lust:

> That cannot be; since I am still possess'd
> Of those effects for which I did the murder –
> My crown, mine own ambition, and my queen.
>
> (III. iii. 53–5)

---

1 *What Happens in Hamlet*, 1937, pp. 104–8.

O

After his final cry – 'Help, angels. Make assay' – comes Hamlet's most unpopular speech:

> Now might I do it pat, now 'a is a-praying;
> And now I'll do't – and so 'a goes to heaven,
> And so am I reveng'd. That would be scann'd:
> A villain kills my father; and for that,
> I, his sole son, do this same villain send
> To heaven.   (73–8)

The reason Hamlet gives for not killing Claudius has always seemed to commentators bad; so it was natural that this should be interpreted as a delaying tactic, a crude form of self-deception. Yet it has also persistently worried commentators, for it is a strong speech, and impressive; and Hamlet himself never criticizes it. Now in terms of the play, as distinct from the character, I find this speech quite intelligible: Claudius has (seemingly) moved into the drama of heaven and hell, and it is in that context that Hamlet's speech is set. It echoes the ghost's first speech, and is itself later echoed by Laertes (IV. vii; especially ll. 124–7). As long as it is uttered by other characters, this aspect of Christian revenge is apparently acceptable to us, as no doubt we should find it acceptable in any other play of the time. It becomes so evidently shocking only when Hamlet himself adopts it. It is, in fact, essential to the structure of the play that it should be so: the other extreme, the chaotic world of Hamlet's scepticism, is easily seen to be repulsive as well as (intellectually at least) attractive; it is far too easy to assume that the world of traditional order is entirely desirable, if only it were valid. The truth is that the image of Christian cosmology offered by, say, the ghost has always been as repulsive as its opposite; and it is that which we are forced to realize here. Technically, one may agree that this idea is not 'Christian', because revenge is in any case forbidden by both testaments; but the fact is that this springs from Christian beliefs, and was hallowed by a considerable tradition, at least in literature. It is fully and exuberantly elaborated in the last part of Nashe's *The Unfortunate Traveller* (1593). The ambivalence of the play is fully realized only when we understand that the oscillation between its two worlds is governed, equally on both sides, by

attraction *and* repulsion; and that Hamlet himself can be involved
in both. Here, therefore, the Christian order is not directly
questioned just where it is most questionable, most ethically
repulsive.

The point surely is that this delay is not due to the futility of
scepticism, but is precisely the result of accepting the order of
heaven and hell. The irony is made finally and devastatingly clear
after Hamlet's exit, when the king confesses his failure to pray:

> My words fly up, my thoughts remain below.
> Words without thoughts never to heaven go.   (97–8)

Hamlet could have killed him then, conscience (since that is what
it was) need not have stopped him. This scene, then, is a fully
coherent part of the play; but it remains difficult to stomach
about the person, for its shocking quality is not allied with
hysteria – Hamlet's own utterance does not contain even that
recognition that it *is* shocking. But this does not call for subtle
psychologizing, only for a recognition of dramatic weakness here.
It is, I think, true that a modern audience (and modern here extends at least from Samuel Johnson onwards) tends to undervalue
the 'orderly' drama that is half of *Hamlet* and so prejudges this
issue; but in any case the extraordinary convincingness of the man
Hamlet makes this intrusion of the play at his expense awkward.
In *Titus Andronicus* or *Richard II* we would not have been disturbed; but it is a measure of how far his perceptiveness in the
presentation of people *as* people has developed, that here Shakespeare has limited his own freedom more than he himself recognized.

VIII

Against that climax of the revenge play comes the climax of the
play's concern with solid or sullied flesh, Hamlet's scene with his
mother. It ends with rather unsatisfactory commonplace moral
advice:

> Refrain to-night;
> And that shall lend a kind of easiness
> To the next abstinence . . .   (III. iv. 165–7)

That blandness is destroyed in the exposure of what Hamlet really sees:

> Let the bloat king tempt you again to bed;
> Pinch wanton on your cheek; call you his mouse;
> And let him, for a pair of reechy kisses,
> Or paddling in your neck with his damn'd fingers . . .
>
> (182–5)

The sense of imbalance is again very strong: this sensuality is, to a prurient imagination, all sensuality – there must be no more marriages.

In this scene, in direct contrast to the last, the purposive chain of cause and effect is lacking: it is strongly ironic that whereas in the last scene Claudius was *not* killed for 'good' reasons, in this Polonius *is* killed for no reason at all. The appearance of the ghost marks this contrast of the play's two worlds very clearly: his presence reminds us of the *other* play, and provokes in Hamlet the reflection:

> Do you not come your tardy son to chide?   (106)

Hamlet is reminded of the need for deliberate action, as distinct from purposeless rashness; the ambivalence which he explored between being and not being emerges in action between doing and not doing, and he comments on it in his two important dialogues with Horatio. The first was before the play scene:

> thou hast been
> As one, in suff'ring all, that suffers nothing . . .
> Give me that man
> That is not passion's slave . . .   (III. ii. 63–70)

The second, very differently, comes after his return from destroying Rosencrantz and Guildenstern:

> Rashly,
> And prais'd be rashness for it – let us know,
> Our indiscretion sometime seves us well,
> When our deep plots do pall . . .   (V. ii. 6–9)

This both echoes, and comments on, the last soliloquy, when he had encountered Fortinbras' army:

                        I do not know
Why yet I live to say 'This thing's to do',
Sith I have cause, and will, and strength, and means,
To do't.

ending

                    O, from this time forth,
        My thoughts be bloody, or be nothing worth!
                                        (IV. iv. 43–66)

'Cause' and 'will' ought to produce effect; but in this play they do
not, and we move through the bloody thoughts (or thoughtless-
ness) of Laertes into the graveyard scene, a grotesque comedy of
the pointless cycle of birth, copulation, and death.

This oscillation between a purposive orderly world and a purposeless world of chance is sustained, then, at an extraordinary
variety of levels (I have said almost nothing of Ophelia's mad
scenes, or of Laertes' classic revenge which projects him into
Claudius' criminality, both of which parallel and contrast with
Hamlet). The action of the play is worked out on the interactions
of this ambivalence, and its ending makes a final transition from
one polarity to the other. A silly fop is used to persuade Hamlet
into a farcical duel which grows suddenly (and with appalling
haste) into the full stature of the final dénouement. The ambiguity
remains present to us in the sense of a shabby muddle in the circumstances which have to become, somehow, heroic. Hamlet's
apology to Laertes – 'His madness is poor Hamlet's enemy' – is a
psychologically rather weak stage in the slightly clumsy transition.
But the end, when the transition is complete, is magnificent: the
cannons fire, and the plot rebounds on the plotters, until everyone who matters is dead or dying. The full revenge tragedy of
heaven and hell is rapidly re-established, via Hamlet's words:

        Had I but time, as this fell sergeant Death
        Is strict in his arrest, O, I could tell you . . .

and:

        If thou didst ever hold me in thy heart,
        Absent thee from felicity awhile,
        And in this harsh world draw thy breath in pain,
        To tell my story.   (V. ii. 328–41)

which leads to Horatio's response:

> Now cracks a noble heart. Good night, sweet prince,
> And flights of angels sing thee to thy rest!   (351–2)

We are moved into the world of heaven and hell in which Hamlet's end is decisively tragic, and that sense is completed, as I said before, by Fortinbras:

> Bear Hamlet like a soldier to the stage;
> For he was likely, had he been put on,
> To have prov'd most royal.   (388–90)

On that the last peal of ordnance is shot off, leaving in its echoes the assurance of a supremely dramatic conclusion. Another Hercules hero has opposed a sea of troubles, and died heroically, noble in the mind.

IX

But there, of course, is the rub: Hamlet never was fully Hercules before, and this tragedy is made out of only one half of the play. The two worlds have not been resolved, it is only that one of them has been brought superbly into full focus so that we shall almost forget the other where no such satisfactory finality would be possible. Almost, but not quite: most critics, and most audiences, emerge from *Hamlet* with a residue of dissatisfaction. The cause can be seen, I think, in the selectiveness of treatment at the end. The play, as I see it, grows out of contrasted worlds; one of order, a pattern of human life that is honourable, active, patient, creative, and the other the negation of that in a bewildering experience of disorder in world and personality, where life is a chaotic disease whose result is destruction. It is out of that opposition that the sense of tragedy has its full growth: we have seen glimpses of a noble Hamlet throughout, seen the greatness of what is destroyed. As long as the ambivalence is in balance, the tragedy can be fully felt; but it isn't in balance. The profound scepticism in the play always criticizes the orderly and creative: the world of heaven and hell is so far questioned (and presented in unpleasant aspects) that it cannot finally gain full confidence; the picture of sexual relationships is always completely overlaid by the image of lust and disease; the sense of futility and death is the dominant one in the play.

Hence the final assertion of a tragedy whose positive values are the soldier and royalty, or Horatio's noble stoicism, leaves out too much, and relies on what has been too profoundly questioned, to be complete. We underrate the play's greatness if we do not recognize that it *is* ambivalent, that an orderly world is seen and felt as well as a disorderly; but it is wishful thinking not to see also that there is in it a fundamental imbalance, a sense of negation in which the clear definition of tragedy is not finally possible. In *Troilus and Cressida* a very similar ambivalence is felt, but there the end ridicules the idea of tragedy, and stresses just what is denied by the end of *Hamlet*, the futile continuance of life, and the revulsion against sexuality.

Nevertheless, this tragic assertion, the final sense of nobility and therefore of faith, is at least partly real. The effect is achieved, I think, by a reversal of the earlier structural principle: again and again I showed an orderly normality presented first, and then blasted; here it is the chaos, the cheap futility of the end which is first shown, and as before we learned to see things two ways round, so here we see, surprisingly, that this muddled failure can also be felt as triumphant success; and that this is at least partly justified by the play because as much as that has been nullifying, deadening, it has also been characterized by extraordinary energy, vitality.

Hamlet is an immensely impressive play, on a scale quite beyond that of any other that I have discussed in this book. Its copiousness of speech and action explore the range of social human life, and it arrives at an assertion of positive value in tragic terms. But the tragic bearings are not taken with full confidence, and its final sense is unstable if we compare it with *King Lear*, a play which explores less widely but more completely the root of human value. Like *Hamlet*, *Lear* presents its story in two radically contrasted forms: but it clarifies the distinction by doubling the action in two apparently similar plots, the orderly world of poetic justice in Gloucester and his sons, the ultimately chaotic world in Lear and his daughters. The double structure that I have analysed in *Hamlet* is less clear because it is less schematically organized; it depends, as I have tried to show, on grasping the radical contrasts of utterance, of *kinds* of poetry, which the play includes. In this it resembles the doubleness I found in *Julius Caesar*, and in the earlier plays as well; but the form has now to present experience and ideas more subtle and more sophisticated (aided, no doubt, by the reading of Florio's Montaigne), and so, as it becomes more complex and obscure, begins to need the separated plots of *King Lear*.

Selective Bibliography

The term 'selective' is a relative one: there is comparatively little to select from in the case of *Titus Andronicus*; but with *Hamlet* the amount is absurd, and even from periodicals since 1960 I can mention here only a tiny proportion.

GENERAL

W. FARNHAM: *The Medieval Heritage of Elizabethan Tragedy*, 1936.
M. C. BRADBROOK: *Shakespeare and Elizabethan Poetry*, 1951.
W. H. CLEMEN: *The Development of Shakespeare's Imagery*, 1951.
B. STIRLING: *Unity in Shakespearian Tragedy*, 1956.
M. M. MAHOOD: *Shakespeare's Wordplay*, 1957.
A. P. ROSSITER: *Angel with Horns*, 1961.
I. RIBNER: *Patterns in Shakespearian Tragedy*, 1960.
J. R. BROWN: *Shakespeare's Plays in Performance*, 1966.

TITUS ANDRONICUS

H. T. PRICE: 'The Language of *Titus Andronicus*', *Papers of Michigan Academy*, 21, 1935, 501–7.
H. BAKER: *Induction to Tragedy*, 1939.
R. A. LAW: 'The Roman Background of *Titus Andronicus*', *Studies in Philology*, 40, 1943, 145–53.
E. M. WAITH: 'The Metamorphosis of Violence in *Titus Andronicus*', *Shakespeare Survey*, 10, 1957, 60–70.
A. SOMMERS: ' "Wilderness of Tigers": Structure and Symbolism in *Titus Andronicus*', *Essays in Criticism*, 10, 1960, 275–89.
A. C. HAMILTON: '*Titus Andronicus:* The Form of Shakespearian Tragedy', *Shakespeare Quarterly*, 14, 1963, 201–13.

RICHARD III

R. A. LAW: '*Richard III:* A Study in Shakespeare's Composition', *P.M.L.A.*, 60, 1945, 689–96.
E. M. W. TILLYARD: *Shakespeare's History Plays*, 1948.
W. H. CLEMEN: 'Tradition and Originality in Shakespeare's *Richard III*', *Shakespeare Quarterly*, 5, 1954, 247–57.
M. C. BRADBROOK: *The Rise of the Common Player*, 1962.
C. LEECH: 'Shakespeare, Cibber, and the Tudor Myth', in *Shakespearian Essays*, ed. A. Thaler and N. Sanders, *Tennessee Studies in Literature*, 1964.

A. C. SPRAGUE: *Shakespeare's Histories*, 1964.
R. B. HEILMAN: 'Satiety and Conscience: Aspects of Richard III' *Antioch Review*, 24, 1964, 57–73.
W. H. CLEMEN: *A Commentary on Shakespeare's Richard III*, 1968.

ROMEO AND JULIET

J. W. DRAPER: 'Shakespeare's Star-crossed Lovers', *Review of English Studies*, 15, 1939, 16–34.
L. E. BOWLING: 'The Thematic Framework of *Romeo and Juliet*', *P.M.L.A.*, 64, 1949, 208–20.
B. EVANS: 'The Brevity of Friar Lawrence', *P.M.L.A.*, 65, 1950, 841–65.
H. MCARTHUR: 'Romeo's Loquacious Friend', *Shakespeare Quarterly*, 10, 1959, 35–44.
I. RIBNER: ' "Then I Denie You Starres": A Reading of *Romeo and Juliet*', in *Studies in the English Renaissance Drama*, ed. J. W. Bennett, O. Cargill, V. Hall, Jr., 1959.
H. LEVIN: 'Form and Formality in *Romeo and Juliet*', *Shakespeare Quarterly*, 11, 1960, 3–11.
P. N. SIEGEL: 'Christianity and the Religion of Love in *Romeo and Juliet*', *Shakespeare Quarterly*, 12, 1961, 371–92.
J. LAWLOR: '*Romeo and Juliet*', in *Early Shakespeare*, ed. J. R. Brown and B. Harris, 1961.
D. LAIRD: 'The Generation of Style in *Romeo and Juliet*', *Journal of English and Germanic Philology*, 63, 1964, 204–13.

RICHARD II

W. PATER: *Appreciations*, 1889.
C. E. MONTAGUE: 'F. R. Benson's *Richard II*', *Manchester Guardian*, 1899, reprinted in *Specimens of English Dramatic Criticism*, ed. A. C. Ward, 1945.
M. DORAN: 'Imagery in *Richard II* and in *Henry IV*', *Modern Language Review*, 37, 1942, 113–22.
R. D. ALTICK: 'Symphonic Imagery in *Richard II*', *P.M.L.A.*, 62, 1947, 339–65.
E. M. W. TILLYARD: *Shakespeare's History Plays*, 1948.
T. BOGARD: 'Shakespeare's Second Richard', *P.M.L.A.*, 70, 1955, 192–209.
D. TRAVERSI: *Shakespeare from Richard II to Henry V*, 1957.
J. A. BRYANT, JR.: 'The Linked Analogies of *Richard II*', *Sewanee Review*, 65, 1957, 420–33.
E. H. KANTOROWICZ: *The King's Two Bodies*, 1957.
M. QUINN: ' "The King is Not Himself": The Personal Tragedy of Richard II', *Studies in Philology*, 56, 1959, 169–86.
S. K. HENINGER, JR.: 'The Sun-King Analogy in *Richard II*', *Shakespeare Quarterly*, 11, 1960, 319–27.

P. G. PHIALAS: 'The Medieval in *Richard II*', *Shakespeare Quarterly*, 12, 1961, 305–10.
R. F. HILL: 'Dramatic Techniques and Interpretation in *Richard II*', in *Early Shakespeare*, ed. J. R. Brown and B. Harris, 1961.
A. C. SPRAGUE: *Shakespeare's Histories*, 1964.
T. YAMAMOTO: 'The Verbal Structure of *Richard the Second*', *Zeitschrift für Anglistik und Amerikanistik*, 12, 1964.
D. C. HOCKEY: 'A World of Rhetoric in *Richard II*', *Shakespeare Quarterly*, 15, 1964, 179–91.
J. R. ELLIOTT, JR., '*Richard II* and the Medieval', *Renaissance Papers*, 1965, 25–34.
A. R. HUMPHREYS: *Shakespeare: Richard II*, 1967.

JULIUS CAESAR

G. WILSON KNIGHT: *The Imperial Theme*, 1931.
L. KIRSCHBAUM: 'Shakespeare's Stage Blood and its Critical Significance', *P.M.L.A.*, 64, 1949, 517–29.
R. A. FOAKES: 'An Approach to *Julius Caesar*', *Shakespeare Quarterly*, 5, 1954, 259–70.
R. ORNSTEIN: 'Seneca and the Political Drama of *Julius Caesar*', *Journal of English and Germanic Philology*, 57, 1958, 51–6.
A. BONJOUR: *The Structure of Julius Caesar*, 1958.
V. HALL, JR.: '*Julius Caesar:* A Play without Political Bias', in *Studies in the English Renaissance Drama*, ed. J. W. Bennett, O. Cargill, V. Hall, Jr., 1959.
M. CHARNEY: *Shakespeare's Roman Plays*, 1961.
E. SCHANZER: *The Problem Plays of Shakespeare*, 1963.
N. RABKIN: 'Structure, Convention and Meaning in *Julius Caesar*', *Journal of English and Germanic Philology*, 63, 1964, 240–54.
N. SANDERS: 'The Shift of Power in *Julius Caesar*', *Review of English Literature*, 5, 1964, ii, 24–35.
M. E. HARTSOCK: 'The Complexity of *Julius Caesar*', *P.M.L.A.*, 81, 1966, 56–62.

HAMLET
(Critical and Stage History)

A. J. A. WALDOCK: *Hamlet: A Study in Critical Method*, 1931.
P. S. CONKLIN: *A History of Hamlet Criticism 1601–1821*, 1947.
C. LEECH: 'Studies in *Hamlet*, 1901–1955', *Shakespeare Survey*, 9, 1956, 1–15.
H. JENKINS: '*Hamlet* Then Till Now', *Shakespeare Survey*, 18, 1965, 34–45.
H. CHILD: 'The Stage-History', in *Hamlet*, ed. J. Dover Wilson, 1934.
A. C. SPRAGUE: *Shakespeare and the Actors*, 1944.

(Criticism)

S. T. COLERIDGE: *Shakespearean Criticism*, ed. T. M. Raysor, 1930 (rev. 1960).

A. C. BRADLEY: *Shakespearean Tragedy*, 1904.

T. S. ELIOT: *'Hamlet'* (1919), in *Selected Essays*, 1932.

G. WILSON KNIGHT: *The Wheel of Fire*, 1930 and 1949; *The Imperial Theme*, 1931.

E. E. STOLL: *Art and Artifice in Shakespeare*, 1933.

F. FERGUSSON: *The Idea of a Theater*, 1949.

E. JONES: *Hamlet and Oedipus*, 1949.

D. G. JAMES: *The Dream of Learning*, 1951.

M. MACK: 'The World of *Hamlet*', *Yale Review*, 41, 1952, 502–23.

R. A. FOAKES: '*Hamlet* and the Court of Elsinore', *Shakespeare Survey*, 9, 1956, 35–43.

G. C. THAYER: '*Hamlet:* Drama as Discovery and as Metaphor', *Studia Neophilologica*, 18, 1956, 118–29.

H. LEVIN: *The Question of Hamlet*, 1959.

C. C. CLARKE: 'A Note on "To be or not to be" ', *Essays in Criticism*, 10, 1960, 18–23.

L. C. KNIGHTS: *An Approach to Hamlet*, 1960.

J. LAWLOR: *The Tragic Sense in Shakespeare*, 1960.

J. SWART: ' "I Know Not Seems": A Study of *Hamlet*', *Review of English Literature*, 2, 1961, iv, 60–76.

J. HOLLOWAY: *The Story of the Night*, 1961.

A. RIGHTER: *Shakespeare and the Idea of the Play*, 1962.

SISTER MIRIAM JOSEPH: '*Hamlet*, a Christian Tragedy', *Studies in Philology*, 59, 1962, 119–40.

ed. J. R. BROWN and B. HARRIS: *Hamlet*, 1963 (Essays by P. Ure, D. William, J. K. Walton, G. K. Hunter, P. Cruttwell, E. A. J. Honigmann, R. A. Foakes, J. R. Brown, T. J. B. Spencer, S. Wells).

K. MUIR: *Shakespeare: Hamlet*, 1963.

C. R. FORKER: 'Shakespeare's Theatrical Symbolism and Its Function in *Hamlet*', *Shakespeare Quarterly*, 14, 1963, 215–29.

J. KOTT: *Shakespeare Our Contemporary*, 1964.

R. B. HEILMAN: 'To Know Himself: An Aspect of Tragic Structure', *Review of English Literature*, 5, 1964, ii, 36–57.

C. E. NELSON: 'Power and Politics in *Hamlet*', *Research Studies* (Washington State University), 32, 1964, 217–27.

M. DORAN: 'The Language of *Hamlet*', *Huntington Library Quarterly*, 27, 1964, 259–78.

W. T. HASTINGS: 'Is *Hamlet* a Hoax?', in *Shakespeare 1564–1964*, ed. E. A. Bloom, 1964.

K. MUIR: 'Imagery and Symbolism in *Hamlet*', *Etudes Anglaises*, 17, 1964, 353–63.

R. HAPGOOD: 'Hamlet Nearly Absurd: The Dramaturgy of Delay', *Tulane Drama Review*, 9, 1965, 132–45.

E. HANKISS: 'The Aesthetic Mechanism of Tragic Experience in *Hamlet*', *British Journal of Aesthetics*, 5, 1965, 368–81.

R. L. COX: '*Hamlet's Hamartia:* Aristotle or St. Paul?', *Yale Review*, 55, 1966, 347–64.

Index